AF600704

# ADORNO, POLITICS, AND THE AESTHETIC ANIMAL

# ADORNO, POLITICS, *and the* AESTHETIC ANIMAL

Caleb J. Basnett

UNIVERSITY OF TORONTO PRESS
Toronto Buffalo London

Toronto Buffalo London
utorontopress.com

ISBN 978-1-4875-4144-6 (cloth)
ISBN 978-1-4875-4146-0 (EPUB)
ISBN 978-1-4875-4145-3 (PDF)

---

**Library and Archives Canada Cataloguing in Publication**

Title: Adorno, politics, and the aesthetic animal / Caleb J. Basnett.
Names: Basnett, Caleb J., author.
Description: Includes bibliographical references and index.
Identifiers: Canadiana (print) 20210218479 | Canadiana (ebook) 20210218525 | ISBN 9781487541446 (cloth) | ISBN 9781487541460 (EPUB) | ISBN 9781487541453 (PDF)
Subjects: LCSH: Adorno, Theodor W., 1903–1969 – Criticism and interpretation. | LCSH: Human-animal relationships – Philosophy. | LCSH: Humanism.
Classification: LCC B105.A55 B37 2022 | DDC 179/.3–dc23

---

University of Toronto Press acknowledges the financial assistance to its publishing program of the Canada Council for the Arts and the Ontario Arts Council, an agency of the Government of Ontario.

Canada Council for the Arts
Conseil des Arts du Canada

Funded by the Government of Canada
Financé par le gouvernement du Canada

*For Taiyo and Hazuki*

# Contents

# Acknowledgments

In thinking back on all the twists and turns that led to these ideas becoming a book, I find it difficult to separate the gratitude I feel toward those who helped along the way from the "unstable events" that entangled our respective trajectories. These entanglements sometimes seemed rather brief; in other cases, we've yet to be untangled.

At any rate, it is perhaps best to use this page in the conventional manner, naming individuals rather than events. First and foremost, I would like to thank Asher Horowitz for guiding this study, and Shannon Bell and Martin Breaugh for reading a rather lengthy early version of it and for the helpful comments and criticisms they offered. I must also thank Stephen L. Newman, J.J. McMurtry, and Andrew Biro for similarly wading through the earlier version and for the insightful commentary they provided.

My past colleagues at York University also deserve honourable mention for their efforts as interlocutors and critics. They include Jordan Brennan, Cohen Brown, Elliott Buckland, Karl Dahlquist, Jason Harman, Paul Herbert, Christopher Holman, Arthur Imperial, Nadia Hasan, Rachel Magnusson, Paul Mazzocchi, James McMahon, Devin Penner, and Daniel Ross. To this list I must add professors at the University of Alberta whose teaching contributed to shaping my ideas, almost certainly more than they realize: Don Carmichael, Catherine Kellogg, Stéphanie Martens, and Sylvia Vance.

I need also to thank Sheela Subramanian, Maxime Capelliez, Alexander Buchinski, Ian Mackell, Craig Warner, and of course Nagisa, Taiyo, Hazuki, Yoko, Wendy and Richard, and Caitlin and Cassandra.

Thanks also to Michael Blézy for his editorial advice, the procurement of unexpected pastries, and all the extremely important discussions about coffee.

Lastly, I would like to thank Daniel Quinlan at University of Toronto Press for his efforts and patience with this project.

A portion of the introduction was previously published in "Animals and Human Constitution: Greek Lessons, Posthuman Possibilities," in *Posthuman Dialogues in International Relations*, edited by Erika Cudworth, Stephen Hobden, and Emilian Kavalski, 15–31 (London and New York: Routledge, 2018).

Portions of chapter 2 appear in "Without Banisters: Adorno against Humanity," *Contemporary Political Theory* 16.2 (2017): 207–27.

ADORNO, POLITICS, AND THE AESTHETIC ANIMAL

*Introduction*

# What Is an Aesthetic Animal?

This study retrieves a theory of the subject from the work of Theodor W. Adorno adequate to the current political juncture, one in which the humanist legacy has become inextricable from social and political domination. I examine Adorno's critical theory in terms of the neglected role animals play in his writings and find that it harbours a theory of the *aesthetic animal*, a subject opposed to the humanist constructions of subjectivity that have facilitated the most comprehensive forms of domination in the modern world.

Despite its modernity, this humanist legacy can be traced as far back as Aristotle and the particular way in which he theorizes the conceptual divide between human and animal. Aristotle profoundly remodels the concepts and imagery of the world of Greek myth, laying the foundations for what will become the Christian tradition. Breaking with the cosmos of Greek mythology informing Homer, the tragedians, and even to an extent Plato, Aristotle inaugurates a new relation between humans and animals based on natural potentials stretching up toward the divine. Yet Aristotle establishes this identity of the human being as the most divine animal through a conception of nature dependent upon aesthetic representation and metaphor. By failing to recognize the role art plays in shaping the identity of the human being, Aristotle preserves the sociopolitical domination that orders his world, which finds expression in his hierarchical conception of natural capacities where some humans are found to be more human than others. This way of understanding political possibility as a knot binding art and nature, human and animal, I call *the Aristotelian problematic*.

Despite the antiquity of this formulation, it continues to resonate in much of the thinking about politics today. To recognize and recover the power of the arts to transform this relationship between human and animal, and the understanding of political possibility with it, is to move beyond Aristotle and his modern humanist variations. I contend that it is Adorno's thought that offers us the surest guidance in this endeavour, enabling the theorization of the possibility of art playing a moral and political role in realigning the relation between human and animal so as to enable life to be lived free of domination. It is this promise, the promise of life lived free of domination introduced and betrayed by Aristotle, to which Adorno might speak. Exactly how this is so demands some attempt at justification, by way of a cursory overview of the role the human/animal distinction and its relation to art and aesthetics has played in political theory.

## Humans, Animals, and Art in Political Theory

The history of political thought in the West has frequently been characterized by attempts to pair theories of politics with what we might call "philosophical anthropologies": theories of what a human being fundamentally *is* that shape what is understood to be possible and thus serve as guides to theories of politics. If the human being is such and such a creature, so these arguments go, then its life ought to be organized in such and such a fashion. Yet this "such and such" of humanity has itself frequently depended on figures of animality for its definition: *unlike* lions, tigers, bears, and wasps, wolves, cranes, and ants, *humans* are such and such a creature, so human politics must be organized in the following manner "x." So these arguments go: *unlike animals, humans ...*

In this way, philosophical anthropologies have deeply coloured inherited understandings of politics operative today, and the figures of animality these anthropologies contain are part of our political inheritance. While I argue below that the clearest and most influential formulation of this division between human and animal is to be found in the work of Aristotle, this particular pairing of theories of politics and philosophical anthropology remains tragically operative in the modern hope birthed from Enlightenment thought that the modern nation-state, organized along rational lines, would at last provide a home for the higher, rational dimension of the human soul. Unfortunately, this hope was dashed on the rock of history: human reason expressed through the institutional structure of the modern state and its bureaucracy led the world into wars more horrible than had previously been imagined, culminating in the Holocaust and the atomic bomb.

While it is common to view these events as lapses in humanity, the pairing of philosophical anthropology and political theory shows that this is not the case. The Holocaust and the invention and deployment of the atomic bomb required all the most ingenious innovations of the modern state and its bureaucracy, and both were likewise bound up in this tradition of humanism that sees the human as being divided between more and less human parts, between parts that are uniquely human and others considered animal, and where the uniquely human might sacrifice the less human or animal for the sake of preserving what is best in the human. This logic of division, hierarchical organization, and sacrifice for the sake of self-preservation, whose shoots are rooted in the soil of the Aristotelian problematic, finds its most brutal expression in these events. Yet the solution to this problem, as will be discussed below, cannot be simply to absorb all that is animal beneath the human banner, for this absorption not only would fail to acknowledge the ways in which the human itself must change but also would contradict the claims to uniqueness of the human even while effacing the concrete differences between different forms of animal life.

Moreover, important features of the political juncture that made the Holocaust and the atomic bomb possible persist to this day. Since the end of the Second World War, humanity has seen amazing growth in its technological capacity both to perpetuate destruction on an ever-greater scale and to manipulate life at every level, without any fundamental shift in the way it understands itself or the relation of humanity to politics – the humanism of the Holocaust and the atom bomb retain their ideological dominance. Echoes of this dominance are audible today whenever humanism is marshalled toward justifying air strikes or "boots on the ground" that concatenate with the march of strategic security and business interests, as well as in humanity's lumbering steps toward its own extinction through studied indifference to the fate of other species and our environment. Humanism has been, and continues to be, entwined with the violence and domination whose practices have to a great extent built the world in which we live and that continue to structure our current political juncture.[1] Here, anyone who has ever taken the Socratic dictum seriously that it is better to suffer harm than inflict it might well prefer to be an animal other than human.

Yet for all the ideological dominance of humanism, these events have not been without their effects in political theory. The twentieth

1 There is a growing interdisciplinary literature that tries to assess this growth of human power on a geological scale, understanding it as part of a new age: *the Anthropocene*. For recent considerations of Adorno's work relative to the concept of the Anthropocene, see Luke, "Reflections from a Damaged Planet"; Nagelhout, "Nature and the 'Industry that Scorched It'"; Weißpflug, "A Natural History for the 21st Century"; and "Special Issue on Adorno and the Anthropocene," in *Adorno Studies*.

century and its legacy have called into question what we understand to be human and its possible vocation, and consequently its place in political theory, thereby dissolving consensus about the link between political theory and philosophical anthropology, even if much of humanism's prominence has been retained. In their introduction to *The Oxford Handbook of Political Theory*, Dryzick, Honig, and Phillips claim that while political theorists "share a commitment to the humanistic study of politics," thus placing some version of humanism at the heart of political theory, this shared commitment comes with "considerable disagreement over what [it] means."[2] Concerning this "considerable disagreement," most broadly we might isolate within contemporary political theory three overarching positions with respect to "humanism," understood not simply as the promotion of human rights around the globe but also as the theoretical underpinnings of a project found in philosophical anthropology. The first and easily largest position gathers those who understand the vocation of politics to be to establish the best framework for humans to be human, one that enables activities that promote the flourishing of natural capacities while protecting the space for this flourishing in a regime of rights. This position encompasses liberals, communitarians, deliberative democrats, and civic republicans in ways that might overlook important differences between these respective positions; I make the association here not to neglect these differences but simply to highlight their common humanism. To this end, it is worth noting the role that philosophical anthropologies play among certain prominent theorists within this category.

For instance, the early work of MacIntyre and Nussbaum illustrates this humanist position in terms of the promotion of humanist politics; indeed, their respective political programs are direct expressions of their philosophical anthropologies. For them, politics is nothing if not the practices through which humanity might flourish, and its prescriptions are entirely oriented to this end.[3] Likewise, thinkers as different from these Aristotelians as they are from one another, such as Fukuyama and Habermas, also rely on particular conceptions of human nature

2 Dryzek, Honig, and Philips, "Introduction," 4. I thus interpret "humanistic" here to refer not simply to methods of textual analysis or reflection upon current and historical events characteristic of those disciplines found in the Humanities, as opposed to more empirically inclined methods found in the sciences, but also to normative and speculative ideas concerning humanity, for the "humanistic" tradition has for the most part always insisted on their inseparability.

3 MacIntyre, *After Virtue*; Nussbaum, *The Fragility of Goodness*; Nussbaum, "Human Functioning and Social Justice."

and dignity in order to promote particular political aims, which in their cases concern the political consequences of biological engineering.[4] Perhaps most stridently, Kateb has taken up the banner not only of a revitalized conception of human dignity but also of an explicit philosophical anthropology, and behind that banner he rallies to theorize not only the human good but that of the planet as well.[5] Though both MacIntyre and Nussbaum have in more recent works revised the most ecstatic elements of their anthropocentrism, they have done so in order to expand the notion of human dignity and the moral consideration bound to it to other kinds of beings, not to displace the fundamental importance or even centrality of their conceptions of humanity for political theory.[6] Thus, for the aforementioned thinkers, *anthropos* remains the measure, even if *anthropos* is acknowledged as being constituted through its relation not just to itself but to other animals as well.

In contrast to the humanist position, which might be said to define the mainstream of political theory, we have what might be called the "post-humanist" position, descended from the anti-humanism of thinkers such as Althusser, Foucault, and Deleuze. Unlike the variations on humanism found among the members of the aforementioned group, post-humanism denies the necessary centrality of humanity as a concept. Instead, post-humanism focuses on the ways in which humans are entwined with non-human entities, including the myriad agencies of animals, machines, and systems that inform and destabilize the concept of the human and the possibility of promoting its self-same ends.[7] For post-humanists, it is possible to speak of conditions that give rise to what we call humanity and with it humanist aims, or a "human predicament,"[8] but the integral stability of the concept of humanity and its humanistic promotion is considered suspect if not rejected outright. For post-humanists, philosophical anthropology is an antiquated relic of the history of political thought that serves only to obstruct more

4 Fukuyama, *Our Posthuman Future*, chs. 8 and 9; Habermas, *The Future of Human Nature*.

5 Kateb, *Human Dignity*. Cf. Rosen, *Dignity*.

6 See MacIntyre, *Dependent Rational Animals*; Nussbaum, "Beyond 'Compassion for Humanity.'"

7 Bennett, *Vibrant Matter*; Braidotti, *The Posthuman*; Haraway, *Simians, Cyborgs, and Women*; Wolfe, *What Is Posthumanism?*

8 Connolly, *A World of Becoming*, ch. 4. Connolly has recently moved away from a post-humanist position to one he calls "entangled humanism," though the basic feature of post-humanism noted here, its displacement of the centrality of the human being in politics and the unique coherence of its concept, remains consistent with "entangled humanism." See Connolly, *Facing the Planetary*, esp. ch. 6.

creative ways of understanding politics as they relate to the material universe.

The last position I want to outline in contemporary political theory relative to humanism is a trend emerging in some sense from the post-human position: what is being called by some "agonistic humanism." Rather than viewing politics as an expression of natural human capacities or as directed toward necessarily humanistic ends, as the humanists do, or rejecting classical humanism outright, as the post-humanists do, "agonistic humanism" recognizes that defining the human is itself a political act: "humanism is," Honig claims, "implicated in political divisions it claims to transcend."[9] In this sense, Honig might be seen as creatively developing the kind of *practical humanism* that Rancière invokes against the *theoretical humanism* condemned by Althusser's anti-humanism.[10] For Rancière, humanism refers to a set of politically contested concepts that both dominator and dominated attempt to appropriate and so direct toward their own aims as they struggle against each other.[11] Instead of rejecting philosophical anthropologies, agonistic humanists concern themselves with locating the political or rhetorical function of those anthropologies and their value as political practices, and tend to avoid ontological claims concerning their correctness or lack thereof. Practical or "agonistic" humanism, then, strives for an appropriation of humanism that remains mindful of the anti-humanist and post-humanist critiques concerning the political constitution of the concepts of humanism. In this way, it preserves the concept of humanity while cancelling its foundational status.

While these three broad positions do indeed constitute "considerable disagreement," it is interesting to note that even more conventionally minded or "anthropocentric" humanists have come to understand humanistic politics as having an important ecological dimension and to recognize the importance of reconciling humanism with inhuman nature. Kateb explicitly attempts to revitalize philosophical anthropology and insists that human stature is something fundamentally different from that of an animal, yet he does so in order to endow humanity with the stewardship of the natural world and the planet on which it flourishes.[12] We thus find that contemporary political theorists share a broad acknowledgment that the humanism of the past is wanting in at

9 Honig, *Antigone Interrupted*, 17. Cf. Rossello, "'To Be Human, Nonetheless.'"

10 See Althusser, "The Humanist Controversy," 253. Cf. Althusser, "La querelle de l'humanisme," 469.

11 Rancière, *Althusser's Lesson*, ch. 4.

12 Kateb, *Human Dignity*, 5, 17, 23, 115, 122.

least certain respects and that politics today must involve a changed understanding of the relationship between human beings and the natural world, even if the precise nature of these changes and the theoretical underpinnings that ought to inform them remain contested.

Of those attempting to explicitly reformulate the relation between humans and the inhuman world, we might identify two broad camps. The first is made up of those who consider it necessary to formulate a more expansive conception of humanity so as to render human beings morally responsible to other forms of life, especially the lives of animals capable of suffering in ways analogous to humans. Again, though the most prominent approaches vary significantly between the utilitarian view advanced by Singer, the modified version of the capacities approach championed by Nussbaum, and the rights-driven approach formulated by Donaldson and Kymlicka, their respective positions are united through their attempts to show an important identity between humans and certain animals, which ought to endow the latter with basic rights and privileges analogous to those claimed by humans.[13] In attempting to expand the conception of humanity, personhood, or selfhood in this manner, these authors all accept that the change humanity needs can be accomplished through political reform and that the kinds of conscious-raising necessary for such reform to gain popular appeal are more or less in line with how one might go about gaining support for any kind of political reform, even if the scope of animal rights is vastly greater than for most other kinds of political reform. In this sense, these authors appear to be in agreement with a generalized version of Habermas's famous critique of Adorno: that the philosophy of the subject and of "consciousness" has been exhausted[14] and that the question that most urgently concerns humanity is not, in fact, how humanity has been constituted through the domination of nature; rather, it relates to the structural possibilities for the democratic production of consensus on substantial issues – such as animal rights, in this case.

It is against this general notion that the concept of humanity can simply be expanded by fiat in order for violence against other animals to wither that I would reintroduce Adorno into this debate. In downplaying the role of violence and the domination of both other animals and other humans in the evolution of human constitution and its ongoing reproduction in the current political juncture, approaches that would

13 Singer, *Animal Liberation*; Nussbaum, "Beyond 'Compassion for Humanity'"; Donaldson and Kymlicka, *Zoopolis*.

14 Habermas, *The Theory of Communicative Action*, 386.

simply expand the concept of humanity fail to address the violence at the heart of the human subject and human society. Such approaches are attempts to alleviate the suffering of some while neglecting its sources and thus the continuation of that suffering through the domination of others. A central contention of this study is that Adorno's work helps us understand how the violence of this concept of humanity is reproduced and might be transformed. To this end, I advance a version of the philosophy of subjectivity whose exhaustion was announced by Habermas, in order to theorize a possible transformation of the human subject, even if Adorno himself did not, so they say, "tell stories about a 'new subject.'"[15] If domination is not simply oppression in the sense of external control suffered by one individual or group at the hands of another, but concerns a psychological dimension whereby the oppressed internalize their oppression so as to naturalize it, thus obliterating even the ability to imagine other ways of living,[16] then the transformation of society based on violence against animal others cannot be separated from subjective transformation.

In this respect, the second broad trend concerning the reformulation of the human/animal distinction appears to offer more promise, though it too is hampered by significant shortcomings. Works in this trend by thinkers such as Agamben and Derrida have attempted to show how what we call human has depended on a corresponding conception of "the animal," whose separation from the human is produced and maintained through systematic violence and domination; this in turn places the focus on the production of the human – production that is often taken for granted by advocates of animal rights and well-being.[17] This attempt to inject the idea that the human is itself a rather precarious concept into the question of our relations to other animals, and the concomitant attempt to trace the history of the theoretical underpinnings of this distinction, are to my mind welcome theoretical innovations in our understanding of the political import of the human/animal distinction. However, these innovations as they are found in Agamben and Derrida misconstrue the manner in which the human/animal distinction has been inherited in the West, for they overlook important aspects of the work of Aristotle. While both Agamben and Derrida recognize the importance of Aristotle's influence on this question, they do not sufficiently appreciate Aristotle's writings on biology or on poetics, which

15 Habermas, "Theodor Adorno," 104.

16 Kontos, "Domination," 219.

17 Agamben, *The Open*; Derrida, *The Animal That Therefore I Am*; Jacques Derrida, *The Beast and the Sovereign*, vols. 1 and 2.

should be seen as modifying his more famous statements on human capacities and their relation to politics.[18] If Aristotle can be shown to offer a more nuanced appraisal of the political nature of human beings, one that might include other animals, as he does in his *History of Animals*, and if nature itself can be shown to depend on artifice, as suggested in the *Poetics*, then the path leading from this point must lead in another direction, even if this direction will, ultimately, move beyond Aristotle.

In returning to the scene of the crime, as it were – that is, to the Aristotelian problematic – we gain a more nuanced understanding of the human/animal distinction: we find that much of what is human is also found in other animals and that drawing and ordering this distinction is heavily dependent upon the arts. Three important consequences are to be drawn from these insights. The first is that if the arts can be seen as playing an integral role in how the human/animal distinction is drawn, then the recent resurgence in the interest of the relation between art and politics acquires a whole new dimension, related as it is to the kinds of philosophical anthropologies that have been employed in the history of political thought, and thus divergent literatures in political theory might be found to relate to one another in new ways.[19] Second, and more urgently, this insight reveals an important potential aid or obstacle to the democratic consensus-building that is necessary if the animal rights and animal well-being movements are to succeed. If the arts play a part in constructing the subjectivity that informs the moral and political decisions involved in supporting these movements, then an important dimension of both the movement's success and the persuasiveness of its theory are being neglected – and that neglect can only be remedied through attempts to grasp how subjects are produced in ways that are not being effectively addressed through the focus on the formal sociopolitical structures that theorists of animal rights and well-being tend to adopt.

Third, in the light of the Aristotelian problematic, the argument stating that "the animal" is something like the *ur*-subject of domination, that is, that people oppress and dominate one another in the same way they oppress and dominate animals, and consequently, if humans come to treat animals better they will treat one another better,

18 On another set of problems with Agamben's Aristotle, see Finlayson, "'Bare Life' and Politics in Agamben's Aristotle."

19 See Panagia, who similarly claims that "our understandings of political life are informed by our aesthetic sensibilities," though Panagia offers this insight by way of different sources. Panagia, *The Poetics of Political Thinking*, 2. Cf. Kateb, "Aestheticism and Morality."

is unfortunately too simple to describe the historical record.[20] The human/animal distinction can be drawn in a number of different ways that would legitimate different human/animal and human/human relations which are not inherently part of trajectories of liberation or domination. Or more bluntly: humans are quite capable of oppressing other humans while relating to other kinds of animals compassionately. Derrida acknowledges this when he notes – in an address on the work of Adorno – that the Nazis related Jews, Romani, communists, and homosexuals to animals, but that they also *loved* their animals, "even to the point of vegetarianism," as in the case of the *Führer* himself.[21] Thus, a more nuanced appreciation of the human/animal distinction and its relation to morality and politics is necessary, one that acknowledges how different ways of drawing the human/animal distinction have political consequences that are not predictable from their outset, and consequently require the arts to mould and shape them. Unfortunately, Derrida himself does not go on to develop this point further in his other writings on animals.

It is Adorno, I argue, who provides a critique of the humanist tradition fitting to this nuanced re-evaluation of the human/animal distinction, while also providing in his writings on aesthetics a practical moral and political guide to the construction of a transformed subject. Though Adorno's writings on aesthetics are well-known, he produced no treatise on "the animal," nor does he appear to have made any substantial attempt to study animals. Yet images of different animals appear provocatively throughout his writings, marking the points at which humanity falters – the points at which the cracks in its veneer become visible and a different set of subjective possibilities are intimated. The animal is for Adorno what is non-identical to the human. Adorno's animals are images of those possibilities repressed and excluded from human constitution in the different instantiations of its drive for self-preservation since the time when Aristotle's conception of the human being formulated its systematic difference *from* and superiority *to* the animal.

In this sense, Adorno provides the combination to the lock forged by Aristotle, a way of appropriating the promise of the Aristotelian problematic as the possibility of radically redrawing political and even natural possibilities through the arts, while managing at once to work

20 This argument is commonly repeated today, though its sources appear to be as old as the Pythagoreans. See Sorabji, *Animal Minds and Human Morals*, 7.

21 Derrida, "Fichus," 181.

toward extricating this process from the logic of violence and domination that animates both. It is this promise, the promise of new subjective possibilities, which is invoked in the term *aesthetic animal*. An aesthetic animal would be a subject constituted through an aesthetic education that might bring about a different relation between animal senses or bodily comportment and human reason, one that might trouble this distinction and its identification of specifically human and animal capacities, one for which self-preservation is no longer the point around which all else must gravitate. Such a subject would demand a qualitatively different form of society, one likewise no longer constituted through violence and domination. Only in such a society, one wherein the relations between humans have been radically transformed, would a comparable transformation in human/animal relations become a concrete possibility. A large part of this book is devoted to retrieving the promise of the Aristotelian problematic by way of constructing a theory of the aesthetic animal from Adorno's work. However, in order to better appreciate how this promise is formulated and betrayed in the tradition Adorno inherits, I must now present the Aristotelian problematic.

## The Aristotelian Problematic

Even more than giants of antiquity such as Homer or Plato, it is Aristotle who has given us the most lasting and influential concept of the human being and its relation to politics. However, contemporary interpretations of Aristotle's famous claims that "a human being is by nature a political animal" and that only "a beast or a god" can live outside the political community[22] all too often ignore their relation to his biological and zoological writings. Aristotle's comprehensive re-evaluation of the knowledge of the natural world is said to have provided both the questions asked and the terms with which such questions were answered for over two thousand years.[23] Such wide-ranging conceptual innovation did not ascend to theoretical hegemony without provoking crisis; indeed, Sorabji argues that Aristotle's work in biology and zoology led to a massive re-evaluation of the psychic capacities thought

22 Aristotle, *Politics*, 1253a1–6; 24–30. Cf. *Politics* 1278b19–22; Aristotle, *Aristotle's Nicomachean Ethics*, 1097b11; 1162a16–19; 1169b16–19. All English citations refer to these translations unless otherwise noted, abbreviated hereafter as *Pol.* and *NE*.

23 Arnhart, "Aristotle, Chimpanzees, and Other Political Animals," 485; Lloyd, *Early Greek Science*, 99; Lloyd, *Greek Science after Aristotle*, 8; Lloyd, *Magic, Reason, and Experience*, 201, 264; Pratt, "The Essence of Aristotle's Zoology," 267.

to be distinctly human.[24] Consequently, there is a political dimension to Aristotle's zoology that cannot be ignored. Grasping the insight to which "the whole of Aristotle's *Politics*" is addressed, namely, that humans are political animals,[25] must therefore involve grasping this re-evaluation of the human being by way of Aristotle's zoology. Only through an understanding of this proto-scientific conception of other animals and how they are similar to and different from humans might Aristotle's claims concerning the necessarily political nature of human beings be grasped, and with it, the way in which the Aristotelian problematic conceives humanity.

A first step in this direction begins with noting that while Aristotle claims the human is by nature a political animal, he does not claim politics to be *exclusive* to humans.[26] Though he does link the practice of human politics to the exclusively human capacity for reason or speech (*logos*),[27] this should not indicate that all politics is necessarily linked to *logos*: in his *History of Animals*, Aristotle claims that animals such as bees, wasps, and cranes are also political. This contention that non-human animals might be political has been seen as something of a curiosity in the modern tradition of Aristotle interpretation, which has often seen fit to translate the word *politika* Aristotle uses to describe these animals as "social."[28] As Arendt notes, however, what is frequently today called "social" is bound up with certain historical developments alien to both the conception of politics held by the Greeks and even the kind of gregariousness Aristotle claims for other, not quite political animals.[29]

Consequently, to understand this passage one must consider the specifically political nature of these other animals. However, the definition Aristotle gives politics here, of sharing a common work (*ergon*), is somewhat different from the one he uses in his explicitly political writings, being more suited to the range of capacities he allots to other animals. For Aristotle, an animal is constituted through the bundle of capacities (*dynamai*) that compose its soul (*psyche*). The soul is the principle of movement: it is what animates and actualizes the otherwise inert

24 Sorabji, 7, 12, 103.

25 Garver, *Aristotle's Politics*, 1.

26 Depew, "Humans and Other Political Animals," 162.

27 *Pol.*, 1253a6–20.

28 Aristotle, "History of Animals," 488a6–10. All further citations refer to this edition (cited as *HA*) unless otherwise noted. See also Peck's translation of Aristotles's *History of Animals*, 15. Cf. Steiner, *Anthropocentrism and Its Discontents*, 61.

29 Arendt, *The Human Condition*, 22–38.

potential of the body. Like a wide range of other animals, humans are largely constituted through their capacities for imagination (*phantasia*), memory (*mneme*), and voice (*phone*), which together make it possible to be political in the sense of sharing a common work.

A work (*ergon*) is the activity that makes a given thing the thing that it is, and though complex animals can have many different works relative to the different aspects of their lives or even bodies,[30] the work considered most definitive of a given animal will be the work that most completely actualizes the capacities inherent to that animal's soul. A political animal is thus gregarious in a particularly intense fashion: it is an animal that shares in common the work that makes it what it is. The capacity for common experience is thus inextricably entwined with the work of political animals, and in his biological and zoological writings, Aristotle shows how capacities such as imagination, memory, and voice form the basis of common experience entwined with politics – a shared experience of space and time in which animals are capable of orienting themselves toward others – and that these capacities are found in a wide variety of animals.[31] In this light, the claim that animals other than humans can also be political becomes a little less mysterious.

Yet Aristotle's zoology undermined the manner of distinguishing between humans and other animals relied upon in the culture of his day. Consequently, if Aristotle is to avoid a total collapse of the conceptual distinction between human and animal, such that human communities would not be meaningfully distinct from those of other political animals, he requires that the capacities capable of making animals political operate differently in humans. He accomplishes this through the concept of *nous*. *Nous* is for Aristotle divine thought: unlike forms of practical knowledge, related as they are to experience, the senses, and hence animality, *nous* for Aristotle does not, strictly speaking, require a body.[32] *Nous* is thought thinking itself, sovereignly independent of the animal world, and for this reason it can be considered divine (*theion*).[33] Humans are unique among animals in that their souls are open to *nous*, and this power serves to reorient the capacities they share with other animals so as to distinguish them from other animals, just as the power of sensation serves to distinguish animals from plants.

30 E.g. Aristotle will write of the *erga* of hands and feet (*NE*, 1097b26ff).

31 On this point, see Basnett, "Other Political Animals," 290–309.

32 *OS*, 429a22–27; 429b5. For a clear discussion of this difficult idea, see Gerson, "The Unity of Intellect," 348–73. Cf. Kullmann, "Man as a Political Animal in Aristotle," 115.

33 Aristotle, "Generation of Animals," 736b27–28, hereafter *GA*; *OS*, 429b31–430a2, 431b17.

The human openness to *nous* is the precondition for a host of uniquely human capacities, which come to mediate the otherwise animal capacities of imagination, memory, and voice. With *nous* come *logos, logismos* (calculation), *syllogismos* (inference), *bouleusis* (deliberation), and *proairesis* (choice), all of which serve to transform how the sensory objects woven together in the imagination relate to one another. In this way, we can say that humans perceive space differently than other animals. Also with *nous* comes the capacity for recollection (*anamnesis*), which makes human memory different from the capacity for memory found among other animals, in that it is bound – claims Aristotle – to the intellectual capacity for investigation (*zetesis*) rather than to something closer to lingering sense perception.[34] Thus, Aristotle distinguishes between the way humans perceive time and the way other animals perceive it.

Lastly, Aristotle views the capacity for human speech, *dialektos*, as animal voice mediated by *nous*. Animal voice serves as the vocal expression of imagination in non-human animals; human openness to *nous* allows for the mediation of imagination by reason (*logos*) and its related intellectual capacities so as to reorder animal voice according to their dictates. Just as the intellectual capacities allowed for a more refined perception and awareness of the objects of sensation, so do they as speech allow for a much more finely articulated expression of themselves than voice. In this way both the space-time occupied by the human and its ability to express, communicate, and organize itself with others has much greater breadth and depth than the space-time occupied by other animals, thus endowing the human with a much wider range of potential ways of orienting itself to others through meaningful activity.

In this way, we find that though humans are political animals just as are cranes, the rudimentary community we share with other animals through our overlapping psychic capacities is not really shared at all: it is as if humans occupy a different dimension of the same world as other animals, one determined by unique ways of reasoning and speaking. Aristotle writes that human politics differ from those of other animals in that their unique capacities allow them to know and deliberate about the good and the just,[35] and he affirms with Plato that justice is the good of the other, of the entire political community,[36] but the way in which he parcels out psychic capacities among humans and other animals renders other animals invisible to human consideration in their

34 Aristotle, "On Memory," 453a6–13.

35 *Pol.*, 1253a6–20.

36 *NE*, 1129b30–1130a5; *Pol.*, 1253a37–38.

deliberations upon justice. Aristotle's zoology can thus be seen as a kind of *ur*-politics, determining, through its account of the composition of animal souls, who might be considered a member of the community in advance of any other political decisions. Furthermore, if humans are to distinguish themselves from one another, they must strive toward the divine, and this involves developing their intellectual capacities – those most uniquely human capacities, according to Aristotle. Unlike in Homer or even Plato, for whom certain animals serve as aristocratic and even divine sigils embodying the kinds of traits humans might strive to imitate, after Aristotle's zoology the good human life becomes a life lived in imitation of what is best in humanity – poetic links between animality and divinity that enabled a wide variety of possible relations between humans, other animals, and the gods, are severed.[37] Through Aristotle's comprehensive reformulation of natural philosophy in his study of animals, the human thus emerges as a conceptually unique being, and politics becomes the organization of the community so as to perpetuate its reproduction.[38]

Modern science has long since surpassed Aristotle's zoology, yet his work continues to resonate in the way that the separation between "human" and "animal" continues to be drawn by modern theorists. For instance, politics are routinely understood to be rooted in natural human capacities and so restricted to human community; indeed, even attempts to overcome anthropocentric politics by formulating just relations between humans and other animals typically endow animals considered to be more biologically complex with greater moral and political value. This is the case not only with contemporary Aristotelians[39] but also with utilitarians[40] and liberal rights theorists.[41] The basis for the unity of these otherwise very different positions continues to be the kind of comparison each insists on making between humans and other animals: where other animals can be found to be sufficiently similar to more "advanced" humans, so their needs can be considered by the human political community, and they can be afforded something like membership status if not outright citizenship.

37 Cf. Vernant, *Myth and Society in Ancient Greece*, 149, 117.

38 Cf. Gellrich, *Tragedy and Theory*, 129.

39 MacIntyre, *Dependent Rational Animals*, 39–49; Nussbaum, "Beyond 'Compassion and Humanity,'" 361.

40 Singer, *Animal Liberation*, 20.

41 Donaldson and Kymlicka, *Zoopolis*, 25. On the arbitrariness of deciding which organisms are more complex than others, see Levins and Lewontin, *The Dialectical Biologist*, 17.

In this way, Aristotle provocatively establishes the possibility that animals other than humans might share a community and act in concert in such a way as to be considered political – that is, that there are *other political animals*. However, he never seriously considers the possibility that humans and other animals might share the same political community, for his account of human capacities is mediated by the divine that serves to establish human nature as qualitatively different from the natures of other animals.[42] Recent attempts to argue the cases of other animals have attempted to show that at least certain other animals are similar enough to humans as to be offered similar kinds of consideration, but Aristotle's method for differentiating the naturally human from other forms of animality in order to establish a political subject remains unchallenged. Yet this division, and Aristotle's concept of nature upon which this division depends, is itself deeply dependent on performative action and identification mediated by the arts.

As we have seen, the Aristotelian conception of humanity depends upon a wide-ranging re-evaluation of natural potentials in order to establish which potentials are exclusively human and which are shared with other animals. Yet insofar as potentials cannot themselves be directly observed, they must be inferred from actions. Consequently, identifying humans involves identifying human actions, and the best humans will, in their actions, display those potentials thought to be most paradigmatically human. In this sense, the human is a kind of performance, one that must be identified and striven toward, and therefore depends upon a humanist education – that is, an education in *human things*, one wherein the pupil is acquainted with the vicissitudes of human life and possible human responses to its dilemmas. The kind of humanist education needed to supplement Aristotle's conception of the human is provided most clearly through ancient Greek tragedy. The account of tragedy given in Aristotle's *Poetics* illustrates this pedagogical function as well as how tragedy is intimately bound to Aristotle's conception of the human being.[43] In this way, we see the other side of

---

42 A variation on this manner of distinction has recently been called "species aristocratism." See Rossello, "All in the (Human) Family."

43 *Contra* Lear, who contests the centrality of pedagogy in Aristotle's conception of tragedy. Though Lear's discussion of tragedy concerns primarily the role of catharsis, whereas mine focuses on the political implications of Aristotle's analysis of tragedy more broadly, a key objection Lear brings against the pedagogical reading of tragedy is that the spectator of tragedy is a "virtuous man" and thus has no need of such education. However, while Aristotle does think that tragedy is a mimesis of the actions of the best human being, there is little evidence to suggest that Aristotle

the Aristotelian problematic: the human is that which is split off from and elevated above the animal, and furthermore, accoutrements of artistic practice are what make this split possible. Tragedy is thus responsible for staging the concept of the human and making possible the performance of its break with other animals, while at once reconciling humanity to a certain image of itself, one wherein not all humans are equally human.

Aristotle begins his account of poetry by noting that what is common to the plurality of poetic forms is *mimesis*, or imitation.[44] He claims that humans are naturally prone to imitate, that they are the most imitative of all animals, and that imitation is the means through which humans begin to learn.[45] Combined with the claim that humans "by nature desire to know,"[46] these statements suggest an anthropological foundation to poetry that would make it another outgrowth of natural potentials; however, a closer look at the concept of imitation troubles this point of view. Of imitation, Barnes writes: "Gibbon represented a degenerate Empire – and there was a degenerate Empire which he represented. Manet represented a lunch, but there was no lunch which he represented. To imitate, let us say, is to represent not in the Gibbon fashion, but in the Manet manner."[47] In other words, Aristotle's *mimesis* is an imitation or representation not of the world as it is, but of the world as it might be – imitation gives flesh to objects of the imagination, which are themselves *interpretations* of the empirical objects that compose the world.[48]

To imitate in the Aristotelian fashion is thus to make oneself and others accord with one's interpretation of the world – it is to endow the world with an openness to knowledge, aims, and desires so as to make this world the means of their realization. It can therefore not be said that the human existed *as human* prior to the human world constructed in imitation. Through poetry, the world becomes a stage – a theatre for human life – but this does not mean that what is human exists prior to this performance. Other animals also engage in imitation by

thought that only the best kinds of people would form the audience, and this was certainly not the case in Aristotle's Athens. See Lear, "Katharsis," 315, 321. Cf. Curran, "Feminism and the Narrative Structures of the *Poetics*," 294; Euben, *The Tragedy of Political Theory*, 51.

44 Aristotle, "Poetics," 1447a14–17.

45 "Poetics," 1448b5–9.

46 Aristotle, *Metaphysics*, 980a21–27. Hereafter *Meta*.

47 Barnes, "Rhetoric and Poetics," 275.

48 Labarrière, "Imagination humaine et imagination animale," 22.

transforming the world around them in accordance with the interpretation they give this world through their life activity – imitation is not a uniquely human attribute. We must thus say that *mimesis* serves to crystallize certain potentials that are shared with other animals, such as sensation and imagination, giving them shape and so organizing them in a particular manner, which only subsequently come to be understood as human.

It is to this poetic or *mimetic* transformation of the given into the human world that Aristotle refers when he claims that "tragedy is an imitation of personages better than the ordinary man"; like a portrait painter, tragedy reproduces "the distinctive features of a man, and at the same time, without losing the likeness, [makes] him handsomer than he is."[49] By assigning tragedy the power to create an image of the human animal better than the reality, and better than the others that surround him, Aristotle is assigning tragedy the power to mark a break – both between humans and between humans and other animals. It is this poetic break that establishes the human as a distinct animal possessed of its own ends, actions, and virtues, and so its own good, all of which become identifiable beneath a single concept: human nature. Through tragedy, humans are distinguished from other animals, and furthermore, insofar as the tragic hero is a more complete articulation of human nature than an ordinary human being, tragedy offers a way of distinguishing between people – between those more like the hero, the embodiment of human nature, and those more like other animals. Thus, for Aristotle, "the poet's function is to describe, not the thing that has happened, but a kind of thing that might happen, i.e. what is possible as being probable [*eikos*] or necessary [*anagkaion*]." This function distinguishes the poet from the historian, placing him next to the philosopher as one concerned with "universals [*ta katholou*]."[50]

In providing an image of that which might be, of potentials not yet realized, poetry is more than simply an expression of human potentials: it must be viewed as endowed with the creative capacity to transform our knowledge of potentials and as providing a framework for formulating our interpretations of the world. Through this reinterpretation of our animal potentials, we come to understand our own potentials as different from those of other animals – we understand them as being uniquely human. We then endeavour to shape and transform ourselves according to this new image and so become human. Thus

49 "Poetics," 1454b8–11.

50 "Poetics," 1451a36–1451b10.

*mimesis* serves not only to create the world as a human world but also to create the human as the kind of animal that might populate this human world. In this sense, *mimesis* is not simply the expression of human potentials; it is also the activity that gives shape to that which is identified as human potential in the first place. Though what is properly human only distinguishes itself through human activity, human activity requires the mimetic tropes of tragedy to become intelligible. Thus it is only through artifice that human nature comes to be and be called natural. In this sense the human potentials staged in tragedy cannot be said to pre-exist tragedy – the artifice of poetry is not the expression of nature; rather, what is known of nature is bound to the artifice through which it is revealed.

We might thus say that tragedy for Aristotle is an art that allows for the organization of action as speech and gesture so as to create an image of the human being to serve as a normative ideal worthy of imitation, one that presents what is best in human life. Yet this ideal human being is precisely that – an ideal, if not an *Idea*. Even if we grant that, unlike Platonic Ideas, this human ideal is rooted in actually existing things, it represents an image of humanity that is not simply an expression of something already existing in the human world. It is only in striving toward this ideal, and in the particular capacities this striving is seen to express, that something like the human comes to exist and distinguish itself from the animal. We might thus see tragedy as a kind of "human guise" that teaches certain animals to be human through assuming a human role,[51] either directly as the actor on stage, or indirectly as a spectator identifying with the actions performed. While the speech and gestures may be nothing but "play-acting" at first – nothing more than a game – it is precisely through this game that what is human comes to differentiate itself from what is "animal" and becomes an evaluative measure that can be applied to hierarchically rank people as being closer or farther from this human ideal.[52] Politically speaking, tragedy as Aristotle conceives it thus serves to accomplish and perpetuate a division between higher and lower human types, rather than support the egalitarianism often associated with democratic Athens. The capacities Aristotle so painstakingly set out to differentiate humans from other

51 Cavell, *The Claim of Reason*, 380.

52 This break accomplished through tragedy bears a close relationship to theories of "speech acts." On how such theories relate to Greek thought and politics more broadly, see Ober, *The Athenian Revolution*, 11. Cf. Ober, *Political Dissent in Democratic Athens*, 38; Vernant, *The Origins of Greek Thought*, 49–50.

animals in his zoology, capacities that enable the human to emerge as a unique being, rest on an ideal of humanity set forth in Greek tragedy. It is thus by way of art that human nature can be identified as something other than simply animal.

Yet Aristotle does not himself acknowledge the creative dimension of the arts implied by his own analysis of tragic poetry; rather, he tends to treat human nature in his other writings as something inherent to humans. Furthermore, that the human is thought to differ from the animal according to capacities understood as superior to those of other animals enables a hierarchical relationship between human and animal that at the same time applies to differences between humans. Insofar as differences make some humans more and less fluent in the articulation of the most human capacities – closer to and more distanced from the human ideal displayed in tragedy – this hierarchical relation is now found to apply to human differences, making some humans more human than others.[53] In giving this hierarchical relation the appearance of nature, art serves to reconcile the human to the arbitrary limitations of its own concept, and the violence and domination upon which this hierarchy is based is conjured away. Unfortunately, it is this dimension of the Aristotelian problematic that has been its most enduring legacy.

**A Forecast**

Notwithstanding the violence and domination concealed in the Aristotelian problematic, Aristotle offers important insights for any attempt to transform the human/animal distinction. Chief among these are the following ideas: that other kinds of animals can be political, and therefore that other subjective possibilities might be politically drawn upon that are not, strictly speaking, human; that a life of leisure and beautiful activity shorn of the dictates of self-preservation is highest, as is found in Aristotle's philosophical ideal; and that art is political in that it might serve a role in producing both these other subjective possibilities and a life of leisure and beauty. I argue in the subsequent chapters that Adorno's work enables the theoretical recovery of these insights and, with them, the recovery of the promise found and betrayed in the Aristotelian problematic.

As for the manner in which my own discussion of Adorno's work will proceed, I treat Adorno's *oeuvre* as more or less a coherent whole. I do this not in alliance with the view that sees Adorno's philosophical

53 Heath, *Talking Greeks*, 32.

concerns, from his earliest work until his last, to be "monolithic, hewn of a single block,"[54] nor in necessary opposition to the view that sees a break between his early and late work,[55] and certainly not to ignore the objective contradictions that Adorno's individual works attempt to articulate that may be said to resist their reduction to a systematic or even non-contradictory whole.[56] Rather, I aim to examine Adorno's work as constellated around the Aristotelian problematic, so as to reveal a way to unbind the knot found therein. I aim to theorize a way of transforming the relation between human and animal, art and politics, so as to think the possibility of the subject transformed, the subject no longer constituted by and through the violence of self-preservation and the domination that frequently accompanies it – one for whom the word "human" would be an anachronism.

In this way I broadly follow Adorno in his "method" of arranging a combination of concepts around a centre that will, through their combination, be opened up to the patient reader. I do not, however, adhere to these dictates as strictly as does Adorno: the reader will find, perhaps to her relief, that I proceed much more linearly and progressively than does Adorno, making no sadomasochistic attempts to ensure that each line is equidistant from the constellation's centre. Moreover, the centre has been explicitly stated – another luxury Adorno denies his readers. In this way I have perhaps made too many concessions to the instrumental necessities of communication at the expense of truth: it might be objected that aping Adorno's "method" in this manner fundamentally misunderstands him, for what I am calling Adorno's "method" is not a method at all, but a technical response to the taboos placed on communication by society itself, entwined as it is with violence and domination.[57]

If thoughts and actions and the identities to which these are tied are all the expressions of a social whole organized around the requirements of domination, then to simply state one's aims and pursue them is to fall precisely into the trap laid by domination and thereby to articulate oneself in ideological terms. Because he refuses to declare the centre to be revealed, and rigorously attempts to bring each of his statements into line with that centre so that his argument grinds to a halt, Adorno's texts remain open to reinterpretation, for their grounding centre must be posited anew by each successive interpreter, who in so positing casts

54 Savage, "Adorno's Family and Other Animals," 105.
55 Bennett, "Modernity and Its Critics," 219.
56 Jay, *Marxism and Totality*, 266.
57 Cf. Hullot-Kentor, "Suggested Reading," 225, 230.

new light on the constellated statements. In this way Adorno attempts to use the cunning of reason to outwit himself, the ideological self that is the expression of sociopolitical domination. This is what it means to structure one's philosophy as a "message in a bottle": a note for the future that might, in revealing the historical contradictions captured in the message, reveal the distortion in their own time and thus the necessity of transforming it. For my part, I am simply trying to read this message in light of the Aristotelian problematic I have outlined, and so offer a way of theorizing a response. I leave it to the reader to decide whether these measures are sufficient to accomplish their aim.

Another theoretical problem arising from the use of Adorno's philosophy concerns the individual status of his concepts. The importance of concepts such as dialectic, non-identity, and *mimesis* for Adorno is difficult to underestimate, not only because of their frequent appearance throughout his writings, but also because he tends to resist giving his concepts independent treatment or definition. It might even be said that individual concepts are woven so deeply into the texture of his thought that any attempt to isolate one of them – to pull at it, as if it were a loose thread – would threaten to unravel the fabric in which it is found. Consequently, the discussion of individual concepts is something of a delicate process: too analytic an approach would only serve to isolate discrete threads, telling us little about the coat Adorno weaves, while too diffuse an approach would give us only a glance at that coat and so deny us the opportunity to grasp it and get a feel for its texture.

Adorno provides a clue for solving this problem in his discussion of the émigré in a foreign country learning to speak its language: overwhelmed by the ubiquity of strange words, one must learn to read without appealing to the authority of a dictionary or the rules learned in school, which serve only to formalize and inhibit direct contact with the foreign. Instead one must learn to recognize correspondences between words, combinations of words, and their different contexts. Such a passage will inevitably entail errors and blind alleys, but only through this kind of foundationless engagement with particulars can the meanings of words in their interrelation begin to take shape.[58] I will thus be placing my treatment of Adorno's concepts in relation to other statements in Adorno's work, and also to those of a variety of other authors, in order to weave these threads into similar garments, albeit

58 See Adorno, "The Essay as Form," 13. Cf. Adorno, *Gesammelte Schriften*, vol. 11, 21, hereafter *GSB11*. Adorno, *Hegel: Three Studies*, 107, hereafter *HTS*. Cf. Adorno, *Gesammelte Schriften*, vol. 5, 341.

different from the one Adorno presents, and so test the durability of his in smaller, more concentrated articles: more of scarf here, and a pair of mittens there, to continue with this metaphor, which, hopefully, will complement Adorno's coat.

It will be remarked that the various articles I weave in this book downplay some of the more prominent of Adorno's materials: Marx, Freud, and Weber, as well as other members or associates of the Institute for Social Research, such as Horkheimer and Marcuse. I do not deny the importance of these figures for Adorno's ideas, or even their relevance to the Aristotelian problematic, but their relation to Adorno's thought has already been much commented upon, and while that in and of itself does not indicate a saturation point, I have opted instead to illuminate other aspects of Adorno's thought and will be focusing on some of the many other thinkers referenced in his writings, along with a few others who have sought to engage directly with Adorno or whose works relate thematically or conceptually to his project. In interweaving discussions of these various thinkers I intend no definitive statement about what is of canonical importance in Adorno's thinking; instead, I use each only to help illustrate more localized problems as they emerge in my discussion of the concepts at hand.

I begin chapter 1 with an account of Adorno's relation to Aristotle and the way in which his ideas of dialectic and negative dialectic, identity and non-identity, thinking in constellations, and solidarity with metaphysics all can be seen to relate to the Aristotelian problematic and what they suggest as a possible response. In chapter 2, I apply Adorno's theoretical innovations to the concept of humanity by examining different ways in which "human" and its related terms appear in Adorno's work, arguing that Adorno uses humanity in multiple senses. I claim that it is only his idea of a "reconciled humanity" that represents for Adorno genuine progress, which is for him the possibility of a subject constituted through objects not beholden to self-preservation, violence, and domination. Yet insofar as humanity was constituted by and maintains itself through violence and domination, Adorno's "reconciled humanity" must be understood as a subject that is not, strictly speaking, human.

Chapter 3 develops the claim that reconciled humanity would not be human. It does so by examining the different roles animals play in Adorno's thought, in an attempt to show that animality is the non-identity of the human that the human must repress in its self-constitution, and thus that if this future subject is to be one not constituted through the kind of repression bound up with violence and domination, it must become some other, new kind of animal. I attempt to show

how one might strive toward this future animal subject by attempting to live *as if one were a good animal,* and with this in mind, I discuss the moral and political dimensions of this subjective transformation, thus offering a means by which mindfulness of suffering nature can be translated into practice.[59] It is here that the importance of art in moral/political education is ironically revived by Adorno, no longer to be used to produce what is human out of the animal and to reconcile that within an ordered, hierarchical whole as it was in Aristotle, but instead to liberate the animal from the human through aesthetic experience.

Adorno's solution to the Aristotelian problematic is the production of an *aesthetic animal,* and the practices that compose this production are the subject of chapter 4. An aesthetic animal is an animal constituted not simply through its senses (*aisthesis*), but through its relation to art, so as to build solidarity between subjects that might make possible the kind of sociopolitical transformation that could displace the centrality of violence and domination and usher in new forms of life. This is the future toward which Adorno's theoretical contributions gesture, constellated around the Aristotelian problematic. In this way, Aristotle appears less as a figure from which Western philosophy descends and more a messenger from its possible future, one in which humanity has become an animal for whom life is no longer constituted through its breaking upon the wheel of its own history.

59 Gandesha, "Homeless Philosophy," 273.

# PART ONE

---

## The Remnants of the Greeks, the Ruins of Humanism

*Chapter One*

# The Perils of Dialectic

But the *aporia* of our thinking points to a knot in the object.

– Aristotle, *Metaphysics*

## Adorno's Aristotle

Adorno is not known as a reader of Aristotle or as a scholar of the Ancients. Though affinities between Adorno and Aristotle are beginning to be noted,[1] Aristotle and the Greeks are still largely viewed as at best peripheral to the concerns that animate Adorno's work.[2] The use made of Homer in *Dialectic of Enlightenment*, and of Aristotle in *Minima Moralia*'s "ironic inversion" of the teaching of the good life,[3] are less attempts to elucidate antiquity (as with most classical scholarship) than attempts to understand modernity. It is modernity, not antiquity, that fascinates Adorno. Geuss goes so far as to claim that for Adorno, "relevant 'history' starts with Haydn in music, Goethe in literature, and Kant in philosophy." Apart from occasional mentions of Bach and Homer, and "isolated throw-away remarks about Plato and Aristotle," readers

1 The most sustained study of this affinity to date is Freyenhagen, *Adorno's Practical Philosophy*, ch. 9. See also Schweppenhäuser, *Theodor W. Adorno*, 49; Brassier, *Nihil Unbound*, 40. On the relation between critical theory and Greek tragedy more broadly, see Rocco, *Tragedy and Enlightenment*.

2 Indeed, a number of the major works that introduced Adorno's thought to the English-speaking world make no particular reference to the possible importance of Aristotle or the Greeks. See for instance, Buck-Morss, *The Origin of Negative Dialectics*; Jay, *Adorno*. Others, such as Seyla Benhabib, claim that any pretention to similarity between critical theory and Greek philosophy are "seriously misleading." See Benhabib, *Critique, Norm, and Utopia*, 6.

3 Bernstein, *Adorno*, 40–1.

will find "no discussion of any work or figure before the middle of the eighteenth century." Indeed, Geuss claims, "it was precisely the *absence* of the Greeks from Adorno's mind and philosophy" that gave him the freedom to focus on the themes that he did.[4]

That a kind of productive forgetfulness lay at the heart Adorno's thinking is a provocative claim. Geuss's remarks suggest that Adorno's philosophy is structured around the absence of the Greeks – of the very origins of philosophy – and thus emphasizes the anti-foundational aspects of his thought as well as his attempt to think "the new," in music and elsewhere.[5] But such a reading risks making the Greeks into the repressed that must return, a vast reserve of vital drives upon which Adorno's philosophy perches precariously, unconsciously following their directives. If Adorno's philosophy is only possible through the absence of the Greeks, then their appearances in "isolated throw-away remarks" amount to nervous tics, symptoms perhaps of the repressed trauma of origins that Adorno would all too happily escape if he could. The return of the Greeks then, would spell either Adorno's destruction, or his reform, as the therapeutic intervention he needs to overcome the damages of life, to put down roots, and to cultivate virtue. In other words, the entrance of the Greeks into Adorno's thought would make a good Greek of him, lending foundation and system to his thought and to the moral and political practices Adorno claims have been set adrift. In this vein, to read Adorno in light of the Greeks is either to dismiss him outright or to find in him a reluctant colleague of contemporary Aristotelians such as MacIntyre and Nussbaum. But another view of this relationship to the Greeks, and to Aristotle in particular, is possible.

We might say that antiquity for Adorno is not *forgotten* at all, but *alienated* – the Greeks, and Aristotle in particular, are appropriated less as the sources of philosophy, and thus as necessary precursors from which Adorno's own thought organically grows, than as objects foreign to it. The Greek *thaumazein*, or "wonder" that in Aristotle precipitates philosophy, is in Adorno a "shock" that serves not as the origin but as a disruption and reorientation of thinking around the object that impinges.[6]

---

4 Geuss, "Outside Ethics," 61n56.

5 In his early essay, "The Idea of Natural History," Adorno provisionally defines history not as a search for origins, but as the movement in which that which is qualitatively new appears. See Adorno, "The Idea of Natural History," 111. Cf. Adorno, "Die Idee der Naturgeschichte," in *Gesammelte Schriften*, vol. 1, 347, hereafter *INH* and *GSB1*.

6 Aristotle, *Meta.*, I.2 982b12–13; for an equation between *thaumazein* and shock, see Adorno, *INH*, 118; *GSB1*, 357.

As "isolated throw-away remarks," references to Plato and Aristotle in Adorno's work are like the scattered contents of a thief's pockets: torn from their own context and placed into one they could scarcely have fathomed, Plato and Aristotle are alienated from their traditional place of authority in the history of philosophy, becoming foreigners in Adorno's texts.[7] As such, references to them might be treated as Adorno does foreign words.

In an early text, Adorno claims that against the "purism" that sees language as a natural or organic growth, foreign words must be defended as "foreign bodies assailing the body of language."[8] True words are not "buried ur-words" that can be "mythically evoked," that is, they do not lay at the origin through which what is has come to be, and whose discovery is therefore necessary in order to understand what has come to be. Rather, true words can for us only be "the artificial words," the "made words," which serve to express the alienation of language from itself, the alienation of language split between the demands of communication and the possibility of a true name.[9] For Adorno, communication mobilizes words as tools for working upon things and is ruled by an authority that assigns its means and ends, while the possibility of a true name is the possibility of a peaceful accord between words and things, and thus a language not treated as an instrument. It is this later conception of truth, an excess irreducible to the exigencies of communication, which gives foreign words their force. Foreign words capture this division at the heart of language, but the antagonism they express toward the body of a language can only be legitimated in a different conception of language, the true naming that for us exists only in the negative, in the fragments of the disintegrating body of language. These fragments continually undermine and threaten to overtake this language, as though they were "the language of the future" germinating.[10]

7 Cf. Adorno, "The Actuality of Philosophy," 35; *GSB1*, 341.

8 Adorno, "On the Use of Foreign Words," 288; *GSB11*, 642. Cf. Adorno, "Words from Abroad," 186; *GSB11*, 218.

9 While Benjamin's influence has been noted here, one can also find Hegelian reasons to praise foreign words. In his *Science of Logic*, Hegel notes that Latin terms often serve as technical terms in philosophy due to their less immediate and more "reflected" character. The dual pull Benjamin and Hegel exert on Adorno's thought will be further discussed below. See Weber Nicholsen, *Exact Imagination*, 67; Lee, *Dialectics of the Body*, 64; Hegel, *Hegel's Science of Logic*, 107. Hereafter *SL*.

10 Adorno, "On the Use of Foreign Words," 288–91; *GSB11*, 642–6. Cf. Adorno, "Words from Abroad," 190; *GSB11*, 221. For a more thorough consideration of Adorno's ideas on language than is possible here, see Gandesha, "The 'Aesthetic Dignity of Words,'" 137–58; Hohendahl, "Adorno"; Larsen, "The Idiom of Crisis."

If references to Greek philosophers like Plato and Aristotle in Adorno's texts can be treated in the same way he treats foreign words, then they are not meant simply to point backwards, to what philosophy has been, and so to explain the present as their descendants. If foreign words exist as fragments at the fraying edges of a language, and stand, as Adorno claims, not for a past from which this language has organically grown, but for the possibility of the language transformed, of its future incarnation, then Plato and Aristotle appear in Adorno's writings as messengers from the future. But for what future might Adorno's references to the Greeks possibly stand? Ironically, it is in an attempt at communication that a possible answer to this question is given clearest definition. Adorno gives his most sustained treatment of any Greek thinker in a series of lectures he delivered on metaphysics in 1965: for a good portion of the first two-thirds of these lectures, Aristotle is Adorno's object of study.

For Adorno, the relevance of Aristotle's *Metaphysics* revolves around two related issues: (1) the manner it relates the universal to the particular, or form to matter; and (2) the possibility of change.[11] Neither of these are for Adorno purely theoretical questions; indeed, they have strong moral and political implications.[12] With respect to the first issue, Adorno claims that Aristotle rejects the Platonic separation between universal Ideas and the world of particular things, attempting instead to bring these two together and so attempt to think the universal through instances of particularity. In thus insisting on the necessity of particulars to grasp the universal, Aristotle opens up the question of *mediation* (*Vermittlung*), the question of how exactly it is that a universal inhabits something particular and can be known through it. Adorno will hold, however, that despite posing the problem of mediation "with extreme clarity [*mit aller Schärfe aufgeworfen*]" Aristotle nevertheless fails to arrive at a genuine concept of mediation.[13] Without a concept of mediation, Aristotle ultimately remains unable to grasp how change is possible.

11 See Adorno, *Metaphysics*, 25, 81. Hereafter *MCP*. Cf. Adorno, *Nachgelassene Schriften* no. 4, *Vorlesungen* vol. 14, 43, 128–9. Hereafter *NSAV14*.

12 In an earlier lecture series on moral philosophy, Adorno claims that "the central problem of moral philosophy" is the relation between the particular and the universal, and that moral philosophy is itself closely connected with practical activity and the political sphere. See Adorno, *Problems of Moral Philosophy*, 18, 2–3. Cf. Adorno, *Nachgelassene Schriften* no. 4, *Vorlesungen* vol. 10, 33, 9–11. Hereafter *PMP* and *NSAV10*.

13 *MCP*, 46; *NSAV14*, 74.

For Adorno, change happens through extremes: it is only in surpassing the limit that binds a thing, the point at which a given object defines itself, that something can be said to change. Dialectic, as the thinking of passage, of the movement between terms, thus presents itself as the means of thinking change. A dialectical understanding of mediation would be one capable of grasping the unity of opposites – the identity of extremes. Only by pursuing these extremes past their limits might a third term, something *new*, appear. Aristotelian mediation falls short of dialectical mediation because it posits a middle term as something existing between the two extremes, not through them. That is, rather than grasping the extremes, and moving through them to see where they lead, Aristotle turns back from these extremes, seeking refuge instead in a "happy medium [*rechten Mitte*]," a point that is not too close to the limits of one end or the other.[14] The mediating term is thus one available among the existing options lying between the two poles, rather than something new arising from the extremes as they surpass their limits. Adorno thus argues that Aristotle is not a dialectical thinker, and moreover that "the dialectic did not exist at that time,"[15] a claim that seems to abruptly contradict much of what is thought about Aristotle and the Greeks today. While vastly different contemporary scholars have referred to Aristotle's dialectical use of concepts,[16] the idea that the dialectic did not even exist in Aristotle's day seems to be an even stranger claim, one that is worth attempting to clarify if we are to understand Adorno's reading of Aristotle and consequently the place of Aristotle in Adorno's works.

In his *Metaphysics*, Aristotle distinguishes between the sophist, the philosopher, and the dialectician (*dialektikoi*). Although all three concern themselves with many of the same objects of study, Aristotle claims that the philosopher uniquely concerns himself with the being (*on*) common to these things, and thus has a claim to real knowledge, whereas the sophist merely imitates the knowledge of the philosopher, differing from him with respect to his choices.[17] The dialectician, by contrast, differs from the philosopher in that he relies on a different

14 *MCP*, 47; *NSAV14*, 75–6.

15 *MCP*, 31; *NSIV14*, 52.

16 See for instance Frank, *A Democracy of Distinction*, 7; Lord, *Education and Culture*, 30.

17 That is, the sophist is a kind of *crude* philosopher, one whose choices show a lack not in philosophical ability but in practical wisdom. In this sense, the sophist is a kind of *upstart* who applies philosophical methods of questioning in ways he ought not. Cf. Aristotle, *Rhet.*, I.1 1355b17–18. Cf. Adorno, *Minima Moralia*, trans. Jephcott, 244. Hereafter *MM*. Cf. Adorno, *Gesammelte Schriften*, vol. 4, 280. Hereafter *GSB4*.

power or capacity (*dunameos*) than the philosopher, remaining "merely critical" of things rather than knowing them in their being.[18] Though Aristotle does not indicate precisely here what capacity it is that the philosopher relies upon that the dialectician does not, if what separates the philosopher is knowledge of the truth of what *is*, then given the discussion of the powers that compose human beings above, it must be commune with the divine *nous* that enables the philosophical grasping of being, and to which the dialectician is indifferent.

That the dialectician engages with the objects of philosophical study in a manner that remains beneath that of *nous* and philosophy would appear to accord with what Aristotle has to say about dialectic elsewhere in his work, especially in the *Rhetoric*. There Aristotle claims that dialectic is closely related to rhetoric: both refuse to be limited by any single branch of study, but concern themselves with virtually all objects of knowledge – all objects "that call for discussion."[19] Dialectic concerns itself with deductions, real and apparent, so it also concerns arguments that, while established among people as reputable, may in fact be spurious.[20] Moreover, Aristotle claims that along with rhetoric, dialectic is the only art capable of drawing opposite conclusions from its premises.[21] In this sense, while dialectic must be closely related to *logos*, it is bound to the particular utterances of language, *dialektos*, which may not necessarily be reducible to that which is, and thus might even be said to speculatively overreach being in a manner similar to poetic fiction.

That the above distinctions appear to relegate dialectic to a space beneath philosophy suggests that Aristotle did not consider himself to be *simply* a dialectician. However, it remains to be seen exactly what is missing in Aristotle's definition of the dialectic to legitimate Adorno's claim that not only did Aristotle not think dialectically, but that such a form of thinking was not available to him. Indeed, much of what Aristotle says about dialectic above resonates with Adorno's ideas concerning dialectic: namely, its critical bent, indifferent to the knowledge of being or *ontology*, along with its close ties to language and to rhetoric.[22] But these similarities are not enough. The crucial element missing in Aristotle's account of the dialectic is the concept of constitutive

18 *Meta.*, 1004b15–26.

19 *Rhet.*, 1354a1–5; 1355b6–9; 1358a10–17; 1356b33–1357a3.

20 *Rhet.*, 1355a8–10; 1355b16–18; 1402a3–8.

21 *Rhet.*, 1355a34–35.

22 Adorno, *Negative Dialectics*, 136; 55–6. Hereafter *ND*. Cf. Adorno, *Gesammelte Schriften*, vol. 6, 140, 65–6. Hereafter *GSB6*.

subjectivity, and for Adorno that is sufficient to say that dialectic did not exist in antiquity at all.[23] That is, the objects available to dialectic are transparent to Aristotle in a way they are not to the post-Kantian Adorno. For Aristotle, dialectic is a way of making deductions concerning speech-objects that are directly connected to the objects themselves. Or put differently: the concepts considered by Aristotle to be available to speech and so to the dialectic are not projected upon objects through the cognitive power of a speaking subject; rather, these concepts inhere in the objects themselves.[24] Objects are what they are because that is what they are: the circularity of the identity of concept and object is what Aristotle's philosopher *discovers* by thinking the object in its being. Identity is not produced by the subject for Aristotle – identity is not simply a way of perceiving or speaking about an object, it is an ontological truth. It is for this reason that Adorno calls Aristotle a thinker of both immediacy *and* mediation, for though Aristotle thinks that universals are necessarily mediated through particulars, he sees this mediation as existing simply and immediately at an ontological level – a particular object is what it is and can be known as such through the inherence in it of a universal concept.[25]

Dialectic is for Aristotle less exacting than philosophy because it focuses on the speech-objects irrespective of their truth or falsity, irrespective of how they relate to being. In this manner, Aristotle reduces the speculative excess of dialectic to falsity: where dialectic draws conclusions about speech-objects that fail to correlate with an object at the ontological level – that is, they refer to something that *is* not – then these conclusions are false. If the speculative excess of dialectic is false, then dialectical deductions are true where their conclusions correlate with what is. Dialectic might thus be said to overlap with philosophy where it concerns correct deductions related to being; but where it speculates on that which does not correlate with anything in being, there it exceeds philosophy to the detriment of knowledge. By reducing the speculative excess of dialectic to the false, and truth to what correlates with being, Aristotle renders dialectic incapable of grasping movement and change, for the coming into being from nothing that is becoming is only intelligible on the side of being – the speculative excess necessary to grasp the passage of something coming into being is excluded in advance as false. Thus Aristotle is capable of writing that one *becomes* a

23 *MCP*, 48–9; *NSIV14*, 77–8.
24 *MCP*, 55–6; *NSIV14*, 88.
25 *MCP*, 31; *NSIV14*, 52.

certain way because that is the way one *is*: "the process of becoming attends upon being and is for the sake of being, not *vice versa*."[26] Change is thus not transformation, but the successive revealing of what already is. Dialectic as the compulsion of thinking to grasp change is thus denied in Aristotle, making him an undialectical thinker. However, this does not preclude the possibility of thinking dialectically through Aristotle, as Adorno does, by looking to that which Aristotle's thinking would exclude.

Adorno thinks that Aristotle's undialectical conception of mediation fortuitously gestures toward that which is excluded from its conception, and thus the possibility of thinking change. Adorno finds this possibility most readily apparent in Aristotle's formulation of the conceptual pair of form and matter. For Aristotle, form gives shape to matter, which on its own is indeterminate and lifeless: form is the actuality of matter, while matter is the potentiality of form. Yet Adorno claims that in stripping matter down to simple potentiality, to an empty state of potency prior to all determination, Aristotle has given conceptual articulation to something non-conceptual.[27] When matter is defined as an indefinite striving toward definition, as something *unformed* without which form could not be, the power of form as actuality is made dependent on a second power, the power of matter to become actualized in form.[28]

Insofar as the actual is what *is*, and the potential is what *might be*, or that which has the power to be something other than it is, it would appear that Aristotle has here inadvertently subordinated form to matter. The concept of matter refers to the non-conceptual in form, or what is non-identical to form. The question of change and transformation, whose mythical articulations in the concepts of fate and chance were banned by "the Greek enlightenment" and its philosophical inquiry into being, returns in the concept of matter.[29] Adorno will claim that

26 *GA*, 778b4–6.

27 *MCP*, 67; 80; *NSIV14*, 107, 127.

28 This discussion bears a striking affinity with Ernst Bloch's work around the same time, and what he calls the "Aristotelian Left," whereby figures such as Avicenna led the way in reformulating the relation between form and matter as it had been inherited from Aristotle, placing a greater emphasis on the potency or even agency of matter. See Bloch, *Avicenna and the Aristotelian Left*, 21, 23, 37, 39. Indeed, there is a good chance Adorno had this text in mind. Bloch's book was published in German in 1963, just two years prior to Adorno's lectures, and we know that Adorno and Bloch were in personal contact during this period. See Müller-Doohm, 420–1, 432.

29 *MCP*, 75; *NSIV14*, 117–19.

matter (*hyle*) becomes a kind of repository for mythical categories displaced by form: namely, fate (*anagke*) and chance (*tyche*). As the indeterminacy upon which determinate form depends, matter contains the potential for the actualization of form to go awry, to fail to hit its mark or realize its *telos* in the fully flourishing actuality of form. Thus it is through matter that form may be disrupted and its impermanence revealed. Aristotle's *Metaphysics* fails to grasp the concept of change, yet its failure indicates the point of departure from which a possible solution to the problem of change might spring: one must look to that which is excluded from the concept, the indeterminate array of material that Adorno will call the non-conceptual, or the non-identical.

It is in the light of the non-identical, of that which the concept excludes, that the isolated references to Aristotle and the Greeks scattered throughout Adorno's writings must be interpreted. Adorno's references to the Greeks point toward the future in which they might be redeemed, both as obstacles to the realization of this future and as promises of its possibility. That is, Aristotle's philosophy has an ideological function, which in supporting the status quo in which it was conceived erected conceptual barriers to social and political change; yet at the same time, his philosophy's manner of erecting these barriers produced remainders that undermined itself, pointing toward its own transcendence. For instance, Aristotle is guilty of being complicit with domination for his insistence on the superiority of contemplative to practical activity. As the greatest good, contemplation becomes indifferent to the task of changing the world and is thus colonized by the dominant political forces of the day, as witnessed in the fall of the *polis* and the form of *praxis* particular to it that accompanies Aristotle's praise of the life of contemplation.[30] Yet this emphasis on contemplation that allows for complicity between Aristotle's philosophy and the destruction of Athenian political life at once provides a critique of the very life that would replace it: the promise of "blissful contemplation" divorced from "the exercising and suffering of violence" transforms "the resignation of the Hellenistic private citizen" into a protest against the state of the world.[31]

Likewise, Adorno finds Aristotelian aesthetics to be complicit with "ruling interests" in that they theorize the task of art as being to provide an "aesthetic semblance" of the satisfaction of the needs and instincts of the public. In this sense, Aristotelian catharsis is a "substitute

30 *ND*, 244; *GSB6*, 242; *MCP*, 92; *NSIV14*, 146.

31 *CM*, 267; Adorno, *Gesammelte Schriften*, vol. 10.2, 769. Hereafter *GSB10.2*.

satisfaction," akin to what will be appropriated and managed by the culture industry more than two millennia later.[32] Yet in seeking "the effect of art in the affects of individuals," Aristotelian aesthetics preserve a kind of experience that is irreducible to political exigencies, and thus make, notwithstanding their complicity with domination, a promise that things might be other than they are.[33] And perhaps most importantly with respect to politics, while Adorno accuses Aristotle of having fused "inner worth" with the status made possible through property and enshrined in law, thus making the "good man" one "who rules himself as he does his own property,"[34] Aristotle will also limit the power of the rule of this law through his concept of equity (*epieikes*). Against the "abstract legal norm," in equity we see a turn toward the particulars that cannot be subsumed under the generality of the law and thereby assimilated to the order of property over which the "good man" rules. In the light of the non-identical, equity becomes the promise of justice beyond the rule of what can be equalized as property, and this is why Adorno claims that Aristotle's concept of equity is to his "imperishable glory."[35]

In light of the non-identical, that which eludes the concept, Adorno's references to Aristotle form a force field of statements concerning the relation of metaphysics to the possibility of a transformed world. This transformed world, the future of which Aristotle is made to speak, is one he both denies and promises: his conceptual innovations militate against their own transformation, and thus the transformation of the world, yet in doing so they produce a remainder that points in the opposite direction – one that suggests something else is possible. Insofar as Adorno finds in the origin of metaphysics the kernel of its other, the non-identical that carries within itself a compressed history of displaced origins, the origin of metaphysics is found to be no origin at all. Rather, it is a reference point along the trajectory of domination, carrying within it the scars of this domination while at once gesturing toward something else. Just as Adorno writes in the "Finale [*Zum Ende*]" to his *Minima Moralia* that "the only philosophy which can be

32 Adorno, *Aesthetic Theory*, 238. Hereafter *AT*. Cf. Adorno, *Gesammelte Schriften*, vol. 7, 354. Hereafter *GSB7*.

33 *AT*, 202; *GSB7*, 301.

34 Adorno, *MM*, 185; *GSB4*, 210.

35 *ND*, 311; *GSB6*, 305. Cf. *PMP*, 124. For a similar interpretation of Aristotelian equity, see Yack, *The Problems of a Political Animal*, 194. For a critique of the critical capacity of Aristotelian equity sympathetic to Adorno's project, see Menke, *Reflections of Equality*; 193–7. Cf. Menke, *Spiegelungen der Gleichheit*, 174–9.

responsibly practiced in the face of despair" attempts to contemplate all things "from the standpoint of redemption," so his references to Aristotle and his metaphysics are attempts to "displace and estrange" Aristotle's thought and thereby reveal "its rifts and crevices, as indigent and distorted as it will appear one day in the messianic light."[36] So illuminated by the light of its other, Aristotle's metaphysics becomes citable in its relation to this future, to its possible transformation.[37]

Adorno's famous declaration of solidarity with metaphysics "at the time of its fall,"[38] which concludes his *Negative Dialectics,* is precisely this: a solidarity with metaphysics through its determinate negation, which both recognizes the contemporary impossibility of a metaphysical system yet continues metaphysical speculation in the form of attending to that which lies beyond the concept, the point at which, as in Aristotle, the material particulars split their conceptual casing and so compel a transformation of the conceptual world.[39] This determinate negation of metaphysics will have been at the same time a determinate negation of Aristotle's thought, and as such, an attempt to solve the problems concerning the relation between the human and the animal, and the relation between art and politics, as they appear in the Aristotelian problematic. In this way, Adorno must be seen as a critic of Aristotle, but one bound to the Aristotelian problematic – a thinker whose anti-Aristotelianism takes up the challenge Aristotle's philosophy poses and attempts to "string the bow" that Aristotle has left for posterity.[40] How Adorno's fate in this endeavour might differ from that of other "suitors" will depend on his approach. To better elucidate this approach and the possible consequences for the transformed conceptual world Adorno inhabits, along with the place of humans, animals, art, and politics therein, we must now ourselves turn to the non-conceptual, to that which Adorno calls "non-identity," and of course its relationship to identity and to the concepts that form the core of Adorno's contribution to philosophy.

---

36 *MM*, 247; *GSB4*, 283.

37 Cf. Walter Benjamin: "only a redeemed mankind [*erlösten Menschheit*] receives the fullness of its past – which is to say, only for a redeemed mankind has its past become citable in all its moments." See "Theses On the Philosophy of History," 254. Cf. Benjamin, *Gesammelte Werke*, vol. 1.2, 694. Hereafter *GWB1.2*.

38 *ND*, 408; *GSB6*, 400.

39 Or what has been called "a post-metaphysical version of the metaphysical project." See O'Connor, *Adorno*, 101–8.

40 It will not, as we shall see, mean a simple revival of "a no longer tenable ontology of nature." See Benhabib, *Critique, Norm, and Utopia*, 7.

## Non-identity and Dialectic

As seen above, the core problems that Adorno highlights in Aristotle's metaphysics concerning the possibility of change and the relation between the universal and the particular remain unresolved, and the moral and political dimensions of these problems remain for Adorno the most pressing of their kind. Adorno claims that the central problem of moral philosophy is likewise the relationship of "the particular interests," or "the behaviour of the individual," in relation to the universal, and that this question relates to "the question of the organization of the world" and the "quest for the right form of politics," inasmuch as such a politics is possible today.[41] Aristotle's claim that a discrepancy exists between the best human life and the best citizen, thus making the best human life dependent upon political organization, becomes revolutionary in Adorno, for whom "there is no right life in the false."[42] That is, the moral quest for the good life cannot be divorced from the political task of changing the world so that life might no longer be false, that political organization will no longer be an impediment to the good life. To declare one's solidarity with metaphysics at the time of its fall is to take up these problems in their interrelation. But in examining what Adorno understands to be the core problems of Aristotle's metaphysics, it was found that he relies on a conception of dialectic whose relation to non-identity and the messianic requires further development if the particularity of Adorno's use of this term is to be understood.

In the preceding look at Aristotle's metaphysics, it was found that a conception of mediation is required in order to relate the universal and the particular and thereby grasp the relation between things and their concepts and how these relations might change – that is, grasp how to think or conceptualize something that changes. It was also found that Aristotle's conception of mediation fails in its attempt to grasp the relationship between the universal and the particular in a manner that might accommodate the possibility of change, and that consequently a dialectical conception of mediation is necessary, for only a dialectical conception of mediation seeks to grasp things as they are and as they pass beyond the limit that defines them as what they are. In this sense, it might be said that dialectical thinking attempts to think objects both in their identity – that is, in the conjunction of concept and object – and in their non-identity, in the disjunction between concept

41 *PMP*, 18, 176; *NSIV10*, 33, 262.
42 *MM*, 39; *GSB4*, 43. Translation modified.

and object created by changes in the object. As the object changes, it sheds its identity with the concept. Dialectic attempts to think this movement by formulating concepts so as to enable their revision according to the changes in the object. The object is constantly undergoing changes, and dialectical concepts are constantly being revised by these changes so as to re-establish the identity with the object lost through its change. Thus, non-identity in dialectical thought precipitates identity: it is the open door that dialectical thinking is forever closing. But here we must ask: is this continued attempt to re-establish identity within non-identity consonant with what Adorno has in mind with his turn *toward* the non-identical, toward the *other side* of the concept? Is Adorno's attempt to see in things their "rifts and crevices," their indigence and distortion, simply a means to better capture them conceptually and thereby continue the expansion of the conceptual domain?

We must answer that no, Adorno's turn toward non-identity is not carried out in the same vein as past dialectical thinking – his aim is not to seek identity in non-identity and thus simply to better conceptualize the world. But this is not to suggest that Adorno then makes a fetish of indigence and distortion, celebrating the failure of the concept to establish identity with its object, as if freedom lay in their discord.[43] Rather, what Adorno denies is the separation between thinking and acting that would make possible the peaceful concord of concept and object in a thinking subject, despite the discord of a world in which that subject's actions are the result of compulsion.[44] So long as our sociopolitical world remains organized in such a way that we must act in accordance with the exigencies of our unequal standing in that world – either as dominated or as dominator – then the very texture of our thinking will be coloured by this organization. For Adorno, to think that an object is sufficiently captured by a concept is to legitimate its place in the prevailing conceptual order bound to its sociopolitical order – it is to deny that either the object or the order in which it has definition could be otherwise. To perpetually seek out identity in non-identity, to set out and attempt to conceptually capture that which lies outside the concept, is from a normative perspective to support the status quo, the world as it exists characterized by domination, even beyond one's intentions or explicit professions of support or condemnation.

43 Indeed, it is worth noting here that one of Adorno's earliest uses of the term "non-identity" is in describing Auschwitz as a remainder that cannot be assimilated to the Hegelian conception of history or concepts of civilization and progress as they have been inherited. See Silberbusch, *Adorno's Philosophy of the Nonidentical,* 11.

44 Adorno, "Marginalia to Theory and Praxis," 261; Adorno, *GSB10.2,* 761–2.

Yet to recognize a compulsive and even violent element in thinking should not then lead us to the conclusion that it would be better not to think at all – such a life is not possible or desirable. Rather, thinking can only abjure violence to the extent that the society in which it takes place abjures violence. In a society where violence is deemed abhorrent yet is perpetuated in multifarious forms each day, we should not be surprised to find that thinking presents a peaceful accord between concept and object that denies the existence of its remainder. This identity would hide anything that falls outside of the concept, just as public denunciations of violence unconnected to sociopolitical change that might inhibit future violence only serve its perpetuation. To turn toward this remainder, the non-conceptual or non-identical, in the manner Adorno would is to use the violence of thought against itself in order to reveal the radical insufficiency of the prevailing conceptual order and thereby compel its reorganization. This thinking is the cognitive equivalent of what would be for the prevailing sociopolitical organization a revolution. However, it is worth asking at this juncture: how is it possible to *think* a revolution that is not being enacted at the sociopolitical level, if Adorno denies the separation of thinking and acting that would allow each a sphere independent of the other?

It is here that we must return to the "messianic light" that illuminates the other side of the concept in the "Finale" of *Minima Moralia.* When one posits the future as a utopia in which the struggles that animate the present are no more, one is capable of seeing in these struggles what *will have been* the promise of their redemption, a promise that would otherwise go unrecognized. It is for this reason that Adorno can write that "the question of the reality or unreality of redemption itself hardly matters,"[45] for redemption is itself *posited* by thinking in order to think against the thinking bound up with compulsion – it is a conceptual trick made at the expense of concepts, possible thanks to the historical possibility of thinking's own redemption in a changed future. Insofar as the future remains unknown, the possibility of its being radically other than the present cannot be disproven, so the ruse lives in this unknown, drawing interest from a principal that may or may not prove redeemable. In this way thinking is able to orient itself to the world and its own activity so as to work against the compulsion that animates their organization, instigating a revolution in thought that might, one hopes, contribute in some way to a revolution in the organization of society. The political ramifications of this thinking, including its relation

---

45 *MM,* 247; *GSB4,* 283.

to art and aesthetics, will be taken up in chapter 4. At present, it must be seen what this "revolution" means for the dialectic.

Just as certain concerns of Aristotelian metaphysics are illuminated by this messianic light and made Adorno's own, so is dialectic, especially the Hegelian variety, illuminated and harnessed toward Adorno's project. Throughout his texts, Adorno repeatedly notes Hegel's affinities with Aristotle,[46] yet by placing Hegel in relation to Benjamin's messianic conception of history, he also draws Hegel away from Aristotle and toward Benjamin in a manner that allows for the redemption of the promise of the dialectic that had been denied by the dominion of identity. We might say, following a simile used by Adorno to describe Benjamin, that just as "everything that fell under the scrutiny of his words was transformed, as though it had become radioactive,"[47] so the Hegelian dialectic too becomes "radioactive," mutating or decaying so as to be transformed from what it was in Hegel. This mutated form of the dialectic, one turned not to establishing identity in non-identity, but rather to finding the non-identical in the identical, is what Adorno calls *negative dialectic*.[48]

However, Adorno makes little attempt to forge an analytical distinction between negative dialectic and the traditional understanding of dialectic, and he will frequently refer to the dialectic and his negative dialectic interchangeably. For instance, in *Negative Dialectics* he claims that dialectic says simply that objects leave a remainder beyond their concept, so the attempt to conceptualize an object produces a contradiction in the conceptualizing subject between the object of experience and the conception of it. To think dialectically is to persist in this experience of the non-identity between concept and object, driven by the "inevitable insufficiency" of our thinking to erase this contradiction.[49] Or put

46 See for example, *MM*, 185; *GSB4*, 210; *MCP*, 79; *NSIV14*, 124; *ND*, 25, 135, 337; *GSB6*, 36, 208, 331; *AT*, 108; *GSB7*, 165. For a more sustained and systematic attempt to link the philosophies of Aristotle and Hegel than anything attempted by Adorno, see Ferrarin, *Hegel and Aristotle*.

47 Adorno, "A Portrait of Walter Benjamin," 229; Cf. Adorno, "Charakteristik Walter Benjamins," in *Gesammelte Schriften*, vol. 10.1, 238. Hereafter *GSB10.1*.

48 *Contra* Jay, who acknowledges the importance of Benjamin for Adorno's negative dialectic yet claims that Adorno's relation to Hegel often serves to bring him closer to Lukács than to Benjamin. On my reading, it is precisely through Benjamin's conception of the messianic that Adorno will appropriate Hegelian dialectic. See Jay, *Marxism and Totality*, 251, 254. On this influence more generally, see Jameson, *Late Marxism*, 52; and more comprehensively, Buck-Morss, *The Origin of Negative Dialectics*.

49 *ND*, 5; *GSB6*, 17.

differently: to think dialectically is to conceptually reflect upon the gap in our experience that both divides concept and object and promises their possible reconciliation. Defined in this manner, if only imperfectly and provisionally, Adorno's understanding of dialectic appears to differ little from the Hegelian one. The dialectic that animates Hegel's philosophy, Adorno writes, is "the permanent confrontation of the object with its concept ... the unswerving effort to conjoin reason's critical consciousness of itself and the critical experience of objects."[50] Hegel himself, supposedly in a conversation with Goethe, called the dialectic "the organized spirit of contradiction,"[51] and in taking up these contradictions, Hegel's philosophy attempts to express the non-identical, even if this very attempt identifies it in the process.[52]

But here is where the difference between Hegel's dialectic and Adorno's comes to light. Adorno wants to express non-identity in a way that does not suppress it beneath identity, in a way that turns the conceptual toward the non-conceptual without the latter being simply devoured or "crushed" by the former.[53] While the Hegelian dialectic appears more or less indistinguishable from the one championed by Adorno, the former variety "is untrue when measured against its own concept."[54] Hegel's dialectic opens up the possibility of thinking through the passage between contradictory particulars with neither foundation nor origin remaining permanent or fixed,[55] yet his idealism forbids this passage, seeking instead to make an absolute subject the foundation of this movement. For Hegel, it is only through the activities of consciousness culminating in an absolute subject that all particulars find unity and so are assigned fixed identities in a totality. The absolute subject, or spirit, is at once found to be the origin of the process and its goal – the constitutive conception of the subject needed for dialectic noted by Adorno above becomes in Hegel the ultimate guarantor of objects in their particularity, for the subject does not simply project concepts onto objects;

50 Adorno, *HTS*, 9–10; *GSB5*, 258.

51 *HTS*, 43; *GSB5*, 287. Cf. Bernstein, who writes: "Negative dialectics, austerely thought, is nothing other than the reflective version of the experience of contradictions." Bernstein, "Negative Dialectic as Fate," 37.

52 *HTS*, 101–2; *GSB5*, 336.

53 Hegel compares thought's negation of the given to eating and claims that what "human beings strive for in general is cognition of the world; we strive to appropriate it and to conquer it. To this end the reality of the world must be crushed as it were, i.e., it must be made ideal." See G.W.F. Hegel, *The Encyclopaedia Logic*, §12; §42, *Addition 1*. Hereafter *EL*.

54 *HTS*, 17; *GSB5*, 264.

55 *HTS*, 13; *GSB5*, 261.

rather, the truth of the objects themselves is for Hegel to be found in these projections, in their *ideality*.[56] Thus there is a preponderance of the subject and the concept over the object in Hegel that, like Aristotle's metaphysics, falls back into a static conception of the totality of the world and of the positive identities of the objects therein.[57]

The image of the circle employed so frequently by Hegel underscores the stasis of totality: things are not transformed into new things, but rather preserve an identity with what they become *concretely* (or, as Aristotle says, in their *actuality*) with what they always already were *abstractly* (or, as Aristotle says, *potentially*) through the successive stages of the development of consciousness.[58] Though we might say that Hegel approaches Benjamin's messianic conception of history with his insistence that the beginning is only found to have been the beginning at the end, and thus is always already mediated by the end in which it will be discovered to have been the beginning,[59] this retroactive positing of foundations ensures that the end is likewise mediated by its beginning and thus is never something alien to it. Insofar as the beginning retroactively posited by the end is never "an arbitrary or merely provisional assumption,"[60] recognizing that the development of a thing is at its end depends upon a version of that end already having been present in the beginning.[61] The end must grow out of the beginning, even if the beginning can only be fully known in the end, and the necessity of this organic link serves to transform Hegel's messianic moment into theodicy. Hegelian theodicy ensures that rather than being caught in a messianic light that illuminates their radical otherness from themselves, things necessarily progress along a given trajectory, developing into the complete form of what they always already were in embryo.[62] In this way, Hegel's idealism arrests the passage of his dialectic in a static system of identity.[63] Adorno's turn to Benjamin and the messianic is thus an attempt to split

56 Hegel, *EL*, §11–12, §14; Hegel, *Phenomenology of Spirit*, §802.
57 Adorno, *ND*, 7, 27; *GSB6*, 18, 37.
58 *ND*, 156; *GSB6*, 158. Cf. Hegel, *EL*, §15.
59 Hegel, *SL*, 71–2.
60 Hegel, *SL*, 72.
61 Hegel, *SL*, 74.
62 On Hegel's expanded use of the concept of theodicy and its relation to reconciliation, see Geuss, "Art and Theodicy," 83. For presentations of Hegel in the context of Adorno's work that attempt to avoid theodicy or metaphysics, see Shuster, *Autonomy after Auschwitz*, ch. 4; Bowie, *Adorno and the Ends of Philosophy*, ch. 3.
63 Or as Hegel writes concerning the transition from becoming to determinate being, but which can be seen as a summary of the movement of his dialectical idealism generally: "Becoming is an unstable unrest which settles into a stable result." See *SL*, 106.

the unity of dialectic and idealism found in Hegel and thereby open up the possibility of a dialectical experience in Hegel's "freedom toward the object"[64] irreducible to idealist categories and the circle of their organic development. Indeed, Adorno rests the very possibility of philosophy having any future at all on the possibility of there being dialectical experience "independent of the idealistic machinery" emphasized by Hegel.[65]

Thus, while Adorno's negative dialectic owes a great deal to Hegel's dialectical idealism, he is not, as Bernstein claims, simply continuing the Hegelian tradition beyond the point at which Hegel had left it, in the manner available to one attempting to do so "after Marx, after Nietzsche, and above all after two centuries of brutal history in which the moment to realize philosophy … was missed."[66] Though the contradictions found in a world shaped by organized compulsion and domination ensure that dialectic remains the shape of thinking, in order to turn toward the non-conceptual and thereby separate dialectic from idealism Adorno must do violence to Hegel – violence that brings Adorno closer to grave-robber than legal heir.[67] Bernstein fails to grasp this, for he fails to distinguish between Hegelian dialectic and Hegelian idealism: Bernstein claims that though Adorno's Hegelianism is *unorthodox*, he nevertheless "accepts the rudiments of Hegelian idealism."[68] While there remains some argumentative flexibility in the term "rudiments," we have seen above that Adorno's approach to Hegel, though deeply indebted to the Hegelian dialectic, is equally opposed to the idealism in which the Hegelian dialectic is framed. For this reason, Adorno's negative dialectic must be seen not as an organic growth pushing itself up through the fertile soil of Hegelian idealism, but as an attempt to think against Hegelian idealism by introducing into it the messianic, as *a foreign body assailing the body of this philosophy*. So, rather than perpetuate Hegelian philosophy, Adorno, through the immanent critique of the dialectic this foreign intrusion precipitates, "explodes Hegelian idealism."[69] Freed from idealism, the remnants of the Hegelian dialectic

---

64 Adorno, "Opinion Delusion Society," 110; *GSB10.2*, 579.

65 *ND*, 8; *GSB6*, 19; See also O'Connor, "Adorno's Reconception of the Dialectic," 541.

66 Bernstein, "Negative Dialectic as Fate," 20. Nor does this make Adorno a Nietzschean, as we shall see below. Cf. Rose, *The Melancholy Science*, 71.

67 Indeed, for those who view Hegel's philosophy as inextricable from his idealism, Adorno's modification of terms such as contradiction, mediation, reflection, and determinate negation amounts to a rejection of the Hegelian project as such. See Rosen, *Hegel's Dialectic and Its Criticism*, 161–2; 176–7.

68 Bernstein, "Negative Dialectic as Fate," 19.

69 *ND*, 329; *GSB6*, 322.

might pursue their passage between contradictory particulars bound by neither origin nor foundation.

## Constellation of Objects

But what might be the moral and political import, if any, of Adorno's immanent critique of the dialectic, and how might these relate to the concerns of metaphysics? And moreover, how can negative dialectic be an "immanent" critique of Hegel's dialectical idealism, if it employs a concept *foreign* to Hegel? If the messianic comes from outside the body of his philosophy, then how can it at once be "immanent" to it?

Most generally, one might call Adorno's critique of the dialectic "immanent" insofar as he employs the dialectic to engage in critique of the dialectic. However, there is more to this critique than simply the self-application of the dialectic, for Adorno also claims that Hegel's philosophy "is untrue when measured against its own concept."[70] That is, it is not simply a matter of being dialectical where Hegel was not; rather, it is a matter of being dialectical where Hegel *ought to have been*, had he pushed his own philosophy past the limits he set for it. Thus, Adorno's foreign "assault" upon the body of Hegel's philosophy has with it also an element of *recovery*.[71]

For the purposes of this discussion, we can isolate two reasons why Adorno is able to insist that negative dialectic is an "immanent" critique of Hegel's dialectical idealism, even if he must employ a concept foreign to Hegel to accomplish this. The first is that dialectic, as Adorno claims, shows that objects are never subsumed beneath concepts without leaving a remainder.[72] The implication here is that dialectic is always pushing beyond itself, always creating a limit whose recognition already presupposes some notion of what lies beyond the limit. Thus to claim that knowledge has been realized in the totality of a system is, dialectically speaking, to gesture toward what might lie beyond the limits of that system, what remains unknown, as the remainder produced in the movement that establishes the totality of the system. In this sense, the passage of the dialectic that allows for the building of a

70 Recall *HTS*, 17; *GSB5*, 264.

71 That Adorno employs Hegel against Hegel has often been remarked upon, though it remains a matter of debate as to whether or not Adorno succumbs to the same problems he would criticize. For some recent treatments of this question, see Bauman, "Adorno, Hegel, and the Concrete Universal"; Coyle, "The Spiritless Rose"; Schecter, "Unity, Identity, and Difference."

72 Recall *ND*, 5; *GSB6*, 17.

system also makes possible that system's destruction, for the creation of stable knowledge through dialectic at once produces an outside to that knowledge that threatens its stability. Thus the movement immanent to the very concept of dialectic already militates against the closure that idealism would impose upon it, pointing instead toward what lies beyond itself. In this sense, that which transcends the dialectic is already immanent to dialectical movement: dialectic, as self-transcendence, has transcendence immanent to its own concept.

This brings us to the second reason why Adorno's use of "the messianic" or "redemption" can be considered part of an immanent critique of dialectical idealism. That is, the messianic transcendence of the dialectic cannot be said to be completely outside the dialectic's own movement. As a conceptual "ruse," redemption is without positive existence or identity in the present; yet at the same time, it does not forgo the possibility of both of these in the future. Whatever content can be assigned to that which lies beyond the passage of the dialectic can only be a projection of the immanent movement of the dialectic, of the conflicts that animate society in the present. Yet at the same time, insisting on a ban of utopian images – of images of the world transformed beyond its constitutive conflicts – is equally a projection of the movement of the dialectic and the perceived needs of struggle in the present.[73] The very availability of a concept of redemption for Adorno to turn against identity and synthesis, thus allowing for a turn in the movement of the dialectic toward non-identity, is itself a product of the dialectic and the social conflicts it articulates. Its positive instantiation, however, would mean the end of the dialectic, for it would mark the end of the split in experience that dialectic expresses.

The object, in its resistance to the suffering it endures through its identity with the concept, seeks its transformation, its freedom to not be measured against the concept. The suffering of the object here refers not simply to the experience of pain, but to experience as such. Insofar as the experience of the object made identical to a concept is mediated by that concept, the object *suffers* this identity and its concept – identity strives to define the limits of experience available to the object.[74] The

---

73 On Adorno's use of the *Bilderverbot*, see Webb, "If Adorno Isn't the Devil."

74 Though Adorno has been criticized for drawing on an undifferentiated – even "un-dialectical" – conception of suffering, the multiple uses he makes of suffering in his work imply a more complex conception, which would include the meaning I give it here, even if he often does not draw clear distinctions between different kinds of suffering. See Raymond Geuss, "Suffering and Knowledge in Adorno," 128–30. Cf. Freyenhagen, *Adorno's Practical Philosophy*, 144–9.

suffering of this limitation cannot be distilled to a limitation of inherent rational capacities, as Honneth argues, for rational capacities are not inherent for Adorno; rather, they are tied to sociohistorical possibilities that mediate bodily comportment. When they are taken to be inherent, rational capacities are bound up with the limits that identity-thinking would impose on objects and thereby contribute to this suffering.[75] Thus, insofar as its conceptual identity fails to capture its own lived experience – that is, its own persistence and transformation in time – the object desires to be free of this identity, and these desires take the shape of the messianic, or redemption: or rather, redemption/the messianic is the conceptual reflection of the desire for transformed experience – transformed life.[76] Redemption is born in the immanent movement of the dialectic, as the desire that things be otherwise – redemption only *appears* to come wholly from outside, and so be *foreign* to this movement, insofar as idealism, in its attempt to build a closed and complete system, served to relegate the unstable remainders produced by the movement of the dialectic to the outside of this system. In this sense, while negative dialectic is the dialectic illuminated by the "messianic light" of redemption, it is at the same time the *recovery* of the possibility immanent to the concept of the dialectic as a transcendence of itself, a self-transcendence betrayed by Hegelian idealism.[77]

Nevertheless, in turning back to the former set of questions concerning these philosophical speculations and the practical world, it might be said that just as logic, metaphysics, and politics were deeply conjoined in Hegel,[78] so do they remain in Adorno. Negative dialectic

75 Honneth, "A Physiognomy of the Capitalist Form of Life," 60. On some anthropological consequences of these claims, see chapters 3 and 4 of this book.

76 Cf. Hullot-Kentor, "Suggested Reading," 230.

77 *Contra* Buchwalter, who claims that Adorno practises a "transcendent critique" that remains at the level of abstract negation. Buchwalter claims Adorno dissociates any possible meaning between the realms of life and death, thus precluding the possibility of the determinate negation necessary to change the world as it exists, for this would require finding in this world some kind of truth or meaning. Though Adorno does indeed deny the possibility of there being meaning or truth in the Hegelian sense for what transpired in Auschwitz, what this means for Adorno is that it is no longer possible to be Hegelian, not that the world cannot be changed. Compared to one who would be simply Hegelian after the transformation of the basic conditions of his philosophy, Adorno's attention to the transformed constitution of the object reflects a *greater* concern with the immanence of critique to socio-historical change and the possibilities available therein, not less. See Buchwalter, "Hegel, Adorno, and the Concept of Transcendent Critique."

78 *HTS*, 95; *GSB5*, 330.

aligns itself with the central concerns Adorno highlighted in Aristotle's metaphysics – namely, the questions of the relation between the universal and the particular and the conceptualization of change – which for Adorno are at once the central problems of moral philosophy and the most salient problems facing politics. Liberated from the foundation of idealist origins that would predetermine its passage, negative dialectic would attempt to think a different relation between the universal and the particular, one that Adorno calls, against the idealism from which he has attempted to separate this dialectic, *materialist*. As Jarvis notes, this materialism is "not a set of fixed metaphysical or methodological commitments," nor is it "a dogmatic ontology stating that only matter is real";[79] rather, it is an orientation to the world, a manner of reinterpreting it in light of the contamination of thinking by its other, by the trace in thinking of what is not thinking but that makes thinking possible. To follow the trace of matter in thinking and to insist on reinterpreting concepts in its sense is to turn against the concept of the constitutive subject that is necessary for dialectical thinking, and that in Hegel's idealism reigns supreme, toward a preponderance of the object.[80]

Adorno calls the object "the positive expression of non-identity," and as such, it is little more than a "terminological mask" for material that can otherwise only be grasped in its particularity.[81] To turn toward the object, to accept its preponderance, is thus to recognize all the particulars in their irreducible variety that form the substance of both thought and the thinking subject, and thus to limit and so end the power of the constitutive subject of idealism. We might say that putting an end to the constitutive subject of idealism is for Adorno the prime moral and political task of philosophical speculation; thus the turn toward the preponderance of the object is at once a philosophical, moral, and political endeavour.[82] While the object can only be conceived by a subject, its otherness to the subject is irreducible: the object is never simply subject; rather, subjectivity remains only a moment of the object. Moreover, what is called subject is itself always also an object – its own objectivity is inescapable. Thus in the subject/

79 Jarvis, "Adorno, Marx, Materialism," 80, 97.

80 For an account of this "preponderance of the object" with respect to contemporary object-oriented philosophy, see Morgan, "A Preponderance of Objects."

81 *ND*, 192; *GSB6*, 193.

82 In its turn toward the object then, negative dialectic is perhaps something more than "the conceptual homage the subject pays the object's resistance." See Gordon, *Adorno and Experience*, 129.

object polarity, object preponderates: it is simultaneously subject *and* object.[83] Yet Adorno insists that the preponderance of the object does not, or should not, establish a new hierarchy between these terms,[84] one where subjectivity is perpetually *reduced* to objectivity, where the concept is reduced to its material conditions, and so explained away. The objectivity of matter is never simply immediate, for *object* is itself a concept, a "positive expression" of the non-conceptual, and hence presupposes the cognition of a subject. A negative dialectical grasp of subject and object, then, involves seeing in each the manner in which their reciprocal permeation fails to coalesce in a stable identity.[85] Subject and object are together an expression of non-identity: they are constituted through their non-coincidence with each other and as such remain "negative throughout."[86]

The negativity of subject and object found in objective preponderance means that the transformation of a given array of objects provokes a transformation of the subject, for the subject is subject through cognition of these objects. That is, the material designated by the concept of *object* includes both the sociopolitical factors that shape the activities available to a given body, and the body itself, predisposing this body to a certain range of relations with its world, including a range of objects of cognition. In relating to the world through its activities and the understanding of these activities, that is, through thinking, a subject is born. To attempt to think the preponderance of the object is to deny the fixed character of subjectivity as itself constituting the objects of cognition, insisting instead on being open to being subjectively transformed through different relations to the object. To be open to the object, to its primacy, is to rend the veil that subjectivity would weave around the object by seeing in the object subjectivity's own contingency. As the subject "is the agent, not the constituent,"[87] of the object – that is, as the subject has an objective core – one must seek after the object not in the absence of the subject but *through* it.[88] Where the subject is found to be at its most particular and contingent, there the object will be.

Thinking toward the object without reducing it to something constituted subjectively thus requires for Adorno that it be placed relative to

83 *ND*, 183; *GSB6*, 184–5. Cf. Adorno, "On Subject and Object," 249–50; *GSB10.2*, 746.
84 *ND*, 181; *GSB6*, 182.
85 *ND*, 139; *GSB6*, 142. Cf. Adorno, "On Subject and Object," 255; *GSB10.2*, 753–4.
86 *ND*, 174; *GSB6*, 176.
87 Adorno, "On Subject and Object," 254; *GSB10.2*, 752.
88 Adorno, "On Subject and Object," 250; *GSB10.2*, 747.

other objects in what he calls, following Benjamin, a "constellation."[89] Here again, we find Adorno making use of a kind of conceptual trick played against concepts themselves, for the placing of objects in constellation is itself a subjective act that works against subjective preponderance. The objects in constellation illuminate in each other the non-conceptual that each on its own would hide. Torn from their organic context and placed in a foreign set of relations established by the thinking subject, they lose the ability to speak their own names, and so to repeat their ideological function, instead becoming readable together as "a sign of objectivity."[90] In unlocking the non-conceptual from the conceptual, like "a safe-deposit box,"[91] this constellation of objects, while itself the work of subjective cognition, at once allows for the release of the grip of the cognizing subject. That is, just as the individual objects are transformed in the relation made possible through the constellation, so is the cognizing subject transformed through its relation to this transformed object. The constellation, through its transformation of the objects of cognition, thus evokes a new subject, one that would possibly replace the subject that served to bring the constellation together in the first place.

Thinking in constellations, this attempt to neutralize the violence of thought by turning it against itself, comes closest to the "distanced nearness" of the non-violent contemplation that would be possible in a transformed world.[92] Releasing the subject from its own grip, it allows for an experience of the *weight* of the object, of the suffering that is

89 Benjamin, *The Origin of German Tragic Drama*, 34. Cf. Benjamin, *Ursprung des deutschen Trauerspiels*, in *Gesammelte Schriften*, vol. 1, 215. The affinities between Adorno and Benjamin have led rightly to the claim that on certain themes "it is difficult to specify the precise location of the boundary between them." See Weber Nicholsen, *Exact Imagination*, 53. Concerning the boundary between these two thinkers on the question of constellations, see Jarvis, *Adorno*, 175–6.

90 *ND*, 165; *GSB6*, 167.

91 *ND*, 163; *GSB6*, 166. Cf. Adorno, "The Actuality of Philosophy," 35; *GSB1*, 340.

92 *MM*, 89–90; *GSB4*, 100. It must be emphasized here that thinking in constellations is not in and of itself non-violent. As noted above, Adorno denies the kind of separation between thinking and acting, or individual and society, that would enable one to simply stop being violent *tout court*, as though through an act of individual will, or as Marder writes, by "*refusing* to reproduce the idealist absorption of the object into the subject" (my emphasis). Insofar as our thinking is social *all the way down*, it is permeated by social violence. Thinking in constellations mimics what would be non-violence in order to point in its direction, but one cannot on one's own pretend to have so mastered one's own powers of cognition – most of which are involuntary – to simply accomplish this through an act of individual refusal. A truly non-violent society is a prerequisite for non-violent cognition. See Marder, "Minima Potentia," 67.

otherwise hidden,[93] and for the possibility of a new subject constituted through this constellation of objects. Yet this power of constellations to transform subjects must itself be seen as being drawn from the "messianic light" projected from the suffering object, rather than as the subject through which a constellation is constituted. That is, as the subject is the agent of the object, not its constituent, a constellation must be seen as the subjectively produced response to the resistance of the object to conceptual capture. In placing objects in constellation, the subject hopes to reveal or even generate non-conceptual affinities among them. A non-conceptual affinity is a relation, either a similarity or a difference, which does not operate at the conceptual level – it is a similarity or difference between objects that it not part of their conceptual identity. Constellating different objects so as to express non-conceptual affinities thus reveals non-conceptual dimensions of the constellated objects, which bring the identity established between these concepts and their objects into contradiction. A constellation of objects thus reveals how objects might relate to one another otherwise, and so reveals the tenuous, fragile, and contingent nature of the conceptual order that presents itself as total, necessary, and complete.

In this way Adorno forges a new conceptual relation between particulars. *Contra* the idealist relation in which the universal exists over and above particulars as their origin and foundation, thereby reducing them to simple moments of the universal's necessary trajectory, Adorno theorizes the universal as emerging only in a particular and subjectively produced constellation of objects. His negative dialectic, which illuminates the reciprocal permeation of subject and object and their instability as tenuous moments in a clash of particulars, serves to think against Hegelian idealism and the absolute subject enshrined therein, theorizing instead the possibility of subjects produced in and through a new constellation of objects, and thus existing against the totality in which the subject is but a relay point in this totality's reproduction. However, while it has been claimed that as in Hegel, dialectical logic, metaphysics, and politics all remain inextricably intertwined in Adorno, some of the more salient consequences of his recasting of the relation between the universal and the particular through negative dialectic must be examined. Specifically, it remains to be seen what exactly Adorno's revolution in thinking might mean for the human/animal distinction as formulated by Aristotle in relation to art and politics. It is to these questions we now turn.

---

93 *ND*, 18; *GSB6*, 29.

*Chapter Two*

# Variations on a Theme: Humanity and Progress

As we have seen, Adorno's negative dialectic, the turn toward the primacy of the object, and thinking in constellations, all have in common an attempt to make clear in thought that which evades thought but makes it possible: that which is non-identical to the concept. This turn toward the non-identical is called by Adorno "an axial turn"[1] of the Copernican revolution in philosophy; but unlike Kant's Copernican turn, which attempted to organize human knowledge into metaphysical categories grounded in a transcendental subject, Adorno's turn toward the object and the non-identical is intended to show the impossibility of such a subject. Adorno thinks that in order for there to be concepts, there must be subjects who think them; however, the primacy of the object means that this cognizing subject is always constituted in relation to these objects and is thus constantly being displaced and transformed by the shifting constellation of different objects. The turn toward the object thus reveals the tenuous and fragile nature of the subject: non-identical with itself, the subject is incapable of serving as the stable ground upon which objects can be definitively known. Even the Kantian categories of *a priori* apperception, space and time, as general as these are, can no longer serve as a stable foundation, for even though space and time can always be found to structure a given subject's cognition of an object, these cannot be abstracted from the subject's particular experience of them in the object so as to form an unchanging substratum of experience. The subject is the *how* of the object,[2] a report on the experience of its

1 *ND*, xx; *GSB6*, 10.
2 Adorno, "On Subject and Object," 250; *GSB10.2*, 746–7.

ever-changing constellation.[3] As such, space and time are always experienced in a particular array of constellated objects and are inseparable from them, just as is the given subject of these objects. To isolate from this experience an unchanging substratum, even one so general as to be constituted only by space and time, is to reduce experience to an expression of *a priori* conditions, making these conditions into a wall standing between subject and object, vivisecting the subject's lived experience of the object.[4]

Yet if Adorno's turn toward the object thus attempts to express the subject's non-identity with itself, what consequences might this turn toward non-identity entail for *political* subjects, specifically, the subject of *humanism*? In the above account of Aristotle's conception of the human being and its relation to other animals, it was possible to isolate different capacities that Aristotle considers to be uniquely human, and those shared with other animals. The uniquely human capacities, such as *nous* and the different capacities bound up with *logos* that underscore

---

3 This is not to make the subject–object relation itself a transcendental condition of experience, and Adorno a transcendental philosopher, as does O'Connor. Though the elegant simplicity of O'Connor's argument is seductive, it must be rejected, for Adorno claims that the very existence of the subject-object relation is "the result of a coercive historical process" that must not be "transformed into an invariant." Subject and object are themselves concepts, and to make them the condition of experience would be to undermine Adorno's turn toward the object, which is precisely an attempt to displace the primacy of concepts, showing that though they mediate experience, they are not its unchanging condition of possibility. However, we must still emphasize that the experience of the non-identical is bound up with conceptual thinking, for the non-identical is experienced as the failure of concepts. For this reason I am wary of Macdonald's term, "primary experience," which seems to suggest an experience outside or even prior to the conceptual, and hence, in rejecting the transcendental position, comes dangerously close to an equally misleading empiricism. See O'Connor, *Adorno's Negative Dialectic*, 15; Macdonald, *What Would Be Different?* 21; 23. Cf. Bernstein, *The Fate of Art*, 189, 250; Adorno, "On Subject and Object," 246; *GSB10.2*, 742.

4 What we might experience as subjective continuity through internal experience such as memory is not, therefore, the product of the machinery of subjectivity, but continuities that persist in the objective constellations of our experience. For instance, insofar as individual subjectivity is bound to a body, the changed constellation of objects that serves to displace and transform our subjectivity still includes our bodies and its changes. The birth of a new subject in a changed constellation of objects is only as different from past subjects as the object is different from past objects. It is worth noting that this conception of the subject bears a striking affinity to certain Buddhist ideas which hold that consciousness of an object should not imply a "self" insofar as we think of a self as a kind of enduring subject with a separate existence. See Thompson, "Self-No-Self?," 168. For a comparison of Adorno and certain Buddhist ideas, see Horowitz, "Adorno and Emptiness."

supposedly human activities such as thinking, speaking, deciding, and recollecting, were found to be unequally distributed among human beings. Though these capacities can be enabled or obstructed through political organization and cultivated or corrupted through the arts, the basic set of capacities available to individual human beings is thought to be fixed and unchanging, at least insofar as Aristotle fails to acknowledge certain consequences of his *Poetics*, as we have seen above. Insofar as Aristotle does not acknowledge the creative power of the arts that he sets out in the *Poetics* to shape and transform conceptions of nature, we can say that Aristotle has a *positive* conception of the human being, in that the plurality of human life can be subsumed beneath a single concept, identical to itself.

To place Adorno in dialogue with Aristotle on this issue, and so to apply Adorno's turn toward the non-identical to this concept of the human being and its difference from other animals, is thus to trouble this concept of the human being. If the subject is without foundation, enthralled instead to the continually shifting constellation of different objects, then what continuity can there be among humans across time and place?[5] What can serve as the transcendental conditions of humanity if transcendental conditions have themselves been called into question? Though Adorno and his colleagues at the Institute for Social Research, what is now called "the Frankfurt School,"[6] have been considered examples of the *Marxist humanism* that emerged philosophically in response to the discovery of Marx's "Economic and Philosophic Manuscripts," and politically against Stalin and the Soviet Union, Adorno's turn toward non-identity must be seen as a critique of the "species imperialism" of humanism[7] and a challenge to the positive Aristotelian conception of human being.

However, Adorno uses the word *human* and its related terms in several different ways. To get a better grasp of what the human being *might be* according to Adorno and his philosophy of non-identity, I will give an account of two of the most prominent conceptions of the human being found in his work. The first, what we might call the *actuality* of humanity, if it were not for its negative character, concerns the ways in which Adorno thinks humanity exists, fitfully and inconsistently, in a world where life is "false." Humanity here is not a positive condition or self-identical subject, but rather exists only in opposition to *in*humanity,

5 See Adorno, "The Problem of a New Type of Human Being," 462.
6 On issues surrounding the term "Frankfurt School," see Wellmer, *Endgames*, 251–2.
7 Jay, "The Frankfurt School's Critique," 296.

as the other of the inhumanity perpetuated by the world. The second form of humanity we might call the *potential* of humanity, if not for the fact that this potential is without any positive existence, nor is it unchanging – it might even be said to be *produced* through the resistance to inhumanity that constitutes the first kind of humanity. This second form of humanity is what Adorno calls "reconciled" humanity. Like Adorno's utopian speculations noted above, reconciled humanity does not actually exist, but rather lives off the promise of a future positivity that may or may not ever be realized. I follow my consideration of this reconciled humanity with an examination of Adorno's often overlooked conception of progress, which I argue is necessary to connect these two different accounts of humanity.

In this way, I use Adorno to begin to formulate a response to the Aristotelian problematic that has shaped our relations to art, politics, and other animals. I argue that, though it would appear that through his condemnation of the inhumanity of the world Adorno gestures toward a humanity *to come*, and thus that the idea of what would be human has remained until now merely a promise of a kind of subject that has not yet been, Adorno's descriptions both of inhumanity and of this reconciled humanity suggest that what would lie on the other side of the struggles of "prehistory" is not human, but a different kind of animal. As such, the concept of humanism, and even the word "human," are deeply misleading and encourage the perpetuation of a cycle of violence, the dialectic of enlightenment, from which Adorno's utopian speculations on the end of humanity would escape.[8]

### Humane Humanity

Adorno's complex relationship to the concept of "humanity" or the "human," and thus the difficulty of referring to him as a humanist,[9]

8 Thus the promise of Adorno's thought is not "emancipated humanity," as Vázquez-Arroyo argues, but humanity *emancipated from humanity*, a point developed below. See Vázquez-Arroyo, "Minima Humana."

9 By "humanist" I mean a more expansive idea than the modern tradition arguably beginning with the French Revolution and the "Declaration of the Rights of Man and the Citizen." "Humanist" and "humanism" in this sense concern not simply the practical promotion of aims considered to be human, or human rights, but the theoretical centrality or necessity of the human being. In this broad sense, the philosophical anthropologies that have underscored much of the political theory of the Western tradition – that is, their ideas of what a human being necessarily is and what they understand to be the political consequences of this – are humanist, even if they do not necessarily promote the kind of practical or political humanism

can perhaps be grasped most starkly by opposing two statements made on the subject in lecture courses he delivered in the 1960s. In a lecture given on 27 July 1965, part of a series of lectures he gave on the topic of metaphysics, Adorno refers to "the infinite possibility [*unendliche Möglichkeit*] which is radically contained in every human [*Menschen*] life," and he even tells his audience: "You may think me an old-fashioned Enlightenment thinker, but I am deeply convinced that there is no human being [*Menschen*], not even the most wretched, who has not a potential which, by conventional bourgeois standards, is comparable to genius."[10] It is hard to find a more succinct statement on humanism than this reference to the "infinite possibility" and even "genius" of every individual human being, merely awaiting realization. Broadly speaking, we might say that these statements are consistent with contemporary interpretations of Aristotelian humanism, such as those of MacIntyre and Nussbaum.

Yet just two years earlier, on 25 July 1963, in a lecture given on the problems of moral philosophy, Adorno told his audience that he "is reluctant to use the term 'humanity' [*Humanität*]" in discussing questions of "the good life," for this term "is one of the expressions that reify and hence falsify crucial issues merely by speaking of them." Moreover, Adorno recounts a story of declining to join the Humanist Union, telling its members: "I might possibly be willing to join if your club had been called an inhuman union, but I could not join one that calls itself 'humanist' [*humanistisch*]."[11] How are we to make sense of the apparent contradiction found between these two statements? Is it possible that by 1965, Adorno's views on humanity and humanism had changed from what they were only two years earlier, and that Adorno's later humanistic statements represent an Adorno who had put aside his earlier reservations? Or is Adorno opposing a progressive form of human being (*Menschen*) to a regressive one (*Humanität*)?[12] As I will attempt to show, Adorno never abandoned his reservations concerning humanism, and though Adorno does describe different forms of humanity in opposition to one another, their progressive and regressive vectors will

---

we see today. In this regard there is a largely unacknowledged affinity between Adorno and that infamous enemy of "theoretical humanism," Louis Althusser. See Althusser, "The Humanist Controversy."

10 *MCP*, 132–3; *NSAV14*, 206–7.

11 *PMP*, 169; *NSIV10*, 251.

12 Or perhaps Adorno, ever the subtle listener, could hear in "Humanist Union" echoes of the "friends of humanity" and their abysmal legacy of colonial violence. See Gilroy, *Postcolonial Melancholia*, 60.

be contextually specific and unstable so as to prohibit being identified by a single term everywhere and always. It is thus necessary to examine Adorno's positive uses of the term human and its related concepts to understand why he expresses more solidarity with the notion of an "inhuman" union than a human one.

Adorno's statements regarding humanity defy any attempt to see in his thought an initial disillusionment with humanity following the Second World War that would eventually give way to a more optimistic view of human life. Rather, Adorno's comments on humanity reveal a curious relation between an extreme pessimism and an extreme optimism that remains fairly consistent throughout his work.[13] For instance, while the apparent pessimism of the major works that Adorno completed during his American exile has been much commented upon, in conversations recorded with Horkheimer in 1956, Adorno insists that he does not "believe that human beings [*Menschen*] are evil when they come into the world" and that humans "are not as bad as all that by nature."[14] Moreover, he claims that "freedom truly consists only in the realization of humanity as such [*der Verwirklichung der Menschheit*]."[15] What he might mean by a humanity that has been realized will be examined further below; first, however, we must confront numerous other remarkably sanguine statements regarding humanity in the present that are scattered throughout his work.

In his role as a public intellectual in postwar West Germany,[16] Adorno frequently employed the terms *Menschen* and *Humanität* and their cognates in outlining the political tasks necessary to build the kind of culture that might resist fascism and its tendencies. In radio lectures delivered in 1965 and 1966, he claimed that the principal task of education was nothing less than the "debarbarization of humanity [*Entbarbarisierung der Menschheit*]"[17] and that this "debarbarization" had been less successful in the German countryside, where democratic and humanistic values had yet to become firmly entrenched.[18] Against the political

13 Freyenhagen, *Adorno's Practical Philosophy*, 1.

14 Adorno and Horkheimer, *Towards a New Manifesto*, 47–8. Hereafter *TNM*. Cf. Adorno and Horkheimer, "Nachtrag zu Band 13," 50. Hereafter Horkheimer, *GSB14*.

15 *TNM*, 50; Horkheimer, *GSB14*, 51.

16 Adorno's reputation in the contemporary Anglo-American world as an aloof cultural mandarin often serves to obscure the degree to which he was in fact a kind of public figure in West Germany, frequently appearing on the radio and publishing in major newspapers. See Huhn, "Introduction," 3.

17 Adorno, "Taboos on the Teaching Vocation," 190. Cf. *GSB10.2*, 672.

18 Adorno, "Education after Auschwitz," 196; *GSB10.2*, 680.

imposition of these values, which remained in the Germany of his day "nothing more than [the] formal rules of the game," Adorno cited the "real humanitarianism [*realer Humanität*]" found in the United States, where the "political form of democracy is infinitely closer to the people [*den Menschen*]" and where daily life was marked by "an inherent element of peaceableness, good-naturedness, and generosity."[19]

"Peaceableness," or freedom from compulsion, appears throughout Adorno's writings as what might be the promise of humanity. He writes that it is the separation between theory and practice, and so the possible disjoining of thinking from the compulsions of practical activity, in which "humanness awakes [*erwacht Humanität*]."[20] The ability to rigorously discipline one's particular actions by applying universal rules in the Kantian fashion would make one "more of a monster than a human being [*Mensch*]."[21] To recognize in an individual only their membership in a universal category, and so ignore their particularity, is precisely to deny them their humanity [*Menschliche*][22] and with it the possibility of non-violent or non-compulsive universality. Indeed, Adorno claims that humanity is nothing but the *resistance to force*, the resistance to violence and compulsion.[23]

In this way Adorno appears to advocate a negative or non-identical notion of humanity.[24] Like his turn towards the preponderance of the object that served to limit the transcendental function of the subject, making it instead the agent of the object rather than its foundation, Adorno's non-identical conception of humanity would make humanity not a transcendental subject whose basic potentials are already given in advance of their actualization, but rather a subject constituted in resistance to the forms of domination that organize the objective world. Humanity, or human subjects, would thus be continually reconstituted around new objective constellations, always pushing against the forces of compulsion found therein. The concept of humanity in this sense would point toward the non-conceptual, the other side of the positive order of domination.

It is perhaps for this reason that Adorno claims that while we cannot know positively what the human (*Menschliche*) or humanity (*Humanität*) is, we can recognize that the *inhuman* (*Unmenschliche*), and thus "the

---

19 Adorno, "Scientific Experiences," 240; *GSB10.2*, 735.

20 Adorno, "Marginalia to Theory and Praxis," 267; *GSB10.2*, 768.

21 *PMP*, 156; *NSIV.10*, 232.

22 *MM*, A116, 182; *GSB4*, 207.

23 *ND*, 286; *GSB6*, 282.

24 Cf. Adorno, "Zu Ulrich Sonnemanns 'Negativer Anthropologie,'" 262–3.

concrete denunciation of the inhuman," is a more appropriate expression of moral philosophy than "vague and abstract attempts to situate man [*Menschen*] in his existence."[25] Positive conceptions of humanity serve the inhuman in two different but related ways. First, positive conceptions present humanity as already reconciled to the existing order, one wherein violence remains among the tools at this order's disposal, and thus rob humanity of its utopian potential by making it the subject of this order and a possible agent of its violence. Second, positive conceptions of humanity establish the human in the place of the transcendental subject, thus making its abstract and eternal qualities the frame of reference through which experience of the object can be reported, thereby dulling the possible experience of this object and rendering humanity deaf to the possible suffering therein. In rejecting these positive conceptions of humanity, Adorno uses the concept of humanity against itself, opposing its promise to its actualization, and in this way attempts to compel it beyond itself, in perpetual dissatisfaction with what the constituted order would represent as humane and good.

This opposition between negative and positive conceptions of humanity might thus allow us to explain the apparent contradiction noted above in Adorno's attitude toward humanity. Adorno's affirmation of the "infinite possibility" and even "genius" of individual human beings concerns not some pre-existing set of possibilities available to human beings *qua* human, but rather possibilities that are themselves historically constituted in relation to that which these possibilities have opposed as inhuman. Likewise, Adorno's refusal to join the Humanist Union reflects his rejection of the positive articulation of human possibilities and their political promotion, which would serve to reify or fix these possibilities at a given moment in history and so deny the possibility of a different instantiation of humanity – of different human subjects.[26]

Yet there seems to be something missing from this explanation. That is, if humanity is nothing but the resistance to inhumanity, then humanity is nothing but the perpetual disruption of the borders drawn by the positive order of the world and its claim to be the realization of humanism, or what is *best*, given the possibilities available to human beings.

---

25 *PMP*, 175; *NSIV.10*, 261.

26 Hence Adorno's opposition to prominent philosophical anthropologies of his day, such as those of Max Scheler, who espouses a kind of metaphysical possessive individualism through his conception of personality, and Arnold Gehlen, who makes personality into a moment of the state's institutions. See Scheler, *Formalism in Ethics*, 480; Gehlen, *Man in the Age of Technology*, 166; Cf. Adorno, "Gloss on Personality," *CM*, 163–4; *GSB10.2*, 641–2.

While such a claim would bring Adorno closer to the "agonistic humanism" of Honig and its roots in the work of Arendt and Rancière,[27] what is extinguished in the above presentation of Adorno and his relationship to humanism, were it to be considered complete, is the messianic light that illuminates the possibility that objects and their concepts are other than they are. That is, the dynamism of the relation between negative and positive humanity, or between humanity and inhumanity, serves to reify the place of struggle in the human constitution, thus presupposing the unchanging nature of political conflict and reviving a mythical understanding of the world as an eternal return of the same, with *agon* as its foundation. If Adorno is to avoid chaining his negative conception of humanity to inhumanity, thereby limiting the possible articulations of humanity to opposing violence and domination, then something must lie beyond humanity as the resistance to inhumanity, toward which this conflict is turned even while remaining irreducible to this conflict. This other, we shall see, is Adorno's conception of a *humanity to come*, that is, a "reconciled" humanity.

**Reconciled Humanity**

Adorno's use of Benjamin's concept of the messianic serves to transfigure concepts in the present and thus make it possible to imagine them being radically other than they are; similarly, he uses the concept of a "reconciled" humanity, a realized or "redeemed" humanity, to separate his negative conception of humanity from its enthrallment to the totality produced through the dialectic of enlightenment. That is, his conception of humanity needs to relate to something outside of the totality in which it is itself constituted in order to remain non-identical to what it would be in this totality, and so avoid absorption into an identity with that with which it struggles. Also, as with Adorno's secularized use of the concepts of the messianic and redemption, this "reconciled" humanity is not a positive reality; or rather, the possibility of its ever becoming a positive reality cannot be definitively demonstrated or rejected in the present.[28]

Adorno posits the *telos* of this humanity as the opposition to inhumanity in a reconciled humanity, not as the necessary unfolding of human potentials but rather as a conceptual device that allows us to see a gap in the struggle between the terms human and inhuman that

27 Honig, *Antigone Interrupted*, 17–19.
28 Cf. Shuster, *Autonomy after Auschwitz*, 41.

makes it possible to imagine a world not constituted by their struggle. Having no positive existence, this future humanity is not a fixed point that will necessarily be realized, nor is it something like a transcendental condition of the negative conception of humanity, the humanity found in opposition to violence. Rather, this "redeemed" humanity arises through the ambiguous promise made by negative humanity to resist the inhuman, but is at the same time a condition that this negative humanity must presuppose in order to maintain its negativity within the circle of perpetual violence and its resistance, through the possibility of a future positivity that may or may not ever become reality.[29] Thus, like the concept of redemption examined above, redeemed or realized humanity is immanent to the struggle between the human and the inhuman even while transcending this struggle in an image of humanity other than what it is. It is this transcendence – the possibility of humanity becoming something fundamentally other than what it presently is – that differentiates Adorno's conception of humanity from "agonistic humanism" or from other theories that might seem similar to his in their opposition to the closure of totality, or the permanent and fixed identities such closure is thought to entail. A brief consideration of such a theory may thus help shed light on some implications and consequences of Adorno's project and the importance to it of this reconciled humanity.

A groundbreaking work that has proved influential in shifting the theoretical focus away from classically conceived revolutionary struggle toward agonism and difference is Laclau and Mouffe's *Hegemony and Socialist Strategy* (1985).[30] From their perspective, the term *humanity* would be not only a discursive construct, but one without clear and definite content. On this view, humanity would be nothing but a "floating" or "empty" signifier, to be filled with whatever content the political partisans who deploy it are able.[31] Of course, Adorno's own

29 In this sense, it is possible to say that Adorno's use of the term *telos* to designate "reconciled" humanity is ironic. Another dimension of this irony, specifically in relation to Hegel's use of teleology, is noted below.

30 Though works such as Connolly, *Identity/Difference*, Honig, *Political Theory and the Displacement of Politics*, and Tully, *Strange Multiplicity* have arguably been more influential on this trend in political theory in North America, none of them make the explicit break between this approach and classical revolutionary politics as explicit as do Laclau and Mouffe, while insisting on the relation between the recovery of agonism and socialism. If agonsim can aid socialist strategy, then agonists can indeed be socialists without being interested in "the purging fire which dominates the revolutionary tradition." See Thomson, "Polemos and Agon," 105.

31 Laclau and Mouffe, *Hegemony and Socialist Strategy*, 171. Cf. Laclau, "Why Do Empty Signifiers Matter to Politics?," 44.

deployment of the concept of a reconciled humanity is itself a political gesture, and as such, Laclau and Mouffe might claim that the concept of "reconciled humanity" is simply Adorno's way of giving content to the "empty signifier" that is humanity. However, this response would deny the *negative* character of reconciled humanity in the present. In contrast to other attempts to fill this signifier, which are made as positive declarations of what humanity *is*, and thus would legitimate the aims of those making the declaration as the *basis* for these aims, Adorno is merely claiming that humanity might be otherwise than it is as constituted through struggle. Thus reconciled humanity would not serve as the content of an empty signifier, but instead serve as an attack on any attempt to fill this signifier, albeit without claiming that the signifier must remain empty or even that the structure producing this signifier will necessarily persist.

Claiming that the attempts of speaking beings to produce meaning necessarily produces empty signifiers, which are then given content through their deployment in various contexts, involves making ontological claims about the structure of society that Adorno tends to avoid. For him, a theory so formulated might at best accurately describe the structure of a given society, or even a group of societies that share common characteristics, but it could not tell us what lies beyond these societies were these characteristics to change, and thus cannot speak for a concept of society *in itself*. In his aversion to making ontological claims about society that might elucidate social features separable from any particular society, Adorno's dialectical critique challenges the predictive power of concepts, compelling their incessant revision.[32] Dialectic, he writes, "is the ontology of the wrong state of things."[33] As such, dialectic shows that concepts are socially and politically constituted and that they can be mobilized to grasp their own social and political constitution. Dialectical reflection thus grasps the particular ways in which the generation and application of concepts is a socially and politically mediated process of grasping. However, dialectic does not allow for the possibility of knowledge that would somehow work above or below this social and political constitution and so be capable of making the kinds of universal claims about society and politics that could apply to particular social or political content, irrespective of history. In this way, Adorno's negative dialectic leaves open the possibility for radical

32 On the difference between this and scepticism, see O'Connor, "Adorno's Reconception of the Dialectic," 540.

33 *ND*, 11; *GSB6*, 22.

change in the elements of both society's constitution and individual cognition as basic as the relation between universal and particular.

Laclau and Mouffe, by contrast, write of "social negativity" as if it were a positive condition, that is, as if society were negative *in its being*, thus making positive identities precarious attempts to construct a whole around an original lack that can never be completely filled.[34] Given that no society has been or ever could be a closed totality, and that social identities are forever subject to slippage or displacement, the most that can be hoped for is the construction of a hegemonic bloc in which different identities are linked through chains of equivalence that allow for their equal coexistence.[35] While the particulars of social relations might change, the basic structure of society and social identity, and of how universals relate to particulars, remains unchanged, whatever type of society is being considered.[36] Moreover, such a theory reduces what Adorno calls "the truth content" of language to the instrumental machinations of what is basically a form of communication, even if Laclau and Mouffe promote the recognition of agonistic differences over the consensus-building of dialogical unity. In this way, the ontology of agonism promoted by Laclau and Mouffe serves as a wall on the other side of which are placed the utopian speculations that inform Adorno's thought and the possibility it holds for radical change. Whereas Adorno binds the relation between the universal and the particular to sociopolitical relations as they are transformed through history, thus leaving open the question of their limits, Laclau and Mouffe's ontology of the sociopolitical outlines the limits to possible sociopolitical change and recommends a socialist strategy that accords with them. Laclau and Mouffe thus reject the utopian, opting instead for a *second sailing* in which the place of conflict as it exists in late-modern capitalist societies is treated as the condition for society as such. By contrast, the possibility toward which Adorno's "reconciled" humanity gestures lies beyond the present structure of society and can appear within it only in the negative and the fragmentary.

Thus Adorno claims that "if humanity [*Humanität*] has any meaning at all, it must consist in the discovery that human beings [*Menschen*] are *not identical* with their immediate existence as the creatures of nature."[37] That is, humanity is not identical with the struggle against inhumanity. This understanding of humanity, made possible through the

34 Laclau and Mouffe, *Hegemony and Socialist Strategy*, 189, 127, 86.

35 Laclau and Mouffe, 178, 182, 258.

36 Laclau and Mouffe, 125.

37 *PMP*, 15. Emphasis added. Cf. *NSAV10*, 28–9.

dialectic of philosophical reflection that places it in relation to a reconciled humanity, thus serves to "smash through human-made constructions [*Menschen Gemachte*]," such as the mythic conception that would identify humanity with endless struggle and suffering. The "human measure [*menschliches Maß*]" to which such constructions "return" [*zurückzuführen*][38] is precisely their relation to this future humanity, the "reconciled" [*versöhnten*] or "liberated" humanity [*befreiten Menschheit*] that does not yet exist[39] but whose realization becomes the guiding light of human activity in its resistance to inhumanity. By positing what would be truly human as something not yet realized, and interpreting all positive articulations of humanity as obstacles to its realization – indeed, Adorno even claims that the potential of the individual human self "stands in polemical opposition" to its reality[40] – Adorno can oppose himself to humanism, allying himself instead with the "principle of being human [*Pinzip des Menscheins*]," which remains "still unrealized."[41] This rejection of humanism in favour of an as yet unrealized "principle of being human" leads him to return to an Enlightenment concept that is taken as a given in some circles, while blithely maligned in others, yet remains fundamental to understanding his idea of a reconciled humanity: *progress*.

## The Question of Progress

The concept of progress expresses optimism concerning the future, and Adorno is not generally known for his optimism. His famous statement in *Negative Dialectics* that "no universal history leads from savagery to humanitarianism, but there is one leading from the slingshot to the megaton bomb,"[42] would seem to militate against a concept of progress. Moreover, Lukács's claim that Adorno occupied a room in the *Grand Hotel Abyss* has proven stubbornly persistent, and for those familiar with Habermas's critique of the supposed nihilism of Horkheimer and Adorno's *Dialectic of Enlightenment*,[43] the idea that Adorno might cling to a concept of progress may perhaps seem surprising. However, in light of Adorno's relation to the concept of humanity outlined above,

38 Adorno, "Why Still Philosophy," *CM*, 10; *GSB10.2*, 465.
39 *AT*, 65; 194; *MM*, 172; *GSB7*, 102, 290; *GSB4*, 195.
40 *ND*, 278; *GSB6*, 274.
41 *ND*, 257; *GSB6*, 254.
42 *ND*, 320; *GSB6*, 314.
43 For a critique of Habermas's interpretation of *Dialectic of Enlightenment*, see Hullot-Kentor, "Back to Adorno," 9–14.

a concept of progress seems necessary for this idea of a reconciled humanity, to the degree that this possible future humanity would be *better* than that which presently exists. So we must turn to Adorno's most concise statement on progress, made in a radio lecture of the same name, if we are to move beyond simple caricatures.

Adorno begins his lecture with terms drawn from *Dialectic of Enlightenment* and the dire pronouncements on human history found in *Negative Dialectics*. For Adorno, the question of the possibility of progress must confront what is humanity's most basic and at the same time most severe challenge: whether it can continue to survive at all. Given the radical increase in the human capacity for destruction made evident in the Second World War, "the possibility of progress" must be understood in terms of "averting the most extreme, total disaster": the annihilation of the human species and perhaps of all life on the planet. Yet here, in the shadow of the possibility of this "total disaster," it may be possible to cite those lines of Hölderlin, in echo of their citation in *Dialectic of Enlightenment*: "But where danger threatens / That which saves from it also grows."[44] The radical nature of this possible disaster, extending as it does beyond any single group to encompass all of humanity, and perhaps even all life on the planet, thus also opens up both the possibility, indeed the *necessity*, of resistance to this disaster on a much larger scale than that on which resistance was conceived in the past. Averting this total disaster requires nothing less than what Adorno calls a total or "global subject" [*Gesamtsubjekt*].[45]

However, despite the temptation to directly associate this "global subject" with the rise of new social movements and the possible emergence of a global civil society – both of which have gained prominence in the years since Adorno's death – Adorno's hostility to positive articulations of humanism troubles any direct or simple association with such movements. Humanity is not for Adorno the *origin* of resistance to this disaster, but the *goal*, and its concept can only be thought through extreme forms of differentiation and individuation – not as a "comprehensive generic concept."[46] Thus one might say that humanity is to be found in the particular activities of various subjects formed in opposition to inhumanity, and perhaps also in the solidarity they express for other subjects formed in opposition to other localizations of inhumanity, but

44 Horkheimer and Adorno, *Dialectic of Enlightenment*, 38. Hereafter *DE*. Cf. Horkheimer and Adorno, *Dialektik der Aufklärung*, 53. Hereafter *DA*.

45 Adorno, "Progress," 144; *GSB10.2*, 618.

46 Adorno, "Progress," 151; *GSB10.2*, 627.

one does *not* find humanity in the sum of these resistances, for as we have seen, only a reconciled humanity would be truly human. To claim that the sum of these resistances is itself an expression of humanity as a whole, that is, a particular instantiation of a universal subject, would be to subordinate their particularity to a universal concept and thereby erase the contexts in which these acts of humanity were actually found, while at once reconciling the concept of humanity with struggle. But reconciled humanity is not an animal constituted through struggle, nor can it be a universal concept that exists above its particular instantiations. The total or global subject that might emerge in response to the threat of "total disaster" is not itself reconciled humanity, but a possible *agent* for the ends, which, realized, would enable the emergence of a reconciled humanity.

Progress, it might be said, is thus the process of different particular subjects constituted in resistance to varying local conditions, aligning themselves with other such subjects so as to crystallize into a global subject. In this way, progress is "measured" in relation to the possibility of a reconciled humanity becoming reality, however indirect this possibility may be. It is important to note, however, that insofar as this global subject does not exist above and beyond these particular instantiations of humanity, it cannot be something for which they might sacrifice themselves. This is where Adorno's Benjaminian mutation of Hegel again becomes evident. The theodicy of Hegelian world spirit is such that particular instantiations of this spirit can be sacrificed for the whole; in fact, particular instantiations of this spirit are really only known insofar as their typically unwitting self-sacrifice serves to further the cause of world spirit. As such, history is a "slaughter bench" – it is the chronicle of the perpetual self-destruction of particulars whose destruction furthers the cause of the universal.

Regardless of what Hegel may have considered the correct disposition of the individual enlightened by this knowledge to political events as they unfold, once transposed into the realm of political struggle, these ideas allow for the most galling violence and barbarity in the name of higher causes, and the submission to the inevitable "march" of history is seen as the realization of progress. We might find in Benjamin's rejection of "moving with the current"[47] of history, then, resistance to the Hegelian view, which, refracted through Adorno's conception of the total/global subject, means a rejection of the theodicy that would allow for the "evil" of the calculated sacrifice of

47 Benjamin, "Theses on the Philosophy of History," 258; *GWB1.2*, 698.

particular struggles for a perceived greater good. If humanity is only found in the particular and differentiated ways in which inhumanity is resisted, then aligning with others in a way that would compel the calculated sacrifice of particular struggles would be a loss of humanity and hence work against the formation of the kind of subject Adorno is outlining.

But for Adorno, the rejection of theodicy alone is not enough to give progress an unambiguous character. Insofar as the activities that serve to build a global subject are bound to activities of resistance, and thus to the forces that compel resistance by precipitating the "total disaster" that must be averted, progress finds itself inextricably bound to the development of the forces of compulsion and domination and to the "total disaster" that looms beyond them. Thus, Adorno must claim that "progress occurs where it ends,"[48] for progress will only truly be realized when resistance to inhumanity is no longer necessary. True progress is progress that would see a qualitatively different form of human life step out of the shadows, and in so doing show human history to have actually been *prehistory*. As such, true progress would itself need to be beyond the progress of this global subject, for the progress of the global subject is bound to the forces in resistance to which it is constituted. Yet if human beings must be liberated from the very power that makes possible their liberation, insofar as humans first liberated themselves from inhuman nature through the exercise of their powers of reason, then it is *this* power from which humans must be liberated: the compulsive and dominating power of *reason*. As we saw in Aristotle, and as Adorno continues to claim, it is the power of reason that enables humans to separate themselves from the rest of the natural world and that allow for its domination toward human ends. Moreover, for Adorno, it is reason that now propels humans toward the "total disaster" through its instrumental exercise divorced of the realization of reconciled humanity.

Yet this possible liberation from reason does not, for Adorno, amount to its rejection. While the shape reason might take in a reconciled humanity is an open question that must be put aside for the moment, as far as Adorno is concerned the question of resistance in the present cannot be divorced from the exercise of reason. Contrary to a view that persists despite the most explicit evidence, Adorno does not see a way beyond the present order of things that does not involve reason, and even an appropriation of the Enlightenment, for only through these is

48 Adorno, "Progress," 150; *GSB10.2*, 625.

Adorno's critique even intelligible.[49] However, to critically reflect on reason and its place in domination, not as simply the capacity that enables humans to lift themselves above domination, but as a capacity that has at once served to facilitate domination, means to displace the centrality of reason in the constitution of what might be a reconciled humanity. Though Adorno claims that there can be no "idea of progress without the idea of humanity,"[50] for, as we have seen, it is only insofar as the cause of a reconciled humanity has been advanced that progress can be said to have taken place,[51] it is worth asking whether this reconciled humanity would itself be human.

If humanity has only ever been the struggle for survival against a hostile natural world, the domination of which has enabled the continuation of struggle and hostility in ingenious new forms, then would not the act of stepping out "of the magic spell" that binds humanity to itself through the domination of nature be to step out of the circle that is humanity?[52] That is, if human identity has always been established in distinction from nature through its mastery – both "external" nature and its own "internal" nature[53] – then would not the end of this mastery make human identity impossible? Is this not the real goal of the progress toward which Adorno points, and whose accomplishment would mean the end of progress as necessary resistance to the inhuman?[54] Yet Adorno does not take this step and abandon the concept of humanity, or at least not completely. Adorno refers to a "definition of humanity as that which excludes absolutely nothing," that is, a human totality that no longer holds within it "any limiting principle,"

49 Despite Horkheimer and Adorno claiming in the preface to *Dialectic of Enlightenment* that they have no doubt "that freedom in society is inseparable from Enlightenment thinking," the view continues to persist that their work is exemplary of a long line of "bitter rejections of our Enlightenment heritage." See Horkheimer and Adorno, "Preface," in *DE*, xvi; *DA*, 3; *ND*, 85; *GSB6*, 92. Cf. Taylor, "Review of Nicholas Tampio," 631. For an account of Horkheimer and Adorno's relation to the legacy of the Enlightenment and how it serves to differentiate them from other prominent critics of it, see McCormick, "A Critical versus Genealogical 'Questioning.'"

50 Adorno, "Progress," 145; *GSB10.2*, 619.

51 For an alternative interpretation of Adorno's concept of progress, see Allen, *The End of Progress*, esp. chs. 5 and 6.

52 Adorno, "Progress," 150; *GSB10.2*, 625.

53 Adorno, "Progress," 148; *GSB10.2*, 623.

54 Tellingly, the most extreme attempt to make Adorno a philosopher of permanent revolution, and so make historical dynamism permanent, also sees the moving force of this permanent dynamism to be humanity itself – "[n]ot animals, not God, not nature." See Holloway, "Why Adorno?," 14.

and is hence free of the coercion that would subject its members to a common standard.[55] Strictly speaking, such a totality would be no totality at all, but simply a collection of different subjects, united only in their difference.[56] Only here, Adorno claims, "would there be humanity and not its deceptive image."[57]

But why must this reconciled humanity, this humanity without any exclusion or "limiting principle," be called humanity at all, if humanity was itself only constituted through exclusion and the establishment and institutionalization of principles of limitation? How might such a humanity even cohere as a concept without some limiting principle? The simplest answer is that these limits and the exclusion they promote also promise their opposite. In establishing limits, the other side of these limits comes into focus, just as acts of exclusion ultimately depend upon those they exclude and contain within them the possibility of inclusion. As the determinate negation of the exclusion and "limiting principle" that served to constitute humanity, reconciled humanity preserves these within itself. In this sense, reconciled humanity is held together as that which no longer must dominate, that animal whose aggressive impulses have been deprived of the objects through which they were made actual. While these aggressive impulses remain in potential, even such potential can be expected to diminish and fade over time, like the loss of prominent canine teeth among anthropoids.

If these impulses were indeed to fade over time, then reconciled humanity, as the determinate negation of humanity, might cease to be any kind of humanity at all, for this animal would cease to be constituted through the contradiction in experience expressed by dialectic through negation – that is, through the instrumental necessity of opposing oneself to others in order to ensure self-preservation. Insofar as reconciled humanity preserves within it the memory of the limiting principle of humanity and the impulses that went with it, then it might be said to be constituted through the contradiction existing between its own peaceful state and the struggle from which it was born. Yet without a constellation of objects to promote their exercise, these aggressive impulses

55 Adorno, "Progress," 145; *GSB10.2*, 619–20.

56 This "Utopia of misfits," as Jameson imagines it, would not quite be the blossoming of "neurotics, compulsives, obsessives, paranoids, and schizophrenics," for these conditions would not all exist, at least not in the same manner, in this utopian future. This is not to say that mental illness would not exist, but simply that how its symptoms relate to various sociopolitical factors would be radically transformed. See Jameson, *Late Marxism*, 102.

57 Adorno, "Progress," 146; *GSB10.2*, 620.

would fade, and so would this contradiction and thus its status as human. In this sense, it is perhaps not as some form of humanity that reconciled humanity serves as the *telos* of the human struggle against the inhuman, but as *some other kind of animal*.

Recall that for Aristotle, the potentials thought to be exclusively human served to elevate humans above other animals, but to differing degrees based on the natural distribution of these potentials found in particular human individuals. In this way the capacities humans share with other animals were made subordinate to those considered exclusively human. This way of formulating the human as the suppression of the animal serves to make "the animal" into the *other* of the human – the non-identical remainder produced through the conception of the human and its flourishing. In this sense, the image of "the animal" might be said to haunt human life as the spectre of life organized otherwise, of life drawing on different capacities than those which served to compel some to recognize others as their betters. In this sense, Adorno's conception of a reconciled humanity and the transformation of human life it entails would appear to proceed through a transformation in our conception of how humans relate to animals.[58]

Thus reconciled humanity cannot be something arising simply out of the struggle between the human and the inhuman, and the progress made through the production of a global subject whose resistance to "total disaster" might propel humanity toward its own reconciliation. Reconciled humanity, if indeed it is a humanity constituted without a limiting principle and hence without exclusion or coercion, is as much animal as human. In this light, the goal of progress is less to produce the conditions in which humanity might be transformed into another kind of *humanity*, that is, another creature that must resist inhumanity, than it is to transform the very conditions that compelled humanity to come into existence in the first place, and so to transform humanity into another kind of animal. This relation between the animal and the human, between the human and its own animality, is thus necessary to grasp the animality of this reconciled humanity and hence the moral and political underpinnings of Adorno's project. To that end, I now consider those underpinnings, specifically by examining Adorno's use of animal imagery, and defend my claim that reconciled humanity would be an animal other than human.

58 Thus the utopian moment of Adorno's thought does indeed gesture toward "solidarity with all the living," though this does not mean we would simply "become what we are" in "a more humane social order," as this process must also transform what the human fundamentally is. See Cook, "Ein Reaktionares Schwein?," 62.

# PART TWO

# Untying the Knot of Humanity

*Much is monstrous. But nothing*
*More monstrous than man.*

– From Hölderlin's translation of the choral ode
in Sophocles's *Antigone*[1]

In his *Philosophy of Right*, Hegel refers to the negative freedom of the abstract will that cancels all particularity as "the freedom of the void." This abstract freedom "becomes in the realm of both politics and religion the fanaticism of destruction, demolishing the whole existing social order, eliminating all individuals regarded as suspect by a given order, and annihilating any organization which attempts to rise up anew."[2] According to Hegel, this situation describes the Terror of the French Revolution.[3] It has since been claimed that the French Revolution introduced an "untimeliness" to historical experience, a kind of "traumatic dissonance" that ever since has marked a split in historical experience: events like the Revolution always happen at once too soon (we are never ready for them) and too late (they are always already long past due). The introduction of this traumatic split and reorientation in the very structure of experience separated past history from subsequent history, thus making the French Revolution "the epochal marker of modernity."[4]

Insofar as Hegel's philosophy can be approached as having been constituted around the experience of the French Revolution, and

1 English translation by Schmidt, *On Germans and Other Greeks*, 269.
2 Hegel, *Elements of the Philosophy of Right*, §5.
3 Hegel, *Elements of the Philosophy of Right*, §5. Addition.
4 Comay, *Mourning Sickness*, 4–7

Hegel himself can be called the "most lucid theorist" of this trauma,[5] we might view the subjective preponderance that Adorno opposes in Hegel as Hegel's attempt to master this trauma. The preponderance of the subject over the object can be seen as an attempt to master the trauma of experience in the modern world, conceptualizing it in such a manner that its shock is deadened and it can be integrated into the order constituted through the subject's own development. Yet it is precisely this deadening and integrating of the shock into a repressive sociopolitical order that Adorno argues enabled its return even more horribly in the violence of the twentieth century. In *Negative Dialectics*, Adorno refers to "the relatively modest horrors of the French Revolution," from which the philosophers of the age were so quick to distance themselves, lauding instead order and the rule of law.[6] If the repressed trauma of the French Revolution that constitutes the unconscious of modernity was able to erupt in events such as Auschwitz and Hiroshima, how much more terrible will the next eruption be, if the trauma upon which the new order sits has so outstripped these past horrors as to render them nothing more than "modest"? It is here again that we see the spectre of "total disaster" that threatens the continued existence of human and other life, in opposition to which we found Adorno's definitions of humanity and progress. Indeed, only in resistance to this "total disaster" may it be possible to psychologically reconstitute the subjects of modernity such that trauma and destruction no longer occupy the central place in this constitution.

Yet if "that which saves" really does grow from "where danger threatens," we might find, as I have already suggested, strange allies in this struggle against inhumanity and in the liberation from this struggle. Adorno, along with the other members and associates of the Institute for Social Research, are known to have been animal lovers; they even gave one another animal pet-names: Adorno was hippopotamus, his wife Gretel was Giraffe-Gazelle, and Horkeimer was Mammoth.[7] A widely published photograph from Adorno's days in Los Angeles shows him at his desk surrounded by figurines made in the images of

5 Comay, *Mourning Sickness*, 4–5.

6 *ND*, 251; *GSB6*, 248–9.

7 Jäger, *Adorno*, 107. This practice of giving one another animal nicknames appears to be the extension of one already in use in Adorno's family from his childhood. See Savage, "Adorno's Family and Other Animals," 107.

his favourite animals, a collection to which he referred as his "household horrors."[8] Might this curious nickname offer a clue to where "that which saves" might actually lie? Adorno's thoughts on nature have become the object of scholarly study,[9] yet little systematic attention has been paid to the role animal imagery serves in Adorno's work.[10]

In his review of the biographies of Adorno by Claussen and Müller-Doohm, Savage argues that these animal-related anecdotes point to the possibility of reinterpreting certain key passages in Adorno's writings that suggest a "structural and functional identity of animality and utopia in Adorno's thought," serving to remind us that "the path to humanity leads *toward* animality, not away from it."[11] However, as I suggested earlier in my consideration of Adorno's conception of humanity, we might push these claims even further. The realization of a reconciled humanity involves not only a transformation of the relation between human and animal but also a transformation of what we think of as human such that this reconciled humanity is not really human, but some new kind of animal, one whose destructive tendencies emerging from the trauma involved in the struggle for survival have been pacified. Reconciled humanity, if it is indeed to embody the promise Adorno claims, must be something fundamentally other than the humanity born and perpetuated in the struggle against inhumanity, the struggle for its own survival.

Defending this claim that Adorno's concept of a reconciled humanity is not human but a new kind of animal will involve demonstrating four separate but related points. The first is that what we call human is a radically constructed creature, one whose constitution is entirely dependent upon the sociopolitical order in which it lives. Here I examine Adorno's thoughts on "anthropology" and its relation to sociopolitical forces, arguing that, contrary to many of his interpreters, Adorno does not have an anthropology, and that his thoughts on the subject must be viewed as a polemic against the various philosophical anthropologies deployed within the Western philosophical tradition. Second, if reconciled humanity would be a new kind of animal, and if the thinking that might orient oneself to society in such a way as to possibly

---

8 Jäger, *Adorno*, 108.

9 See for instance Biro, ed., *Critical Ecologies*; Biro, *Denaturalizing Ecological Politics*; Buck, "The Utopian Content of Reification"; Cook, *Adorno on Nature*; Nelson, "Revisiting the Dialectic of Environment"; and Vogel, *Against Nature*.

10 For exceptions to this rule, see Gerhardt, "The Ethics of Animals"; Gerhardt, "Thinking With"; and Mendieta, "Animal Is to Kantianism."

11 Savage, "Adorno's Family and Other Animals," 109–10.

bring about its creation involves a turn toward the object and the non-identical, then there must be some relation between the concept of the animal and that of the non-identical. Here I argue that the concept of the animal points to that which is non-identical to the human and that this can be understood through the violence done to animals in constructing and maintaining what we call human. Third, insofar as the animal illuminates the non-conceptual side of the concept of the human, to see the "rifts and crevices" in this concept is to see human activity as animal activity, and historically conditioned social activity as natural activity. In this way, the centrality of the concept of the human is displaced, and both the possibility and desirability of its mastery over the animal are brought into question. Fourth and finally, I examine the relation between Adorno's use of animal imagery and his conception of utopia, concluding that a truly reconciled humanity can only be something decidedly other than human, a kind of animal whose life is no longer characterized by the kinds of conflict that served to bring the human into existence.

*Chapter Three*

# Relatively Modest Horrors: Adorno and Animals

## Anthropology, Dialectical and Otherwise

The final section of Horkheimer and Adorno's *Dialectic of Enlightenment*, "Notes and Sketches," comprises twenty-four fragments, most of which relate to what the authors call in the preface of the book a "dialectical anthropology."[1] No further elaboration of this term is given. However, many of the fragments that make up this section explicitly concern the human being and its constitution, especially in relation to animals and the violence done to them. The relation established between humans and other animals through violence will be discussed in further detail in the next section; here I focus instead on the various references to "anthropology" scattered throughout Adorno's other works, often polemically. This "anthropology" should be understood much more broadly than the academic discipline of the same name.

For Adorno, anthropology concerns the theories and popular representations of human life and its possibilities in a given society, as well as how these relate to the structure of society and the activities it compels. Insofar as Adorno considers what we call human to be a product of specific sociopolitical relations, and not a creature naturally possessed of a certain set of potentials, these theories and representations make up an important part of what constitutes human life in a given society. As human constitution is bound up with the form of society in which it appears in this manner, positive articulations of what humanity is have the ideological function of supporting the existing order by imposing an understanding of the possibilities available for living within the terms of this order. The role Adorno attributes to

1 Horkheimer and Adorno, "Preface," in *DE*, xix; *DA*, 7.

anthropology here is one of solidifying a particular constitution of human being and so giving a natural appearance to the set of historically produced sociopolitical relations in which this human being appears. Thus, if progressive change is to be realized, that is, if a given form of sociopolitical relations is to change in a manner that might facilitate the emergence of a reconciled humanity, an important part of the task of theory is to show how what we call human is a function of these relations. In this way, Adorno should not be understood as being engaged in philosophical anthropology as some claim,[2] for he does not attempt to identify what is definitively human or to promote the centrality of its concept. Rather, his work polemically opposes itself to philosophical anthropology, from the Aristotelian variety to those prominent in his own day, such as in the work of Max Scheler or Arnold Gehlen,[3] both of whom were influenced by Aristotle in important ways.[4]

Perhaps Adorno's most concise statement on the ideological role of anthropology is made in *Negative Dialectics*, in reference to Franz Neumann's book about the National Socialist state, *Behemot*.[5] There Adorno calls anthropology "the chemism of humankind."[6] The extreme concision of this statement requires some unpacking, specifically with reference to Hegel's *Science of Logic*, which Adorno is here appropriating in his characteristically fragmented fashion. On the subjective side of Hegel's logic, objectivity is divided among three moments: mechanism, chemism, and teleology. According to Hegel, for an object to be known in its objectivity – that is, known by a cognizing subject, yet known free

2 See for instance, Benhabib, *Critique, Norm, Utopia*, 215; Breuer, "Adorno's Anthropology"; Freyenhagen, *Adorno's Practical Philosophy*, 253; Hammer, *Adorno's Modernism*, 60; Honneth, *The Critique of Power*, 40ff; or Jameson, *Late Marxism*, 17, 64, 68, 104, 109. That the most comprehensive development of Adorno's "dialectical anthropology," Breuer's, focuses primarily on the development of capitalism, rejects any conception of "first nature" and ultimately claims to be "an anthropology without anthropos" (31) leaves one to wonder exactly what remains of Adorno's philosophical anthropology at all.

3 Indeed, Adorno and Gehlen debated each other on West German radio. An account of this can be found in Müller-Doohm, *Adorno*, 378–9; 390–1. Freyenhagen uses this same episode to frame his discussion of Adorno in *Adorno's Practical Philosophy* (2, 242), though he sees philosophical anthropology as a point in common between Adorno and Gehlen, despite their particular differences regarding what is actually proper to human being, whereas I argue that Adorno is critical of the very possibility of philosophical anthropology.

4 See Gehlen, *Man*, 17, 169, 276, 299, 339, 356, 360, 361, 363; Scheler, *Formalism in Ethics*, 481; Scheler, *Man's Place in Nature*, 91.

5 Neumann, *Behemoth*.

6 *ND*, 346; *GSB6*, 339.

of the imprint of the subject's own knowing – this objectivity must be known free of limitation, opposition, or contingency.[7] For example, if the object in question is a work of art, to know this work of art in its objectivity, or call it *objective*, means to know it in its entirety, without remainder; to know it in its individuality, that is, to know how it relates to others in both similarity and difference; and lastly, to grasp its necessity, that is, to know that it is the result of a necessary unfolding that could not be otherwise. The possibility of actually knowing in this manner and thus the coherence of this position will not be considered here; rather, I will restrict myself to explicating this part of Hegel in terms of Adorno's conception of anthropology.

For Hegel, coming to be objective in this manner requires the passage from *mechanism*, wherein the object is seen as an aggregation of parts whose actions on themselves and one another are "extraneous" to themselves[8] – where they are seen to operate without intention, end, or self-direction, such as physical laws in the Newtonian sense – to *teleology*, whereby the actions of the parts of the whole are known by an intelligence that directs itself toward given ends in accordance with some purpose.[9] Chemism serves as the mediating point between these two, whereby the various mechanical processes are synthesized as a whole and known to be the parts of a totality, gaining an added level of particularity through their place and participation in that totality.[10] Yet despite this new degree of particularity, for Hegel, chemism ultimately remains closer to mechanism than teleology, for it is part of an external way of knowing that cannot grasp the self-moving drive toward various ends that is life. Consequently, at the level of chemism, particular objects remain *dead things*.[11]

To call anthropology "the chemism of humankind," then, is to compare anthropology to a chemical reaction with "humankind" as its result. Anthropology is a process of synthesis whereby the various positive instantiations of humanity, the various kinds of human life that appear in different societies, are synthesized into a totality that is, in the Hegelian terminology, a "chemical object" *external* to itself and hence un-*reflective*. Or in other words, the human being, as the object of anthropology, is a general conception that purports to capture what the

7 Hegel, *SL*, 709.
8 *SL*, 711.
9 *SL*, 734.
10 *SL*, 727.
11 *SL*, 740, 767.

human being really and necessarily is, based on these positive instantiations of how humans are *compelled* to live – that is, based on how humans live under domination. As a "chemical object," humanity does not understand its own processes of construction any more than the substance resulting from a chemical reaction can be said to understand what it is or how it has come to be. Humanity as produced by anthropology does not understand how its unity has come to be imposed as a concept through its own practices of knowing, and thus it takes the object – itself, humanity – that it sees distorted through an existing articulation of the subject to be the object in its totality. But to grasp the objectivity of the object, the subject's own role in the object's constitution must be understood. Only through an understanding of how the subject structures the object can its objectivity be known, and can the external unity established through "chemism" be made internal, thus allowing the object to begin to determine its own ends and strive toward them in the Hegelian sense. Thus, humanity as an object of anthropology is not a living, breathing entity, capable of the agency Hegel ascribes to teleological subject/object relations, but a *corpse* produced for dissection.[12]

An example of one such anthropological process can be found in Adorno's criticism of television. Adorno claims that in television dramas, the dramatic changes the characters suffer reveal only what they always already were, their "true nature,"[13] as opposed to the myriad ways in which these sufferings are socially produced. People become only what their nature allows, so the "hidden message" of the various forms of entertainment that compose the culture industry is contained in the view of humanity they promote.[14] In seeing such views of nature and the boundaries it sets to human life so dramatized, viewers come to adopt similar attitudes, and so understand these same boundaries to be those that mark their own lives and possibilities. Insofar as these ideas regarding human life come to influence their own daily decisions and practices – insofar as people come to seek opportunities in their own lives to re-enact

12 Hence Adorno's claim that reconciled humanity is the *telos* of the struggle against inhumanity, for inhumanity includes the positive articulations of the limits of human life enshrined through the "chemism" of anthropology. Adorno's use of *telos* and this Hegelian schema is ironic, however, in that Adorno's reconciled humanity would be free of the dynamism that characterizes the subject–object relation found in the *teleological* moment of objectivity.

13 Adorno, "Television as Ideology," *CM*, 66; *GSB10.2*, 527.

14 *CM*, 61; *GSB10.2*, 520–1.

the narratives they have absorbed through television or elsewhere – these ideas come to have substance in positive instantiations of human life, which in turn serves itself up as fodder for further dramatic representation. In this way, the television drama, as one instance of the "chemism" of anthropology, creates a view of humanity that is incapacitated as well as alienated from other potentials its sociopolitical constitution has made available, in the *opposite* image of Adorno's global subject, which would be constituted as an expression of solidarity between different instances of human resistance to inhumanity.

If anthropology is to a significant extent involved in the creation of its own object, the human being, then the human being must be, as noted above, constituted through sociopolitical relations. We might be tempted to see here a likeness to the argument found in Foucault's *The Order of Things* concerning the discursive construction of the human being through a shift in the social sciences, includiing anthropology. At the end of that work, Foucault famously claims that a discursive transformation might result in the disappearance of the concept of the human being, "like a face drawn in sand at the edge of the sea."[15] Such a transformation is welcomed by Foucault, who, in Heideggerian fashion, would see anthropology destroyed in order to make possible a more primordial relation to language so that we might rediscover "a purified ontology or a radical thought of being."[16] Though Adorno does not appear to have been familiar with Foucault, he did know this argument as it is found in Heidegger, and he expressed deep suspicion of it. For Adorno, though "the current talk of humanism is awful," he sees in Heidegger's turn toward a being loftier or more primordial than human a quietism that would remain unmoved by suffering.[17] Humanity contains both the danger of domination and destruction and the promise of a life free of these, and the task of Adorno's critique of humanity is to resist these dangers in the interest of its promise, even if the promise of humanity will, as I argue, be found not to have been human. So to better grasp this difference between Adorno and Heidegger/Foucault's position on anthropology, we must ask: to *what extent* must humanity be seen as the product of particular sociopolitical relations? What, if anything, remains unchanged through the vicissitudes of anthropology?

15 Foucault, *The Order of Things*, 387.

16 Foucault, *The Order of Things*, 342.

17 *ND*, 89; *GSB6*, 96.

Put most simply, it is Adorno's turn toward the object that distinguishes him from Foucault and Heidegger.[18] Insofar as anthropological processes concern ways of knowing, they can be considered *subjective*. As we have seen, Adorno argues against the absolutely constitutive powers of subjectivity in favour of a preponderance of the object. For Adorno, objects are given and pre-exist subjects, even if they cannot be known *without* subjects.[19] Thus subjective processes such as those of anthropology cannot be said to constitute the human absolutely; rather, there must be some object, some material, that is continually being conceptualized as human but that remains irreducible to this conceptualization. However, just as the subject is also an object, so is anthropology also objective – its existence cannot simply be separated from the objectivity of society, and so removed from it, as a tumour from a body. That is, anthropology must correspond to some need in society, some aspect of its objectivity, as opposed to being a complete and arbitrary construction. To turn toward this need, toward the objectivity of society veiled by the subjective processes of anthropology, is thus to search for the object in the subjective constructions of anthropology. Adorno attempts to accomplish this turn by illustrating the ways in which the different aspects of the subjective constitution of the human being correspond to social needs – to the structure of the object. To answer the questions, then, regarding the extent of the anthropological constitution of the human being, and so what remains non-identical to it and perhaps as such even resists it, we must examine the instances where Adorno locates the object through cracks in the subjective wall.

According to Adorno, "man as a *constituens*," that is, the human subject that not only transforms nature and builds cities but also grounds the objects of cognition, "is in turn man-made," a fact that must displace the creative centrality of the human mind.[20] The "self," "I," or ego (*das Ich*) that is so often taken as the emblem of the individuality particular to humans is "entwined with society," owing to society its very existence, for, as Adorno claims, *all* of the content of this self comes from society, from its relation to the object.[21] Moreover, Adorno claims

18 For an overview of Adorno's differences from the related "post-structuralism," see Peter Dews, "Adorno, Post-Structuralism."

19 That is, though the givenness of an object is not reducible to its conceptual mediations, it is only accessible through them – through the shifting layers of conceptual sediment that make up its history – and is thus never given in its totality. For further discussion, see O'Connor, "Adorno and the Problem of Givenness."

20 Adorno, "On Subject and Object," *CM*, 251; *GSB10.2*, 749.

21 *MM*, 154; *GSB4*, 175.

there is no "substratum" that might lie beneath the social deformations of humanity, no interior upon which social forces exert their pressure from outside;[22] rather, interiority must itself be seen as part and parcel of the particular form of humanity created in the historical transformation of sociopolitical relations.[23] Thus, Adorno holds that no meaningful distinction can be drawn between who or what people are, as particular instances of humanity, and their social roles, for these roles "extend deep into the characteristics of people themselves, into their undermost composition."[24]

These claims directly challenge any positive conception of the human being based on a necessary set of ahistorical potentials, such as those of Aristotle, who attempts to isolate certain fundamentally human capacities. Indeed, Adorno will claim that the attempt to isolate such capacities is itself the product of the division of labour and thus mediated through specific sociopolitical relations.[25] The consequence of such claims is that even capacities that are taken for granted in our society must necessarily be seen as its products. For instance, concepts such as the individual and its freedom, and competition between individuals, must all be seen as the products of social-historical relations, including basic features of the individual, such as the ego, will, reason, and even bodily reflexes. The competition between formally equal individuals that characterizes bourgeois society and that is thought to be the inevitable consequence of certain fundamental human building blocks is thus found to be itself produced by the very set of relations it is held to legitimate. If the individual, at least when taken as an "absolute" as opposed to a result, is indeed "a mere reflection of property relations,"[26] then competition between individuals, "the truly bourgeois principle"[27] that characterizes their relations, is itself a product of the distribution of property. Adorno will even speculate that pre-bourgeois competition, or the antagonism thought to structure human relations at a more fundamental level, is the consequence perhaps not of the human struggle for survival against a hostile natural world, but of the reification of "archaic arbitrary acts of seizing power."[28] In this case, the antagonism that exists between people would be the inheritance of

22 *MM*, 229; *GSB4*, 261.
23 *AT*, 116; *GSB7*, 176–7.
24 Adorno, "Free Time," in *CM*, 167–8; *GSB10.2*, 645.
25 *MM*, 64; *GSB4*, 71.
26 *MM*, 153; *GSB4*, 175.
27 *MM*, 27; *GSB4*, 28.
28 *ND*, 321; *GSB6*, 315.

acts of violence that were themselves contingent and unnecessary from the perspective of human development. In both cases, however, this antagonism is itself maintained and reproduced through sociopolitical relations that might be otherwise, as is the ego, which is part of the architecture of the individual "implanted" by society.[29]

Even reason itself, the very cornerstone of the difference between human and animal, is for Adorno a social product. Reason has frequently been understood as an important, even definitive, capacity in defining human life, yet here again Adorno sees in reason its *artificiality*, or socially *produced* nature. Reason evolved genetically through the "force of human drives,"[30] in the interest of survival. Insofar as there is no human history that is not *social* history – that is, insofar as humans have been social for at least as long as they have been human – the survival that was facilitated by reason was always already survival in the context of human societies and so cannot be isolated as a capacity that pre-existed them. As the most "hypostatized" category, reason or *ratio* in bourgeois society becomes the self-preservation of the individual against the whole and thus serves to perpetuate the antagonisms among individuals.[31] The executor of this self-preserving reason is the will. Yet the act of willing involves the capacity to command the body, and in order to marshal the body to its command, the will must treat the body as an object, as its instrument. In so doing the will separates itself and the *ratio* from the body and its impulses, from its reflexes, which are now seen as alien and mechanical, as divorced from that which is highest and most definitively human.[32] When the body is divided and alienated from itself in this manner, the model of a hierarchical division of labour, or social domination, becomes the model for the inner architecture of the human being. It is for this reason that Adorno writes that perhaps the freedom of a free society would mean being free from the will,[33] for insofar as the will is a mechanism for inner repression produced by the outward repression that structures society, the disappearance of outward repression would mean the transformation of this human architecture.

In this way, Adorno reveals the socially constructed character of anthropological concepts and thus the objectivity of the subjective

29 *ND*, 297; *GSB6*, 292.
30 *ND*, 230; *GSB6*, 229.
31 *ND*, 317–18; *GSB6*, 312.
32 *ND*, 217; *GSB6*, 216–17; *MM*, 231; *GSB4*, 246–7.
33 *ND*, 264; *GSB6*, 261.

constitution of the human being. This manner of finding objectivity through the subject might even be seen to dialectically mediate the positions of Foucault and Aristotle noted above. *Contra* Foucault, Adorno's turn toward the object opens up the discursive constructs of anthropology to their other: the unintentional reflexes and impulses of the body suffering the activities imposed upon it by social organization, the experience of which remains irreducible to the concepts of anthropology.[34] But at the same time, and *contra* Aristotle, these bodily reflexes and impulses cannot be isolated from their social expression or their mediation by language in an unchanging set of potentials that might tell us definitively what a human being *is*. As Adorno writes, "We cannot say what man is. Man today is a function, unfree, regressing behind whatever is ascribed to him as invariant ... He drags along with him as his social heritage the mutilations inflicted upon him over thousands of years."[35] Thus attempts to define the human being serve only to chain human being "to the rock of his past."[36] That the human being evades definition in this manner does not elevate anthropology; rather, "it vetoes any anthropology."[37] Anthropology forges the conceptual manacles binding that which might have resisted inhumanity.

Thus, even if what we consider human is largely a function of anthropology, there remains something non-identical to the conception of human being proffered by anthropology. This "something" is not simply to be found in the discursive slippages produced by an excess of significations; rather, it is the result of the embodied condition of discourse that both enables and limits discursive constructions. That is, what can be said about human beings and its acceptance as plausible depends on the bodily experience of social subjects – if anthropology had no point of contact with objectivity in this sense, it would be without force or even meaning. This *point of contact*, the most basic meaning-making activity that serves to both enable and limit the reach of anthropology, is what Adorno calls *mimesis*: an "indelible ... element in all cognition and in all human practice."[38] Insofar as *mimesis* has traditionally been linked to imitation, Adorno can thus claim that humans are only human insofar as they imitate one another; however, his use of the term

34 A version of this argument is levelled against Foucault in Butler, "Foucault and the Paradox."

35 *ND*, 124; *GSB6*, 130.

36 *ND*, 51; *GSB6*, 61.

37 *ND*, 124; *GSB6*, 130.

38 *ND*, 150; *GSB6*, 153.

suggests a much broader meaning, and commentators have often noted the difficulties of pinning this term down.[39]

While Aristotle's conception of *mimesis* was not limited to direct representation or imitation of objects of observation, but instead allowed for their imaginative transformation – utilizing capacities humans share with other animals, we must recall – it nevertheless remained tied to what Aristotle considered the naturally human desire to know. Insofar as knowledge serves a more important role in human life than in those of other animals, and insofar as Aristotle sees the human desire for knowledge as reaching up toward divine thought, *mimesis* thus shares these associations: just as humans are held to be the most intelligent, so are they held to be the most imitative of all animals.[40] Adorno, however, does not simply adopt the Aristotelian conception of *mimesis*.[41] As Horowitz writes, Adorno's conception of *mimesis*, "primordially," involves "the desire to be what there is contact with before there is a self to make contact." But even this formulation, Horowitz claims, involves too great a separation between subject and object: "'One' is 'the object.' And that is all there is."[42] This conception of *mimesis*, it must be noted, while serving to condition the desire for knowledge and what we call humanity, is reducible to neither.

At its most basic, *mimesis* is a desire for contact, and this desire is not exhausted in the divisions of self and other or subject and object. For this reason, *mimesis* can be considered something like the drive that animates the bodily excess of conceptual organization. It makes possible the process of identification, yet no identification can ever fully encompass it, and consequently it lends itself to a continual series of mediations that retranslate it into new conceptual schemas, of which anthropology is but a set. Thus we might say the dynamism that characterizes human development, the constant transformation of humanity through its own self-organized processes of compulsion, depends on *mimesis*, as would the transformation of this compulsion and of the humanity constituted thereby. However, a full account of *mimesis* will have to wait for chapter 4 and my discussion of how Adorno's conceptions of art, morality, and politics relate to one another. At present

39 *MM*, 154; *GSB4*, 176. Cf. Lee, *Dialectics of the Body*, 109; O'Connor, *Adorno*, 149.

40 Aristotle, "Poetics," 1448b5–15.

41 Though there are indeed similarities, as noted by O'Connor, *Adorno*, 156. For a reading of Adorno's *mimesis* as a response to Kantian aesthetics, see Bernstein, *The Fate of Art*, 201.

42 Horowitz, "Adorno and Emptiness," 272.

it is sufficient to note that what we call human is the product of sociopolitical relations operating on both subjective and objective levels and that the condition of this humanity and its vicissitudes depends on a bodily desire that is not reducible to the human. It remains to elucidate now what relation this construction of the human might have to other animals. How has the human managed to differentiate itself from other animals and maintain its privileged status? To this question I now turn.

## Animal Violence in Human Constitution

Having demonstrated the degree to which the human being is produced through sociopolitical relations, and having highlighted the bodily impulse whose continual mediation informs these relations and the vicissitudes of anthropology, we now return to the "dialectical anthropology" of *Dialectic of Enlightenment*. Like Schoenberg's or Beethoven's "failed" compositions that through their failure bring to light the status of the object more truthfully than a successful composition might have done, Horkheimer and Adorno's failed attempt to write an anthropology – even a "dialectical" one – illustrates the impossibility of the task and thus the status of its object, the human being.[43] Adorno described *Dialectic of Enlightenment* as an attempt to write "a primeval history of the subject,"[44] and it is perhaps for this reason that it might be considered their bleakest work: the authors here attempt to draw the outline of the shadow in which they sit, even while historical events burn this shadow into the ground. Illuminated by this light, the human being is that moment in the history of the subject where the destructive and violent impulses that allowed for its clear distinction from its object through the latter's domination are given their most complete articulation: in the possibility of the total destruction of the natural world.

---

43 Notes made by Adorno around the same time (1941) on the possibility of a new anthropology suffered the same fate: they fail to stand on their own as an independent whole and are instead ultimately divided and cannibalized by other works, such as *Minima Moralia*. See Müller-Doohm, 274, 389. For a later statement on anthropology (c. 1969), see Adorno, "Zu Ulrich Sonnemanns 'Negativer Anthropologie.'" As for success in failure, see Adorno, "Alienated Masterpiece," 317; Adorno, *Philosophy of Modern Music*, 69, 71, 119. Cf. Adorno, *Gesammelte Schriften*, vol. 12: *Philosophie der neuen Musik* (Frankfurt am Main: Suhrkamp, 1975), 69–70, 71, 114. Hereafter *PMM* and *GSB12*. On the direct influence of Schoenberg's techniques for Adorno's philosophy, see Buck-Morss, *The Origin of Negative Dialectics*, 15, 44–5, 188–9.

44 *ND*, 185; *GSB6*, 186.

In *Dialectic of Enlightenment*, Horkheimer and Adorno display the other side of the struggle against inhumanity that constitutes the human being: inhumanity is not merely a kind of brutality perpetuated by humans against one another; it must also be seen as that which is simply not human, such as the natural world and the other animals that populate it. In turning toward the primeval history of the subject, Horkheimer and Adorno find that the human is only a moment of the subject that has been constituted through the violent suppression of nature – most notably, the violent suppression of animals. If the subject is to emerge as something distinct from its object, and so ultimately take up the banner of *human being*, a creature distinct from nature and from other animals, it must master and suppress its own objectivity, its own history and condition of possibility – its *animal* body. As I will show, it is in part for this reason that Adorno's idea of a reconciled humanity cannot be human, for the turn toward the preponderance of the object and the non-identical is, in the case of humanity, a turn toward animality, toward the suppressed animal impulses that inform all human activity and that must continually be suppressed, transformed, and disciplined through the repression of a society organized around the exigencies of domination for the human to be produced. The object for which the anthropological subject is but an agent is an animal, and it is only in recognizing this that the repressive social relations necessary for the reproduction of human life might be relaxed, so that human life might dissolve into a different kind of animal life, free of this repression.

As commentators have noted, sometimes pejoratively, this aspect of *Dialectic of Enlightenment* bears a close affinity to Nietzsche,[45] especially the Nietzsche to be found in the second essay of his *On the Genealogy of Morality*. Here Nietzsche provides something very much like a "primeval history of the subject," wherein human social features and institutions are treated as part of the biological evolution of the species. For Nietzsche, humans came to reason and so possess a degree of mastery over their emotions and drives through memory. It was through memory that a connection between past, present, and future was first forged so as to enable remembering individuals to identify themselves in their past and thereby make calculated projections for their future. For the future to look enough like the present and past to render calculations concerning it useful, human activities had first to be made regular and reliable. Such reliability was produced through a transformation

45 See Habermas, "The Entwinement of Myth and Enlightenment," 106, 110, 120–2, 127. Cf. Rose, *The Melancholy Science*, 71.

of this "necessarily forgetful animal," for which forgetfulness had been a strength that enabled daring, by means of the pain inflicted through "the most horrifying sacrifices and forfeits ... the most disgusting mutilations ... the cruelest rituals."[46] Religious and sociopolitical institutions were the mnemonic devices employed to "breed" this animal capable of making a *promise*, and that animal was possessed of an inner life to serve as the Archimedean point for the vicissitudes of its experience – a *subject*. First among these institutions was the institution of debt: thus the debtor/creditor relation, which established in the human animal the concept of *equivalence*. Insofar as widely disparate things might be made equivalent under certain conditions, the expansion of these conditions involves an increasing number of things coming under the law of equivalence, including these promise-keeping animals, whose equivalence between each other and their values allows for the emergence of their *common humanity*. Thus for Nietzsche humanity is not something that by nature is possessed of certain distinctive capacities; rather, it is the subject of repression as it has been socially organized throughout history.

Much of Nietzsche's genealogy is consistent with what Horkheimer and Adorno say in *Dialectic of Enlightenment*: the idea that the things commonly considered to be naturally human are the product of millennia of social repression, and that this repression might be discernible through a "biological" or "genealogical" standpoint – a "natural-historical" standpoint, for Horkheimer and Adorno – allows for a certain degree of harmony between their respective positions. Yet despite Nietzsche's clear influence,[47] the latter might be said to differ from Nietzsche on three related points that ultimately bring their projects into discord: (1) the place of power in the natural world, (2) the role of reason and its historical possibilities, and (3) the possibilities available for politics and the relations it establishes between animals. Concerning (1), Nietzsche claims that "anything in existence" has come to be the way it is, and continues to be transformed, according to the purpose imposed upon it "by a power superior to it." This continual process of transformation in which old meanings and purposes are "obscured or completely obliterated" is a result of the "overpowering and dominating" forces of which "everything in the organic world" consists.[48]

46 Nietzsche, *On the Genealogy of Morality*, Essay II, §3, 38. *GM* hereafter.

47 Adorno would later claim that "of all the so-called great philosophers I owe him [Nietzsche] by far the greatest debt – more even than to Hegel." See *PMP*, 172; *NSAV10*, 255.

48 Nietzsche, *GM*, EII, §12, 51.

While terms such as "anything in existence," or everything in the "organic world," suggest that Nietzsche is making ontological claims that would hold for any society at any point in history, for Horkheimer and Adorno, as is consistent with Adorno's later philosophy, such ontology could only ever be that of the "wrong state of things."[49] That is, while Nietzsche's genealogical standpoint shows that any power is itself historically constituted, the *relation between* historically constituted powers based on domination and submission that characterizes the "organic world" is held to be unchanging. Yet for Horkheimer and Adorno, not only is the power that overpowers another always a historically constituted power, but the relation between these powers that compels one to dominate another must also be seen as historically constituted. The organic world is thus not an unchanging substratum upon which human society sits, nor is it an unchanging drive that animates continually changing historical entities; rather, nature and natural drives are themselves internally mediated by history through emerging forms of sociopolitical organization. The idea that meanings and purposes are continually being displaced and reinterpreted informs Adorno's approach to concepts in his turn toward the non-conceptual; but as we have seen, this turn is illuminated by a "messianic light" that shows these things might be other than they are, and not simply in the sense that what appears to be a natural power is in fact historically constituted – the structure of domination in which power is exercised might itself be radically transformed. While Nietzsche himself comes close to something like a messianic *impulse* with the notion that his "man of the future" will "redeem" what came before, ultimately the redemption to be found in forgiving debts and renouncing the law of equivalence is for him a new display of power, and with it, a new imposition of values.[50] That the strong will and must triumph, even in redemption, is for Adorno a projection of sociopolitical domination – it does not tell us what might lie beyond a society organized around such domination.

We might consider the first consequence of this differing approach to the place of power in the natural world to be a different relation between Nietzsche and Horkheimer and Adorno with regard to reason and so to the legacy of the Enlightenment. Nietzsche's genealogy undermines the notion of reason as a godlike capacity that distinguishes humans from other animals; it shows reason instead to have evolved as another instance of the biological drive for dominance, and as such, the means

49 Recall *ND*, 11; *GSB6*, 22.
50 Nietzsche, *GM*, EII, §24, 66. Cf. §10, 48.

by which a certain historically constituted animal learned to exercise its power and so dominate others through the imposition of its own standards. Horkheimer and Adorno agree with this exposition of reason to the extent that its nature must also be seen as internally mediated by history, but they also hold that reason as an expression of domination has at the same time made intelligible its opposite, the possibility of freedom, and with it the possibility of a different articulation of reason. To reach this different articulation of reason and the freedom it may enable requires that reason recognize its own complicity in domination and thus its own relation to nature. Insofar as domination is perpetuated by reason unaware of this complicity, to become aware of complicity would be to deprive domination of one of its tools, thus compelling it to perpetuate itself by different means. Through this transformation of social domination, reason would itself be transformed, for, like nature, it is continually subject to the internal mediation of history and the forms of sociopolitical organization that emerge therein. In this way, Horkheimer and Adorno cling to the idea of the transformative capacity of reason and thus can write that "freedom in society is inseparable from enlightenment thinking."[51]

Concerning the prospects of reason in the service of future life, Nietzsche's genealogy is not so sanguine. Reason, calculation, and memory have for Nietzsche served to give the human animal greater depth, perfecting repression in such a way as to create the possibility of a new kind of animal that might relate to the human as the human presently tends to relate to other animals. However, reason, calculation, and memory are embedded in a system of equivalences that has grown so broad as to have become an impediment to the realization of this possibility. For a new, higher kind of animal to emerge that might rule over humanity, what is needed is the ability to posit values, meanings, and purposes that are exclusive – values that not all will be capable of holding. The positing of such values presupposes the power to affirm both one's particularity and one's superiority over and above the rest of humanity as a *singular* individual, and that power has been eroded by the system of equivalences in which reason, calculation, and memory have emerged. If values can be made equivalent, then none can rule, and this would undermine the very principle of life, which is the drive to overpower and to dominate. If life is to triumph over "the great nausea, the will to nothingness," and "nihilism,"[52] then potential rulers

51 Horkheimer and Adorno, *DE*, xvi; *DA*, 3.
52 Nietzsche, *GM*, EII, §24, 66.

must be seduced into exercising their power to distinguish themselves as singular individuals. Insofar as reason is tied to a system of equivalences, distinguishing oneself as singular will involve the emphasis of something other than one's capacity for reason.

The political consequences of these two points mark Horkheimer and Adorno's decisive split with Nietzsche. For Nietzsche one must be seduced into affirming one's singularity against all equivalences, thus making oneself capable of affirming one's life not only in the triumphs but also in the defeats and suffering, so that one might say, "I wanted it thus!"[53] In making one's own life in its singularity the content of the will, and so living as if one had given oneself one's own life, one separates oneself from the humanity that exists in the equivalences established between particular triumphs and defeats, in particular sufferings, subject to external authority. The capacity to withstand being the sole author of one's life becomes the new capacity that elevates one above others – this is what makes the singular individual capable of this performance superior to others. Insofar as the affirmation of the singularity of one's life is a response to seduction, to being seduced by its potential beauty, then Nietzsche can be seen to re-establish the aristocratic rule of the beautiful, the nobility of those who would rule others like cattle by virtue of the strength of their mythic superiority.

Horkheimer and Adorno reject this myth as the perpetuation of domination, even class rule. For them, Nietzsche's "man of the future" is *all too human* in that the order he represents is precisely the same kind of sociopolitical domination that has characterized a prominent strand of human development – that is, one where humans separate themselves from other animals and rule over them as their superiors. While the particularities that Nietzsche would isolate as the ones most important to establish the singularity of a new subject differ from the intellectual powers isolated by Aristotle to differentiate human from animal, this same pattern of separation and domination we find in Nietzsche remains consistent with that found in the Aristotelian problematic. Adorno, however, offers something different. For him, the political problem posed by humanity is the possibility of a world free of domination, and so one where the aggressive instincts that have informed such human development have been pacified. To understand how this pacification relates to other animals, and thus how Nietzsche's own solution is a perpetuation of the order of domination in which humanity emerged and whose continued existence it maintains, we must

53 Nietzsche, "On Redemption," in *Thus Spoke Zarathustra*, 161.

look to the constitution of the human in relation to the animal and at how "the animal" can be considered non-identical to the concept of humanity.

Recall that what Adorno calls identity is a correspondence between an object and its concept. To think is to identify, to establish a correspondence between a concept and an object given in the material world. The animal that became human evolved for self-preservation by establishing such correspondences; thus Adorno refuses to separate thinking and life activity into independent spheres, for thinking evolved as a response to life activity and is itself an activity meant to preserve life. Identity must therefore be seen as a response to the threat that nature posed to early or even prehumans, just as the concept must be seen as the "idea-tool" (*ideelle Werkzeug*), which allowed for the seizure and control of the objects of the natural world.[54] From this standpoint, the non-identical has the appearance of a threat to human survival and for this reason must continually be seized by concepts and identified. Identification must therefore be seen as a compulsive activity born in terror, whose continuation represents both the perpetuation of the human attempt to dominate "the nightmare of nature" and the "dizzying horror of the organic"[55] that spawned this compulsion.[56] Yet just as the natural world is always evading human efforts to seize, control, and manipulate it in myriad ways, so does the object always exceed the concept and undermine its subjectively established identity. Adorno's turn toward the non-identical, then, is a turn toward that which is continually suppressed by the concept in the terror-stricken human compulsion to dominate, in the hope that this terror might be exorcised.

Perhaps nowhere is the violence of this suppression, and so the terror that accompanies it, more evident than in the concept of the human being. With Horkheimer, Adorno writes: "Throughout European history the idea of the human being has been expressed in contradistinction to the animal. The latter's lack of reason is the proof of human dignity."[57] If the concept of the *human* is a way of establishing an identity between the material entity, or body, in the array of a certain set of relationships and activities in which it engages, then the non-identical would be that which falls outside of the concept – all the practices, relationships, and physical features that fall outside this ideal. Insofar as the concept of

54 *DE*, 31; *DA*, 46; *ND*, 11; *GSB6*, 23.

55 As Jameson puts it. See *Late Marxism*, 96; 218.

56 *ND*, 172; *GSB6*, 174.

57 *DE*, 203; *DA*, 262.

the human is "expressed in contradistinction to the animal" and "few other ideas are so fundamental to Western anthropology,"[58] then the concept of the *animal* points to the practices, relationships, and physical features that are non-identical to the concept of the human. The animal, then, appears as a symbol for the rejected possibilities of the life that calls itself human – that which is subject to the ban erected by the concept of the human. It is for this reason, Adorno claims, that identifying certain visible groups of human beings with animals "is the key to the pogrom."[59] When certain humans are identified as animals, their destruction becomes the preservation of the relationships, practices, and features that can be identified beneath a given conception of human and thus the maintenance of the ban this concept imposes on other forms of life.

Insofar as it is specifically intellectual capacities such as reason that have marked the distinction between human and animal, then insofar as reason is not seen as a function of the body, the body becomes a liminal space between the human and the animal. The body is the necessary site of all human endeavours, but it is only as commanded by reason that it performs in ways that are identified by the concept of human – in its involuntary functions, such as the rudiments of perception and experiences of pleasure and pain, the body is animal. Absent reason, the world of the body, like that of the animal, is one without concepts, caught in a flux of drives that conform only to vital patterns, deprived of volition, meaning, and purpose, and produced as such through what might be seen as the other side of the anthropological processes that serve to constitute the human: the treatment of other animals. It is in "the twitching movements of the bound victims" that the human body is found to be "mechanical, blind, automatic," in the same sense as an animal, yet it is precisely this involuntariness of the body that resists identity with the concept of the human. The concept of the animal, in pointing toward what is non-identical in the concept of the human, that which resists life organized under the concept of humanity, bears witness to the possibility of a humanity transformed.[60]

The problem of human constitution in relation to "the animal" and the ethical implications thereof have been taken up by recent philosophers,

---

58 *DE*, 204; *DA*, 262.

59 *MM*, 105; *GSB4*, 118.

60 Thus the attempt to separate in Adorno "impulse actions" from "reflex actions" would serve to perpetuate a humanist reading of Adorno that upholds the ban on the animality of the body. See Shuster, *Autonomy after Auschwitz*, 106.

perhaps most notably by Jacques Derrida, who notes that the concept of "the animal" is itself a *bêtise* that reduces the "heterogeneous multiplicity of the living" to a singular concept in order to facilitate the identification of the human. Yet insofar as this *bêtise* also facilitates *resistance* to the human, we should be cautioned against its simple rejection. Derrida claims that the very act of reducing the multiplicity of animal life to "the animal" in the singular reveals the *animality* of the human, in terms of both its latent aggression and its cognitive limits. This claim is broadly consistent with Horkheimer and Adorno's attempt to expose the non-identical in the concept of the human.[61] However, rather than conclude that this moment of human animality gestures toward the possible transformation of the human, as do Horkheimer and Adorno, and perhaps even the transience of the concept of the human as such, Derrida suggests instead that the dissolution of this concept of "the animal" in the singular into a concept of *animals* in the plural – the "heterogeneous multiplicity of the living" – might inhibit the violence perpetuated through these concepts.[62] However, my discussion of the Aristotelian problematic above suggests serious problems with Derrida's conclusion.

Aristotle shows little interest in the concept of "the animal" in the singular – for him the study of animals and their contrast to human beings is always a matter of grasping animal life in its heterogeneity and multiplicity, and these do not prevent their conceptual capture and hierarchical organization. Derrida's turn to heterogeneity and multiplicity seems to assume that the plural and the singular, or *the Many* and *the One*, are liberating or repressive in and of themselves, rather than attending to the particular instantiations of the singular and the plural at the sociopolitical level as these change historically.[63] Though his apparent intent is laudable, Derrida's attempt to extend "the similar, the fellow, to all forms of life, to all species" and so claim that "all animals qua living beings are my fellows,"[64] serves to advance the empire of

61 Derrida, *The Animal That Therefore I Am*, 31, 41. Indeed, Derrida even acknowledges Adorno as an inspiration for these ideas. See Derrida, "Fichus," 180.

62 Derrida, *The Animal That Therefore I Am*, 47–8.

63 Cook reads Adorno in this same vein, claiming that "Adorno aims to foster reconciliation by overcoming the tyranny of the One to reveal the astounding profusion of the Many" (*Adorno on Nature*, 162). Adorno himself avoids these ontological terms, hearing in them the reverberation of myth: "The illusion of taking direct hold of the Many would be a mimetic regression, as much a recoil into mythology, into the horror of the diffuse, as the thinking of the One" (*ND*, 158; *GSB6*, 160).

64 Derrida, *The Beast and the Sovereign*, vol. 1, 109.

the same, whose subject is positive humanity, the humanity constituted and maintained through violence. Much as with attempts to extend human rights to certain kinds of non-human animals without a concomitant transformation of the human subject, their inclusion in the world of humans ignores the degradation of humanity and the intraspecies violence by which society is maintained.[65] Thus the task is not simply to expand the domain of the human and so make animals into human subjects; it is also to liberate the human from itself and from its own need to dominate others.

As my examination of Nietzsche has shown, however, this recovery of animality, of thinking of humans and their particular capacities genealogically, is on its own not enough to transform the relation between these animals wherein some must overpower and dominate others.[66] In Hegelian terms, Nietzsche's overcoming of the human amounts to its *abstract negation*: it fails to take into account the actual structure in which the human emerged as its object and so fails to transform the conditions of possibility upon which the human depends. Instead we require, again in Hegelian terms, the *determinate negation* of reason and humanity put forward by Horkheimer and Adorno, wherein reason is not lost but rather displaced and transformed in its mediation by its other, the animality of the body and its involuntary impulses. Only mediated by its own repressed animality might the strictures that give rise to the human be relaxed and the human finally be reconciled to its own

---

65 See for instance Singer, *Animal Liberation*; Cavalieri and Singer, "A Declaration on Great Apes"; Martha C. Nussbaum, "Beyond 'Compassion for Humanity'"; and Donaldson and Kymlicka, *Zoopolis*.

66 This dimension of Nietzsche is lacking in Lemm, *Nietzsche's Animal Philosophy*. For Lemm, the shape and development of human life is defined in terms of the antagonism between human and animal life: where humans have defined themselves against their animality or sought to deny this animality "a productive role," so they have dominated and exploited one another (5). Nietzsche's philosophy, in its attempt to give human animality "a creative role in the constitution of social and political forms of life," moves "beyond the political domination of life," striving for "an overcoming of domination toward freer forms of social and political life" (5). While I agree with Lemm that animality is important to Nietzsche's conception of creativity, Lemm assumes an equal capacity for this creativity among different individuals that is completely absent in Nietzsche. Without this equality, it is difficult to see the "promise" of the overhuman (2) as anything other than the establishment of a new sociopolitical order where the distance between overhuman and human is every bit as great as that of human and animal in the present order. See Bull, *Anti-Nietzsche*, 40, 153; and Vázquez-Arroyo, *Political Responsibility*, 116ff. For a farther-reaching critique of Nietzsche than is possible here, see Waite, *Nietzsche's Corps/e*.

animality and thus to other animals. Theorizing this possibility, and thereby the turn to the non-identical of humanity found in the animal, thus involves seeing not the humanity of animals but rather the animality of human constitution. It is to Adorno's account of the animality of human particularity that I now turn.

## Non-identity as Human Animality

In the interest of showing that the reconciled humanity toward which Adorno gestures is an animal other than human, I have argued that the mimetic impulses that underlay human life have been produced as human through what he calls "anthropology" and that the various practices and capacities designated as "animal" should be considered non-identical to the anthropologically produced conception of the human. Adorno's attempt to reveal that which is non-identical to the concept within the conceptual framework of thinking, in this context, thus involves revealing the animal within what we consider human, or showing those aspects of the human that we understand to be most definitively human to in fact be animal – the task I take up in this section. The rudiments of this task can be found as early as "The Idea of Natural-History" (1932), in which Adorno attempts to comprehend what is most historical as being natural and what is most natural as being historical.[67] This attempt to grasp the entwinement of history and nature will find a new articulation in the entwinement of myth and enlightenment in his collaboration with Horkheimer. It will also inform his later work, perhaps most notably in his readings of Hegel and Marx.[68] Yet following this trend in Adorno's thinking and attempting to see in the human its repressed animality brings my interpretation of Adorno into conflict with what is arguably the most prominent interpretation of Adorno's ethical thought, referred to as his "ethical modernism."

The chief proponent of this view, J.M. Bernstein, expounds what he calls Adorno's "ethical modernism" in a rich and complex interpretation of Adorno's texts, a full account of which cannot be pursued here. Broadly put, however, it might be said that for Bernstein, Adorno's "ethical modernism" is an attempt to reconstruct the ethical meaning

67 *INH*, 117; *GSB.1*, 354–5. Cf. Mendieta, "Animal Is to Kantianism," 151; though for Mendieta, this project involves refounding metaphysics and anthropology, in the vein of Bernstein (see below).

68 Horowitz, *Ethics at a Standstill*, 81; Hullot-Kentor, "Introduction,'" 102–3.

lost to the ravages of the Enlightenment, which served to disenchant the world and thereby undermined the traditional objects of ethical life. For Bernstein, this makes Adorno something of a romantic Weberian: Adorno sees the disenchanted or secular world of modernity to be without a "rationally compelling" or "intrinsically motivating" normative account, and Bernstein understands providing such an account to be the aim of Adorno's philosophy.[69] To accomplish this aim, Adorno sets about reformulating how we think about concepts and their relation to objects so that our concepts might once again correspond to those objects that make up the "fundamental structures of ethical reasoning and moral insight" – that is, authority, knowledge, and experience, all of which have been set adrift by the corrosive powers of Enlightenment reason.[70]

With respect to nature, this project orients itself against the Enlightenment view that served to disenchant the natural world by seeing all anthropomorphism as myth. In the interest of purging myth, the Enlightenment drove a wedge between the human and natural worlds, transforming the objects of the natural world into mere fodder for human aims and thereby robbing them of the capacity to make ethical claims upon humans. Insofar as *human* nature is itself part of nature, however, this hard distinction is irrational and requires reconceptualization. To this end, Bernstein sees Adorno as reviving an idea of anthropomorphic nature, albeit a secular one, wherein the objects of the natural world have been *re-enchanted*. That is, the objects of the natural world are understood as being entwined with the human world so that what might be called human is impossible without them, and insofar as human relations need necessarily encompass natural objects, natural objects would form part of human ethical life and so require some degree of ethical consideration.[71] In this way, Bernstein writes, "Adorno pursues romantic ends ... through hyper-cognitive means."[72]

Bernstein's interpretation is attractive for a number of reasons: Adorno is found to provide an answer to important ethical problems raised by modernity and offers a theory concerning the possibility of a more peaceable relation between humans and the natural world, thus making Bernstein's Adorno the (perhaps not so reluctant) colleague

69 Bernstein, *Adorno*, 18.
70 Bernstein, *Adorno*, 32–4.
71 Bernstein, *Adorno*, 191, 197.
72 Bernstein, *Adorno*, 4.

of Aristotelians such as MacIntyre and Nussbaum.[73] Yet, there are significant problems with this view that must be confronted. As Marasco rightly claims, Bernstein's reading risks "attributing to Adorno a generalized nostalgia for enchanted and holistic nature."[74] I shall argue that Bernstein's interpretation fails to capture what I understand to be crucial in rethinking the human/animal distinction and its relation to politics and art. Bernstein downplays the transformative aspect of Adorno's thought, both politically and what we might call *mimetically*, by reifying the place of the human and so attempting to stamp the whole of the natural world with a human imprint in order for it to have ethical weight. Moreover, this view demands of the individual the kind of human activity that is itself linked to its own domination, for it bases the possibilities available to ethical life on an idealized notion of the human subject, one for whom the exercise of its basic capacities is precisely what sustains the order to which it is enthralled. On my reading, Adorno is not trying to find new foundations for the ethical life that modernity has displaced and thereby reconstruct its meaning; rather, he is trying to theorize how one might live a life denied such meaning.[75] To better grasp this life and its relation to animality, it is worth examining a critique levelled at Adorno and his work on Enlightenment with Horkheimer that captures this aspect of Adorno's thought better than does Bernstein.

In *Nihil Unbound*, Brassier seeks to advance the Enlightenment project by arguing that the disenchantment of the world is not a debilitating calamity to be mourned but rather an "invigorating vector of intellectual discovery" that ought to be celebrated and taken to its radical fulfilment. The philosophical fulfilment of the Enlightenment project, Brassier argues, involves affirming precisely the corrosive potential of reason that has disenchanted the world, and the nihilism that is its consequence, by "kicking away" the "pseudo-transcendental props" that persist in supporting the image of the world as possessing inherent meaning and value. With this comes the recognition of the mind-independence of the world and its utter indifference to human aims, which Brassier claims has been the triumph of modern scientific discovery.[76] From this perspective, human beings are less the source of

73 Interestingly, in focusing specifically on Adorno's ethical thought, Bernstein here serves to bring Adorno closer to Aristotle than he was found to be in an earlier study that focused on Adorno's aesthetics. See Bernstein, *The Fate of Art*, 234, 274.

74 Marasco, *The Highway of Despair*, 197n13.

75 Cf. Adorno, "The Actuality of Philosophy," 32; *GSB1*, 336.

76 Brassier, *Nihil Unbound*, xi, 26.

Enlightenment rationality than they are its temporary bearers, a transitory point in a narrative wherein an inhuman intelligence has awoken and is "in the process of sloughing off its human mask."[77] Reading Adorno (and Horkheimer) along the lines traced by Bernstein, Brassier finds their thought, as the rehabilitation of anthropomorphic nature and the "resurrection of Aristotelianism,"[78] to be a romantic and anachronistic attachment to the human being and a pining after a lost nature. For Brassier, to follow the inhuman trajectory of the Enlightenment is to see the *Dialectic of Enlightenment* not in the terms of Homer's *Odyssey*, that is, not as humanity's homecoming in anthropomorphic nature, but rather in the terms of Cronenberg's *The Fly*: "human reason is revealed to have been an insect's waking dream."[79]

To read Adorno *against* Bernstein, as attempting to think the animality of humans and how to live after the loss of meaning, *instead* of as the resurrection of meaning through anthropomorphic nature, is to find, perhaps startlingly, Adorno and Brassier aligned on certain important points. Adorno is not, as Brassier would have it, simply on the side of those who would mourn the disenchantment of the world. Adorno can be said to mourn the disenchantment of the world in that he sees the liquidation of features of the past that served to resist domination, such as individuality, as unhappy developments. Additionally, Adorno remains far less sanguine than Brassier concerning the progressive possibilities of the recent developments of reason. However, Adorno nevertheless *rejects* the idea of returning to some pre-given structure of ethical life seen as fundamental in the way Bernstein would have it, instead aiming to exploit the possibilities that history has made available to thinking in the hope of seeing new life dawn. Of nihilism and its relation to this hope, Adorno writes: "A thinking man's true answer to the question whether he is a nihilist would probably be 'Not enough' – out of callousness, perhaps, because of insufficient sympathy with anything that suffers. Nothingness is the acme of abstraction, and the abstract is the abominable."[80]

To begin unwinding the ideas bound in this quotation, we might note: (1) Adorno thinks that the abstractions of thinking involve anaesthetizing oneself to suffering in ways that can allow one to continue going

77 Brassier, *Nihil Unbound*, 48. A similar argument is made by Lyotard in *The Inhuman*, 8–23.

78 Brassier, *Nihil Unbound*, 40.

79 Ibid., 48. Cf. 244n13.

80 *ND*, 380; *GSB6*, 373.

about one's affairs despite one's own suffering and the suffering of others; however, (2) a *lack* of abstraction can also serve to trap one within one's own particularities and so fail to critically grasp the anaesthetizing role played by abstraction. In this sense, abstraction is the only means of curing abstraction, for it is only through critical thinking – that corrosive element of reason – that the conceptual screen that would shield us from the world becomes visible. To maintain a critical disposition to the world and so continue to press against one's own conceptual capture is, in a sense, to adopt a nihilist posture to the world, one that refuses satisfaction with any positive content: "Thought," Adorno writes, "honors itself by defending what is damned as nihilism." Thus Adorno defends the nihilism that sees the emptiness of all conceptual structures that have accompanied modernity against the "true nihilists," those who try to ignore or flee from this emptiness by championing the meanings and values of the past. Against these attempts to seek solace in past meanings and values, Adorno insists on persisting in the critical negativity of thought that would reject these "faded positivities,"[81] striving instead toward the fulfilment of this critical negativity in the new.

Adorno's thoughts on nihilism gesture toward his critique of anthropology and the concept of humanity produced therein and align his attempt to see the animality of the human with Brassier's comment on human reason being the dream of an insect. Though Adorno will occasionally employ conventional rhetorical tropes that make pejorative reference to human characteristics as "brute" or animalistic in some sense,[82] there is an important tendency in his thought to interpret those capacities that are traditionally held to be most human as in fact animal, thus undermining anthropocentric accounts of the world. For instance, while Adorno and Horkheimer claim that the "hypertrophy of the cerebral organ" in human beings is well-established enough to be considered more than "a freak event in natural history," they nevertheless insist on thinking of human beings as kinds of animals whose technological prowess must be understood as an extension of the aggressive drives mobilized for self-preservation, just as is found in other animals.[83] Likewise, Adorno reads the history of the transformations of economic forms described by Marx as analogous to the rise and fall of different animal species over millions of years.[84] Perhaps most

81 *ND*, 381; *GSB6*, 374.

82 Tellingly, these references occur more frequently in his lectures than in his published writings. See *PMP*, 133, 174; *NSIV10*, 197–8, 259; *MCP*, 77; *NSIV14*, 122.

83 *DE*, 184; *DA*, 234.

84 *ND*, 356; *GSB6*, 349

important for this view, however, is Adorno's insistence on describing the mental life of human beings, that which is traditionally considered to be most definitive of humankind and so thought to separate humans from other animals, in terms of animal life.

For Adorno, ideology can be likened to the rage a lion must have for the antelope it attacks,[85] psychological pathologies can be likened to the mutations suffered by dinosaurs prior to their extinction,[86] and the "sovereign mind" and its subjectivity must be seen to be entirely embedded in "the animal life of the species."[87] As noted above, Adorno thinks that thinking must be understood as the particular way humans evolved in their struggle for self-preservation: establishing correspondences between concepts and objects enabled humans to identify objective continuities in their worlds that signalled possible threats as well as aids to self-preservation. Yet with this capacity has come a kind of mental captivity, one that deadens our experience of particularity, which is to say, one that deadens us to suffering. Recall that to suffer is not simply to experience pain, but to experience as such – to *undergo*: it is at once to persist in time and to be changed by it, in the particular manner that one does as a living creature. In this sense suffering involves an indelibly passive element, for even where we are active, to experience our own activity as self-changing we must be worked upon by this activity – we must *suffer* it, and ourselves, as the complexes we contribute to creating both in resistance to and in adoption of the identities foisted upon us by our societies. Insofar as we tend to experience objects through concepts, the particularity of the suffering we witness is continually mediated and categorized within the forms of thought we have inherited through our cultures and languages, which in turn shape and are shaped by the vicissitudes of our societies.

In this sense, Adorno writes, our "mental captivity is exceedingly real."[88] The structure of individual consciousness and the limits it imposes on experience repeat the social captivity of the individual, whose very notion of the individual freedom being trammelled by society is itself a projection born of these social relations. Adorno links this mental captivity to the carapaces of armoured animals such as the triceratops and the rhinoceros; such carapaces, formed in the struggle for self-preservation, seem to have trapped them beneath their weight, yet

85 *ND*, 349. Cf. *ND*, 22; *GSB6*, 342, 33.
86 Adorno, "Opinion Delusion Society," 111; *GSB10.2*, 580.
87 *ND*, 22; *GSB6*, 33.
88 Adorno, "On Subject and Object," *CM*, 252; *GSB10.2*, 750.

they are compelled to drag them around as a kind of "ingrown prison which they seem – anthropomorphically, at least – to be trying vainly to shed."[89] Adorno even suggests that this "imprisonment in their survival mechanism" might explain the animal's ferocity – both for the rhinoceros and for the human being. Humans, like the rhinoceros, have inherited their conceptual imprisonment as both a defence mechanism and a weapon, and insofar as they are so equipped to defend and to attack, it is really no surprise that they produce societies that require one do both in order to survive. However, in seeing the animality of this condition, that "the human being is a result, not an *eidos*,"[90] a response to certain historical pressures that are, conceivably, subject to change, we might envision the evolution of an animal other than the one we are, one other than the animal constituted in resistance to the threats of starvation, exposure, and violence.

Insofar as the animal can be seen as the non-identical of the human, to attempt to reveal in the identical concept of the human what is non-identical to it is to see human activity as animal activity. Put differently: Adorno uses animal objectivity to limit the pretension to absoluteness of human subjectivity. This turning of the human toward the animal has three important sociopolitical consequences. First, when human activity is viewed as animal activity, human pretentions to sovereignty and autonomy are revealed to be contingent, fragile, and transient. That is, what is understood to be most fundamentally and irreducibly human remains as such only as a response to certain conditions that could be otherwise. Second, and following from this first consequence, the human is most animal precisely where it had thought to make its break from animality, thus revealing a continuity between human reason and animal aggression – that is, we are most *inhuman* precisely where we see ourselves to be most human. Thus to understand ourselves as uniquely human and so uniquely possessing reason, faith, or even historical dynamism is to lock ourselves into a particular

89 *ND*, 180; *GSB6*, 182; Adorno, "On Subject and Object," 252; *GSB10.2*, 749–50. Adorno's use of the image of the rhinoceros here may reflect the influence of Eugène Ionesco's *Rhinocéros*, to which he makes reference at *AT*, 347; *GSB7*, 516. Though Ionesco's play appears to cling to some sort of humanism by giving lines ridiculing humanism to those characters who transform into animals, only Berenger, the character most poorly adjusted to the demands of being human, who claims to lack "will-power [*volonté* ]," manages to resist transforming into a rhinoceros. Those who triumph the will and reason are the first to succumb. See Ionesco, "Rhinoceros."

90 Adorno, "On Subject and Object," 258; *GSB10.2*, 758.

form of life no less free from compulsion than "the industriousness of ants and bees, or the grotesque struggles of the beetle as it carries a blade of grass."[91]

Third and last, if we are to resist the inhumanity of humanity that serves to trap humans as humans, the inhumanity that would reconcile us to societies in which we are compelled to struggle for our survival, then we must then draw upon those capacities seen as *merely* animal – those that would be excluded from the heights of what is considered most definitively human. Drawing on animal capacities in this way is what it means to live in a world where humanity is inhumane, where historical events have ruptured the correspondence between ethical meaning and the daily activities one must suffer to live. It is for this reason that Adorno writes that against the "caricature of freedom" offered by personality, what is left to morality today is "to try to live so that one may believe himself to have been a good animal."[92] Our own animality is the necessary starting point for the resistance against inhumanity, for it allows us to acknowledge our own inhumanity and complicity with its order, while drawing upon that which shrinks from the grammar of that order – that which resists what is seen to be definitively human.

For Adorno, we moderns are all Gregor Samsa – Gregor's triumph is to have realized his own animality, to have come directly into contact with the fact of human reason as the waking dream of an insect. Where Gregor fails is that he refuses to pursue the challenge his animality presents to human compulsion, attempting instead to live his human life as before. The impossibility of living as an insect in a human world, of circulating between the points of what would be human meaning but can no longer apply, is one for which Gregor pays with his life. Brassier in his critique actually follows this particular vector of Adorno's thought more closely than Bernstein. There can be no new correspondence between ethical meaning and the daily activities we pursue for self-preservation without the concomitant transformation of society, and with it, all that is considered human.

## The Utopian Animal

The activities Adorno considers the most definitively human are the spellbound attempts of a human animal to repress animality; thus they

91 Adorno, "Marginalia to Theory and Praxis," 262; *GSB10.2*, 762–3. Cf. *ND*, 369; *GSB6*, 362.

92 *ND*, 299; *GSB6*, 294. Cf. Adorno, "The Problem of a New Type of Human Being," 465–7.

are continuous with the compulsion traditionally thought to animate animal life. This insight underscores the inhumanity of the human and is why Adorno rejects the notion of humanism as the promotion of certain fundamentally human capacities. But to reveal the animality within humanity is not simply to discard humanity *because* of its animality, as if humanity were simply a lie; nor is it to reveal the need to overcome this animal condition in a *truly human* one, for as we have seen, insofar as the promise of humanity is a humanity without boundaries or limitations, it is not humanity.

To better understand this point we might again make reference to Adorno's critique of Hegel. As we have seen, Adorno criticizes the elements of theodicy and teleology in Hegelian philosophy, arguing that these limit Hegelian dialectic to the positive unfolding of that which is originally given. While this unfolding may pass *through* the negative, it *must* conclude with the positive reconciliation of this negativity to a whole that was already contained in its origin as embryo. Adorno claims that his utopian or messianic displacement of the origin and with it the possibilities available to thinking is such that his negative dialectic avoids the false reconciliation of the Hegelian variety: a negation of a negation does not result in a positive, he says, but rather transforms the whole in which negative and positive were opposed.[93]

To think that the negation of inhumanity results in humanity is to follow the logic that Adorno rejects – the idea that the negation of a negation results in a positive – by viewing negative humanity as requiring the passage of history to become what it positively is. However, Adorno thinks what can legitimately be called human, those acts of resistance that gesture toward the arrest of violence and compulsion that I earlier called *negative humanity*, always already were the negation of the inhuman. A second negation, the negation of this negation, is thus not to choose humanity over inhumanity, but to negate the very structure in which each is constituted in opposition to the other. The persistence of negativity here, Adorno's "nihilist" posture, is thus an attempt to transform the very constellation of possibilities in which the human has come to be, and so gesture toward a new form of life. As Adorno requires the third term of *reconciled humanity* to obstruct the reconciliation of negative humanity with inhumanity in a positive order constituted through their permanent struggle, we get intimations of what reconciled humanity might look like through its refractions in instances of resistance and, as I shall argue in the next chapter, in

93 *ND*, 159–61; *GSB6*, 161–3

the experience of works of art. Here, however, we find that the link between Adorno's utopianism and animality, seen in these flashes of animality, confirms that reconciled humanity would be an animal other than human, and that the sociopolitical transformation required to end compulsion would free humanity of its own constitutive fetters.

In understanding Adorno's reconciled humanity to be a kind of animal, it is important to realize that this animality is not a return to some prehuman, animal past. With Horkheimer, Adorno writes that animals are without concepts and as such are trapped in a perpetual present that, uninterrupted by thought, is "dreary and depressive."[94] Though we have seen that human reason must itself be viewed as an animal drive, we have also seen that to view the human as an *eidos* possessed of certain fundamental capacities is to trap what we call human in a state much like this perpetual present. It is reflection that might serve to interrupt this cycle and so propel humans toward their transformation,[95] and for this reflection concepts are necessary. But for this reflection to displace rather than reinforce the conceptual capture of human identity, it needs to stem from an experience of the non-identity of the human, which was found to be the animal, or animality. It is for this reason that Adorno, in conversation with Horkheimer, will claim that although our "animal phase" can no longer be retrieved, animals might nevertheless "teach us what happiness is." To this claim, Horkheimer responds that freedom is to "achieve the condition of an animal at the level of reflection," which he links to the possibility of no longer having to work.[96] Adorno further refines this point in a later conversation: "Philosophy exists in order to redeem what you see in the look of an animal." Adorno links this redemption to the negation of the interests of self-preservation.[97]

In these passages, we see the animal as a symbol of what is blocked by the concept of humanity, but redeeming this blocked possibility requires both conceptual thinking and the transformation of society. Specifically, this transformation would be one to end the struggle for self-preservation in which the human was constituted and that formed the ground on which our interests have been discernible and on which the organization of our lives through labour has depended. The animal in this sense, what is seen in its gaze, is the possibility of living a

94 *DE*, 205; *DA*, 263.
95 *ND*, 345; *GSB6*, 338–9.
96 *TNM*, 16; *GSB14*, 39–40.
97 *TNM*, 71; *GSB14*, 58.

life unsubordinated to instrumental interests. It is for this reason that "Utopia goes disguised in the creatures,"[98] in animal life, for the lives of animals are without human purpose and so are not directed toward necessary ends organized beneath the banner of exchange. In this sense, what the animal reveals is the possibility of *individuality*, that hallmark of the most definitively human, whose gross parody is thought to be what modern Western societies are organized for.[99]

The possibility of this individuality and its denial are visible in the tiger "endlessly pacing back and forth in his cage,"[100] and its promise can be found in zoological gardens, which Adorno claims are the bourgeois equivalent of Noah's Ark, preparing for the flood the bourgeoisie itself is precipitating. The zoological garden, and the imagination it stirs, exhibits the hope that animals might survive "the wrong" done to them by humans and thereby "give rise to a better species, one that finally makes a success of life"[101] – a hope that likewise reflects the human desire for the end of its capture. It is in fact this *human* capture to which Adorno alludes when he writes that the eyes of apes "seem objectively to mourn that they are not human,"[102] for insofar as humans are no less trapped in a form of life they understand to be the measure of good, they might only recognize their own capture through the capture of other animals.

In this way we might liken humanity to the stupidity (*Dummheit*) of which Adorno and Horkheimer write in the concluding fragment of *Dialectic of Enlightenment*. "Stupidity is a scar" that "marks a spot where the awakening play of muscles has been inhibited instead of fostered": it marks "the points where hope has come to a halt."[103] Adorno and Horkheimer take the feeler of the snail, vulnerably stretching out into the world in curiosity, as their "emblem of intelligence," for it is only in seeking out new directions in this manner that the animals that exist came to be as they are, and it is only insofar as this movement into the beyond is repulsed that they must remain as they are, continuing along the same beaten paths. Self-same humanity might in this way be seen as the emblem of stupidity, the ossification of intelligence that would turn away from the possibility of a new form of life dawning,

98 *MM*, 228; *GSB4*, 261.
99 *ND*, 343; *GSB6*, 337.
100 *MM*, 116; *GSB4*, 131.
101 *MM*, 115; *GSB4*, 130.
102 *AT*, 113; *GSB7*, 172.
103 *DE*, 214; *DA*, 274–5.

a form that, through the "feeler" of intelligence, of reflection, "might emerge from the clearly formed species to which the individual creature belongs."[104] Reconciled humanity, then, represents a state in which humanity has laid down its humanity, in which the particular traits thought to be definitively human and those considered to be common with other animals have been drawn upon so as to bring about a new form of life. Though the coring of human meaning by enlightened modernity has reduced the "divine parody" of humanity to its animality, it is here in our animality that hope persists, for only in "the feeble tail-wagging of a dog" might "the ideal of nothingness evaporate."[105] That is, only our animality can cure the nihilism that has reduced humans to animality, and only as some new kind of animal might reconciled humanity become a positive reality and in this way leave the dynamism of struggle behind.

Perhaps the most concise statement of this utopian shedding of human dynamism is to be found in the aphorism titled "Sur l'eau" in *Minima Moralia.* There Adorno speculates on the possible ends of a utopian "true society," claiming that the insistence on the positing of ends and the bustling mobilization to meet them together reflect bourgeois values and the concept of nature these presuppose: dynamism is itself an "anthropological reflex of the laws of production."[106] *Contra* the natural persistence of dynamism, Adorno imagines a world where humans are without want, a world whose enjoyment has thereby been transformed. Rather than throwing themselves into "the conquest of strange stars," such a humanity might be content in an animal existence, "lying on the water and looking peacefully at the sky."[107] This, Adorno suggests, would be true peace, the "eternal peace" of a "fulfilled utopia" – one that is free of sociopolitical domination – indeed, free even of the compulsion that inheres in what we consider the natural psychological structure of humanity.[108] To grasp the two layers of the transformation

104 *DE*, 213; *DA*, 274.

105 *ND*, 380; *GSB6*, 373.

106 *MM*, 156; *GSB4*, 178.

107 *MM*, 156–7; *GSB4*, 179.

108 Though Chrostowska claims that the relation here between utopia and animality cannot be taken literally, it might be asked what "literally" would mean in this context. Though Adorno does indeed rely on simile to illustrate that life in his utopia would be experienced *like* animals experience it, even a humanity transformed into some other kind of animal would still be a particular kind of animal undoubtedly different from other animals as apes, dogs, and porpoises are different from one another. Why this would mean that the subject of Adorno's utopia would not *literally* be some kind of animal is unclear. See Chrostowska, "Thought Woken by Memory," 110n61.

involved in such a utopia, of society and of the individual, Adorno pairs two wildly different texts: Maupassant's account of sailing between St. Tropez and Monte Carlo, "Sur l'eau," from which the aphorism takes its name, and Kant's philosophical sketch, "Perpetual Peace," referenced by Adorno toward the end of the same aphorism. Together these texts form a constellation whose particular combination of terms – like the lock of Adorno's safe deposit box – springs open to a possibility that would otherwise remain hidden.[109] These texts, and the relation between them Adorno constructs, are worth examining in greater detail.[110]

As its title indicates, Kant's essay "Perpetual Peace" is a theoretical plan for securing lasting peace, here understood principally as that between nation-states. To summarize the most important points this essay makes for my present discussion, Kant claims that war is a result of the lawless condition in which states and their interests exist in opposition to one another and that this condition would be ended with the establishment of a world republic wherein each state, like an individual in the state of nature, would renounce the lawlessness of its pure freedom and so bring itself beneath the yoke of public coercion, or international law. However, Kant claims that this solution is unlikely because it runs contrary to the "will of the nations" and their own understanding of their particular rights – that is, their commitment to their own sovereignty and their own particular laws.[111] Consequently, Kant advances a kind of second-best solution, one that might *take men as they are, and laws as they might be.*

---

109 Recall *ND*, 163; *GSB6*, 166. Adorno, "The Actuality of Philosophy," 35; *GSB1*, 340.

110 Schweppenhäuser also remarks on Adorno's use of Maupassant and Kant in this aphorism; however, he does not develop how each relates to the other (such that their meaning is found in this relation) in the way I do here. Moreover, his interpretation of the reference to Maupassant depends on an episode in the 1876 version of the story, rather than the story Maupassant published under the same title in 1888. In the 1876 version, the peaceful experience of being on the water suddenly turns to terror as the sailor finds his boat caught on something below the surface and rendered unmovable. He regains his composure after his boat is dislodged only to discover later that it had been the corpse of an old woman with a stone tied around her neck that had weighed down his anchor. For his part, Adorno makes no attempt to clarify to which version of "Sur l'eau" his own appropriation refers. I base my reading below on the 1888 version and the account of animality therein, though the experience of peace as dependent or bound up with the suffering of others persists in both versions, thus requiring the mediation of Kant, I argue. See Schweppenhäuser, *Theodor W. Adorno*, 87–9.

111 Kant, "Perpetual Peace," 104–5.

Kant's second-best solution is to establish a federation for the promotion of peace that would aim to end all war by securing the sovereign rights of individual states, but without binding them to the coercive power of a higher law, as would a world republic. Kant envisions this pacific federation as balancing the power-seeking and self-serving inclinations of states against one another: each would be held to recognize the sovereign rights of other states and so abstain from waging war upon them, for fear of losing recognition of its own sovereign rights and being attacked in turn. In this way, "peace is created and guaranteed by an equilibrium of forces and a most vigorous rivalry."[112] No longer dependent on moral improvement, but relying instead on the power of nature and the inclinations Kant thinks it has given human beings, such an arrangement would accommodate even "a nation of devils," so long as those devils were sufficiently rational to understand how this arrangement promoted their own particular interests.[113]

While the reading of Adorno I have pursued above places him in agreement with Kant that "perpetual peace" must be the goal toward which humanity strives, and that this peace must inevitably be rooted in something like natural inclinations and would require the transformation of political institutions, Adorno's turn toward the animality of humanity keeps him from fully endorsing Kant's position. Kant's theorization of the possibility of perpetual peace depends on an understanding of the human being as a creature divided between its free will and the capacity for reason on the one hand, and the mechanism of its nature on the other. Consequently, while the world republic requires that humans cultivate morality by aligning their particular wills with the universal exigencies of reason and adapt themselves to law, the pacific federation organizes human life so that nothing more is required of human beings than that the mechanism of their nature pursue the course it is bound to pursue. However, for Adorno this arrangement means Kant has bought peace at the price of freedom, for Kant bases his political recommendations on human nature rather than viewing human nature as a product of the mechanisms of coercion.[114]

Insofar as Adorno understands what we consider natural to be historically produced, to follow the blindly mechanical workings of one's nature is to acquiesce to the compulsions that animate one's society

112 Kant, "Perpetual Peace," 114.

113 Kant, "Perpetual Peace," 112.

114 On the repressive dimension of Kantian humanism, see Rensmann, "National Sovereigntism and Global Constitutionalism," 31ff.

at a particular point in history and that are required for the perpetuation of sociopolitical domination. We might, perhaps, say there is peace in Kant's pacific federation, but it is the peace of the vanquished and unfree. Kant's world republic fares little better: here freedom is found only insofar as one is capable of subordinating one's natural inclinations to those of the whole. Elsewhere Kant candidly puts this process of adapting one's particularity to the necessary universality in terms of the human being requiring "a master to break his self-will and force him to obey a universally valid will under which everyone can be free." Or more bluntly: "man is *an animal who needs a master*."[115] As we have seen, Adorno considers such statements to be the anthropological reflexes of social domination, and for this reason he speculates that a free humanity will be free even of the will.[116] In this light, his turn toward the non-identical of the human, the animal, can be seen as an attempt to draw upon Kant's insights regarding the possibility of a perpetual peace but without having to sacrifice freedom. To this end, he requires an experience of freedom that is animal in the sense of not being subordinated to the exigencies of the will, yet something other than the compulsive activity of natural mechanism. Adorno finds such an experience in Maupassant's "Sur l'eau."

In the 1888 version of "Sur l'eau," Maupassant recounts a leisurely voyage by sail between St. Tropez and Monte Carlo, during which he reflects on everything from the wind, and war, to human nature and society; all of this he prefaces with the comment that his trip provided him with an opportunity to see nothing more than "water, sun, cloud, and rocks," which gave him no more than the simple thoughts one has when borne "drowsily along on the cradle of the waves."[117] This preface recalls Adorno's utopian image of an animal "lying on the water, and looking peacefully at the sky," and in this regard, Maupassant's critical view of humanity and his celebration of animal solidarity resonate deeply with Adorno's turn to animality. With characteristic hyperbole, Maupassant claims that one would need to be "blind and besotted by stupidity and vanity" to think that one is "anything more than an animal." We human beings are, for him, "shut-up, imprisoned inside ourselves" and in our vain sense of superiority: in reality, the human being

115 Kant, "Idea for a Universal History," 46.

116 *ND*, 264; *GSB6*, 261. This point can also be read as a polemic against Gehlen's anthropology, which depends on a radically un-Kantian conception of the will to define humanity. See Gehlen, *Man*, 358, 360.

117 Maupassant, *Afloat*, 2.

is but "a two-legged insect."[118] It is this vanity that blinds us to our own barbarity, which is most clearly visible in the efforts humans exert waging war. Regarding these efforts, Maupassant writes that "among all the species, the human race is the most frightful [*affreuse*] of all,"[119] thus inverting Sophocles's choral ode to the *deinos* of *anthropos* in *Antigone*: in light of this *affreuse*, lacking as it is the double meaning of fear *and* wonder found in *deinos*, Maupassant refuses to celebrate human power, finding in it instead only cause for contempt.

Having rejected humanity in this way, Maupassant can only feel himself to have escaped the dreariness of existence by hurling his body "like an animal" into the pleasures of life, loving the sky, forests, rocky crags, tall grass, and clear water like a bird, a wolf, a chamois, a horse, and a fish without being *uplifted* – that is, without finding in them his humanity, but rather loving these simply as a "brute beast."[120] This love that Maupassant feels for these aspects of the world brings him a sense of peace and solidarity with other animals, and this love grows from his own experience of himself as an animal non-identical to his humanity. This animal experience of peace as solidarity is what is missing from Kant's perpetual peace and its rational cessation of hostilities. But this is not to turn Maupassant into a simple critic of Kant, for in placing "Sur l'eau" in constellation with "Perpetual Peace," Adorno delivers Maupassant the animal to be broken by Kant the master. Though Maupassant spurns the aristocratic love of battle, there remain three elements of his misanthropy and celebration of animality that echo an aristocratic alliance with animals that Adorno uses Kant to disarm: a disinterest in questions of equality; a belief in the unchanging nature of human animality and progress; and a sense of the hopelessness of politics.

With respect to equality, Maupassant's aristocratic sensibilities allow him to praise the life of solitude despite the company of two sailors who obey his orders, to fantasize about a luxurious life including the ownership of slaves and a harem, and to complain about the ugliness of peasants.[121] Insofar as Kant insists that the possibility of perpetual peace is tied to Republican government and the equality made possible by it,[122] the importance Kant places on establishing political institutions

118 Maupassant, *Afloat*, 22, 25–6.
119 Maupassant, *Afloat*, 60. Cf. Maupassant, *Sur l'eau*, 100.
120 Maupassant, *Afloat*, 37.
121 Maupassant, *Afloat*, 9, 53–4, 61.
122 Kant, "Perpetual Peace," 99.

provides a critique of the experience of animality that would fail to translate itself into politics. With respect to politics and the question of progress, Maupassant claims that "man never changes," and for this reason, despite the evils of war and the monstrosities perpetuated by governments of all stripes, which he readily acknowledges, he can only imagine that humans will continue to bear the burden of these "hateful customs" and "criminal prejudices."[123] As in the "Sur l'eau" of 1876, Maupassant finds the experience of freedom toward the object, of peace with nature, tied to human misery like a stone around one's neck.

In opposition to the endless turning of the mythic wheel of peace and violence, Kant links the compulsion of mechanistic nature with progress, arguing that the conflicts brought about through the natural inclinations of human beings can be turned toward human progress and the possibility of perpetual peace, even if Adorno rejects certain details of this conception.[124] Moreover, for Kant, this progress necessarily involves a kind of political solution to the evils of war, one that Maupassant cannot grasp. In this way, Kant "breaks" Maupassant's animality, less in the sense of domestication than in the sense of showing it to be radically incomplete without political direction that would make the experience of this animality more than one only available to some at the expense of others. At the same time, Maupassant's animality shows Kant's conception of peace to lack the experience that would make his perpetual peace something other than empty form, and allows for a freedom that Kant's peace would not permit – a freedom without coercion.

In this sense, the lock is sprung, and the utopian content revealed: we are returned to a concept of a *political animal*. However, this animal can only be the product of political struggle that ceases to be struggle, the utopian possibility that guides and might emerge from political struggle but lies beyond it, not the basic set of capacities that serve unchanging to condition this struggle. In placing Kant and Maupassant in constellation, Adorno works against the tendency that sees politics as a necessarily human affair, as it is in Kant, or that sees animality as a kind of escape from politics, as it is in Maupassant. Both sides of this tendency, it might be said, depend on a flattened understanding of Aristotle that sees the human being as a political animal, to the exclusion of other animals. In bringing Kant and Maupassant together, Adorno

123 Maupassant, *Afloat*, 25, 31.

124 Kant, "Perpetual Peace," 113; Kant, "Idea for a Universal History," 50. Cf. Thomä, "Passion Lost, Passion Regained," 124.

returns to the question of the political animal posed by Aristotle, but that question is now transformed: the problem is no longer how to establish the political supremacy of what is best in humanity, but how to rescue animality from humanity's clutches, a rescue that would entail a radical transformation of humanity. Through Adorno's conception of reconciled humanity we see that a political animal is what we might become, not what we always already were. If Homer's *Odyssey* chronicles the primeval history of the subject in its return to its most fully developed form, humanity, then Maupassant's voyage, read in relation to Kant's "Perpetual Peace," allows us to glimpse a voyage that does not return to its source, but rather arrives at a foreign destination.

If reconciled humanity is itself the concept that preserves the negativity of negative humanity, glimpses of which are revealed in the resistance to force, then even the resistance of negative humanity, in its striving toward reconciled humanity, is already the animal non-identity of inhuman personality. Thus, the realization of reconciled humanity, the creation of an animal heretofore unseen, must require the cultivation of animality in a politically directed manner. For the utopian animal that is reconciled humanity to become a positive reality, we must therefore *learn to live as good animals* – we need a practice of animality directed toward the possibility of future transformation.

*Chapter Four*

# The Politics of an Aesthetic Animal

In a now infamous note to his lectures on Hegel's *Phenomenology of Spirit*, Alexandre Kojève claims that with the realization of the struggles that animate history, the driving force of these struggles, the human being as *Action*, would become superfluous. This cessation of Action would mean the end of revolutions, wars, and even philosophy: the human being would survive itself, in a sense, remaining alive as an animal now in harmony with nature, no longer a Subject opposed to an Object. Of the lives of these post-historical animals, Kojève writes provocatively:

> If Man becomes an animal again, his arts, his loves, and his play must also become purely "natural" again. Hence it would have to be admitted that after the end of History, men would construct their edifices and works of art as birds build their nests and spiders spin their webs, would perform musical concerts after the fashion of frogs and cicadas, would play like young animals, and would indulge in love like adult beasts.[1]

The image painted here shares an affinity with the animal aspect of Adorno's utopian speculations; however, Kojève would later revise this position in two important ways. Rather than seeing this state of post-historical animality as one found in a communist future, as he claims to have thought in 1946, Kojève would come to believe that history had in fact already ended with "Robespierre-Napoleon," and that the subsequent world wars, revolutions, and anti-colonial struggles for independence were merely aligning the rest of the world with the basic system of recognition attained by its vanguard in Revolutionary France.

---

1 Kojève, *Introduction to the Reading of Hegel*, 158–9n6.

However, this revision does not signal Kojève's dismissal of his claim regarding the return to animality. Rather, he is claiming that this return to animality is already an accomplished fact, for life is no longer organized around the existential crisis of recognition and the dynamic negating of the given that defined humanity, but rather has become focused on raising living standards, the acquisition of consumer goods, and the general satisfaction of "animal" needs seen in both the United States and the postwar Communist Bloc. For Kojève, "the Russians and the Chinese are only Americans who are still poor but are rapidly proceeding to get richer."[2] Insofar as American capitalism is thought to be more capable of providing these creature comforts, the American way of life is the life most suited to the post-historical period – that is, it is the most suited to an *animal* way of life, devoid of metaphysical concerns.

The second revision Kojève made after a visit to Japan in 1959. He claimed that Japan had already experienced three centuries of post-historical existence; rather than returning to the kind of animality found in American gratification, the Japanese had adopted a kind of aesthetic "*Snobbery*."[3] That is, the Japanese had embraced formalized values rooted in aesthetic tastes rather than the simple pursuit of animal satisfaction, and this made them human insofar as the separation between form and content maintained the subject/object distinction, yet this humanity was without the historical content that characterized human struggle in the West. Rather than returning to animality, then, in Japan the human persisted – but as a *style*, not a substance.

It may be tempting here to simply dismiss, as most do, Kojève's brand of *high-altitude* history, a perspective from which the complex political entanglements represented in the innovations and failures of Robespierre and Napoleon appear as a single event separated only by a hyphen, or that sees the tumult and horror of the twentieth century to be no more than the worrying of the details of a struggle whose essence was realized a century earlier. Moreover, such broad brush strokes may appear to be out of line in a discussion of Adorno, turned as he was to contact with objects in all their micro-logical detail. However, Kojève's speculations on the end of history, its relation to animality, and the revisions of his position, all present important insights for my discussion of Adorno and the animality of reconciled humanity.

Not only do Kojève's speculations posit a utopia at the end of the history of struggle wherein the human has become a different kind of

2 Kojève, *Introduction to the Reading of Hegel*, 161n6.

3 Kojève, *Introduction to the Reading of Hegel*, 161–2n6

animal than what it always had been, but he then complicates this utopia by claiming that it already exists. He "forces" this reconciliation, as it were. But he accomplishes this forced reconciliation only at the price of producing an excessive remainder, the Japanese example, thus making his post-historical animal utopia only one among at least two alternatives. Thus it appears that for Kojève one might choose to be an animal by adopting ways of life congruent with the satisfaction of animal needs, such as that supposedly found in the United States (or Russia/China!), or one might choose to be human by insisting on living a life mediated by certain formal aesthetic strictures.

We must note that with the word *choosing*, Kojève is not suggesting that one might choose directly between human and animal at an individual level, as if these were simply lifestyles that might coexist within the same society; rather, the choice here is a political one relating to the structure of society and the form of life it makes possible. The distinction between human and animal is here a question of how one would live, not simply in terms of the moral decisions that inform one's daily activities, but also in terms of the political organization that enables these decisions and makes possible different modes of life. In this way, we find that Kojève's speculations on animality also point toward the Aristotelian problematic and the particular way it relates ethics and politics: that is, the question of aligning the best life and the political organization that might sustain it. Though these conclusions, in bringing us back to Aristotle, would appear to raise serious problems for Kojève's claim that history and philosophy have come to an end,[4] we might also see this return as a challenge to Adorno's idea that reconciled humanity would be an animal other than human, and how this animal of the future might be linked to our animality in the present.

In taking our animality as the starting point for the political possibilities available today, and asking how one might live in such a way as to say one had been a good animal, Adorno is suggesting the kind of moral cultivation that produces individuals both alike and unlike the manner advocated by Aristotle. Rather than cultivating those potentials thought to be most definitively human according to their natural

---

4 For does not deciding between an animal and a human life in these senses imply the question that animates the very roots of philosophy, that is, *how ought I to live?* – and further, do not American animals and Japanese humans, if they are indeed two different kinds of being and so other to each other, need to *recognize* each other? That is, if America and Japan do indeed represent two different actualizations of post-historical being, then their otherness to each other demands recognition by each other, and so the continuation of history.

distribution, Adorno, in recognizing that this nature is itself the sociopolitical result of the vicissitudes of history, shows that to cultivate one's humanity in this way is to reconcile oneself to society as it exists and the domination it perpetuates. Consequently, if one is to oppose this order, and strive instead to resist its inhumanity and so work to bring about the global subject that might transform society so that reconciled humanity – a new animal – might come into being, one must cultivate one's animality. Cultivating animality for Adorno is not simply about satisfying animal needs in the sense given by Kojève;[5] rather, it concerns how we might orient thinking and acting in ways that oppose those enthralled to positive humanity, to the humanity that thinks of itself as already having arrived. Elucidating this process of cultivation, as a kind of moral resistance linked to politics through art, is the task of this chapter.

Adorno, like Aristotle, views the possible actualizations of one's animality as linked to the mimetic comportment facilitated by the arts. But for Adorno it is through the arts that moral *resistance to humanity* is made possible, and it is through the arts that this moral resistance might become political in the sense of *precipitating change* – goals that, as we have seen, were not Aristotle's. However, *mimesis* alone is not enough, for while the persistence of the mimetic impulse ensures that humans might become animals other than the ones they are, *mimesis* also serves an important role in making humans human in the first place, and it continues in this role in reproducing the human as it is. Consequently, the mimetic impulse needs to be disrupted and set upon a different course: it needs to enter into a new relation with reason if it is to produce the human as some other animal.

The moral experience of this disruption, the moral impulse to something other than humanity, is what Adorno calls the *addendum* (*Hinzutretende*), the corporal side of the will that relates reflex and activity. The addendum, as a liminal space between the will and reflex, volition and reaction, is a kind of animal impulse entwined with the body – it is the resistance of animality to the imposition of human aims upon the

5 Indeed, Hullot-Kentor claims that Adorno's *Aesthetic Theory* is a book "written in utter opposition to what we [Americans] are." That this book tends be either polemically rejected or "rehabilitated" in various ways, typically rendering it less austere and more friendly to pop-culture and the culinary appropriation of art, speaks of the allergy of American "animality" to the kind of animality Adorno would cultivate. See Hullot-Kentor, "Right Listening," 195. Cf. Raymond Geuss, *Changing the Subject*, 275–6. On this point more generally, see Jenemann, *Adorno in America*.

body. In this way, the addendum both makes possible and undermines human thought and activity. To orient thought and action around the addendum is to attempt to transform humanity through its animality, to orient the identity-producing activity of *mimesis* around the rupture of the non-identical in human constitution.

There are two sides to cultivating animality through the addendum, and both require the intervention of the arts. The first side looks to what I call the *receptive* experience of artworks, which involves relating the passive moment of the "shudder," the aesthetic analogue of the addendum, to the active moment of reflection in such a way as to resist the reconstitution of the human subject and thereby persist in one's animality. This receptive experience, insofar as it involves critical resistance to the violence and domination upon which the empirical world is built, I call moral. The second side looks to what I call the *productive* experience of artworks, which involves building on this reflection through practical activity. Here reason is deployed through technical procedures in order to invent new ways of expressing animal experience. Productively experiencing artworks thus involves creating works in accordance with moral experience, and where these artworks contribute to the creation of a subject who might threaten the established order of the community, this experience can be called political. The receptive and productive experiences of artworks together realign the relation between *mimesis* and reason in what Adorno calls "aesthetic comportment," the subject of which, seen in this light, cannot be considered human – rather, it is a new kind of animal.

Adorno's attention to the experience fostered by artworks through their reception and production is thus closely bound up not only with releasing animality from its human confines, but also with elucidating the specific moral and political dimensions of this project. It is specifically the latter, the productive/political dimension of artistic experience, that has been overlooked in studies of Adorno's aesthetics.[6] Adorno's account of the receptive experience of artworks reverses the Aristotelian attempt to use the practice of *theoria* to reconcile animal to human; it does so by creating instead a *dissonance* whereby the animal might resist the human. However, Adorno requires a productive/

6 For example, Zuidervaart in his classic study overlooks this dimension when he argues that Adorno conceives of *praxis* in *Aesthetic Theory* primarily in terms of contemplation, and thus as more or less equivalent to Aristotle's *theoria*. On my reading, this basic affinity holds for the receptive experience of artworks, wherein Adorno reverses Aristotle, but with productive experience Aristotle is transcended. See Lambert Zuidervaart, *Adorno's Aesthetic Theory*, 148–9.

political dimension in order to break with Aristotle's focus on the effects of art – hence the division between those who embody the (human) ideal and those who can only recognize this ideal. In theorizing a productive/political experience of artworks, Adorno erases the inequality produced and reconciled in Aristotle's poetics, as well as the division of labour between artist and critic, and with it the possibility of drawing an analogy between the artistic avant-garde and a political vanguard. The importance of avant-garde art – or as I call it here, simply *new* art – remains, but it is the prerogative of all to experience it both receptively and productively. Though Adorno himself does not explicitly advocate that all become artists, his aesthetic theory removes the obstacles that ensure the division of labour that produces artists and critics as systematically distinct subjects. His aesthetic theory thus points in this direction, even if it does not announce it with a megaphone.

In this way, Adorno's taking up of the Aristotelian problematic concerning the relation between humans and animals on the one hand, and art and politics on the other, is not a return to or perpetuation of Aristotle. It is not, as Brassier would have it, a regressive slip into aspects of Aristotelianism that the Enlightenment and modern scientific discovery have long outflanked. Rather, it is the utopian recovery of the fragments of Aristotelianism that would allow Aristotle to speak to us from a future wherein the political animal has become at once *an aesthetic animal* – an animal no longer human. In this sense, Adorno provides the determinate negation of Aristotle, in such a way that the promise made in Aristotle's philosophical enterprise is preserved in a transformed constellation of possibilities. Thus Adorno can be seen as ironically reviving the Aristotelian idea of aesthetic education, one in which the arts are marshalled not to cultivate the human and thereby repress the animal, to force the reconciliation of the subject to violence presented as natural, but rather to liberate human animality and create a nature that has never existed. It is through Adorno, then, that the Aristotelian problematic might be appropriated and surpassed, and through him that the shadow of an aesthetic animal might be glimpsed.

## Mimesis

*Mimesis*, of course, comes to us from the ancient Greek. It is thus a foreign word, and all the more so for being part of a dead language – that is, there is no one living for whom *mimesis* is not foreign. Treating *mimesis* as a foreign word according to what Adorno has to say about the role of foreign words in language means that we should view Adorno's use of *mimesis* as an assault on the pretence of language to organic unity: when Adorno writes "*mimesis*," he is not simply referencing a tradition of aesthetic thought connected, in some way, to Aristotle and the Greeks; he is also haunting his own text with the destruction of that world – with the fall of democratic Athens and its absorption by the Hellenic empire, and with the unfulfilled promises these might represent.[7] For Adorno, Aristotle's is an aesthetics of effect, in collusion with the quietist tendencies toward privatization in Hellenism and the idea that art must serve as a kind of "substitute satisfaction," but at the same time Aristotle's aesthetics preserves a conception of individuality that might be turned against its own quietistic tendencies.[8] Insofar as *mimesis* is a central concept in Aristotle's aesthetics, it might be said to display this same duality: *mimesis* is culpable in the production of the world as it is but also retains something irreducible to the world as it is and that might be solicited to transform the world as it is.

In the preceding presentation of Aristotle's conception of *mimesis*, I argued that although Aristotle appears to suggest that *mimesis* is a fundamental human capacity, one of those most definitive in distinguishing humans from other animals, its humanity, or its entwinement with other human capacities, can only be recognized through that which *mimesis* has itself produced: these other human capacities cannot be known, and so cannot be said to exist, prior to mimetic production. In this way, I argued that *mimesis* crystallizes the various capacities that come to be seen as the human ideal and as the measure of what is definitively human. Insofar as capacities similar but non-identical to the human ideal are frequently called animal, it is really a set of certain animal capacities that become human through *mimesis*, thus making *mimesis* a transformative process, not simply one wherein pre-existent potentials become actual. Though Adorno does not devote any specific text to an examination of Aristotle's conception of *mimesis*, his objections to other elements of Aristotle's aesthetics, and indeed, his insistence on its double character, can be understood as the result of Adorno turning a historicized conception of *mimesis* against Aristotle and the tradition strung together by those who would be his descendants. This appropriation of Aristotle comes to Adorno not simply through the channels established through the tradition of philosophical aesthetics, but also through somewhat more occult sources: those of Walter Benjamin.[9]

7 Cf. Hall, "Is there a *Polis* in Aristotle's *Poetics*?," 304–5.

8 *AT*, 202; 238; *GSB7*, 301; 354. Adorno, "Marginalia to Theory and Praxis," 267; *GSB10.2*, 769.

9 Hammer, *Adorno's Modernism*, 59.

In Benjamin's fragment "On the Mimetic Faculty," Aristotle is both present and absent, channelled as if through telepathy or séance, in such a way that what speaks through Benjamin's text bears a resemblance to Aristotle but is not identical to him.[10] Most explicitly, the title of Benjamin's piece invokes Aristotle by calling *mimesis* a faculty (*Vermögen*). Like the English *faculty*, the German *Vermögen* refers to potency, potential, capacity, ability, and power, all of which capture something of Aristotle's *dynamis* and likewise has been used to translate it.[11] In so linking *mimesis* to the psychological structure of human being, Aristotle casts a shadow over Benjamin's fragment. Moreover, Aristotle's voice reverberates in Benjamin's claim that "nature creates similarities" through mimicry and that it is the human being that possesses the "highest capacity for producing similarities." The human being is endowed by nature to produce "similarities," to mimic the world around and so "become and behave like something else," and is most natural when doing so.[12] In this way Benjamin takes as his starting point the rudiments of Aristotelian *mimesis*, along with the relations it would establish among nature, art, and human beings: humans are endowed by nature with certain potentials or *faculties*, which, as we have seen, require artifice in order to become actual and so display that which is naturally human. The goal of artifice is thus to actualize nature, so art must aim to mimic nature. However, as we have seen, what Aristotle calls nature is already historically produced, already mediated by artifice, though he lacks the conceptual tools to express this. It is here that Benjamin's modifications of Aristotle begin.

Benjamin writes that the mimetic faculty, though natural, has a history: "neither mimetic powers nor mimetic objects remain the same in the course of thousands of years."[13] *Mimesis* is here divided between the explicitly natural component, the "mimetic powers" thought to inhere in human beings, and the explicitly historical component, "mimetic objects," which might be considered both those things that one might mimic and the formal rules or general shape taken by the exercise of the mimetic faculty in mimicking these things. As children, humans learn to exercise their natural powers of *mimesis* through play,

10 Interestingly, in a letter to Gretel Adorno, Benjamin drew a connection between this fragment and an essay of Freud's on telepathy. See Rosen, *On Voluntary Servitude*, 238.

11 See Aristotle, *Nikomachische Ethik*.

12 Benjamin, "On the Mimetic Faculty," 333. Cf. Benjamin, *Gesammelte Schriften*, vol. 2.1, 210.

13 Benjamin, "On the Mimetic Faculty."

but this play is historically mediated through the kinds of games – the sorts of play – in which children engage, and the particular things they would mimic: the shopkeeper, the teacher, the windmill, the train. As children grow they are assimilated to society mimetically, by reproducing its objects in their own activity, and through this process society is both reproduced and transformed. As society changes, new mimetic objects are produced that set the boundaries that organize the exercise of the mimetic faculty. The mimetic faculty thus exists in its actualization in history, in mimetic objects, whose transformation precipitates transformation in the mimetic faculty.

For Benjamin, however, mimetic objects are not all alike in relation to the mimetic faculty: some objects demand more of it, encouraging the faculty to develop more broadly, to increase its power, while others demand less, so that the mimetic current diminishes to a trickle. A powerful mimetic faculty is one capable of forging creative connections between widely disparate objects or phenomena, which Benjamin calls "nonsensuous" similarities.[14] Such similarities persisted in earlier societies in the form of magical correspondences and occult practices, but the demands for clarity, precision, and causality imposed since the Enlightenment have radically altered the ability to establish non-sensuous similarities. For Benjamin, the question thus becomes: are the changes wrought by the Enlightenment and modernity bringing about the decay of the mimetic faculty, or its transformation? Benjamin spends the rest of this short fragment trying to locate evidence that might indicate the latter, alighting on the relation the mimetic faculty has long established with language, even claiming that language is "the highest level of mimetic behavior and the most complete archive of nonsensuous similarity,"[15] and suggesting that it is through its "admittance" and expression in language that mimetic production managed to rid itself of its ties to magic.

This last claim is the most significant: if *mimesis* lives on in language, and if it is through its particular relation to language that magic was "liquidated," then magic and the occult on the one hand, and Enlightenment and modernity on the other, might all be distilled as different combinations of particular linguistic conventions and innovations. This insight does not suggest that the principal difference between magical correspondences and Enlightenment rationality is simply their respective ways of using language, however, for at the heart of both of their

14 Benjamin, "On the Mimetic Faculty," 334.
15 Benjamin, "On the Mimetic Faculty," 336.

attempts to read their own "script" in objective phenomena are their ways of establishing non-sensuous similarities. In other words: they must both be seen as forms of *mimesis*. In this way, Benjamin's' fragment appears to curl back on itself, like a snake biting its own tail – the very search for the possibility of a future life for *mimesis* through the vicissitudes of society arrives at the conclusion that *mimesis* is itself the very possibility of its own vicissitudes. The mimetic faculty is revealed as occupying a kind of foundational status in the language, thought, and the reproduction of society, so as to be considered – though Benjamin himself does not explicitly push this far – a transcendental condition of their possibility. Benjamin's attempt to historicize Aristotelian *mimesis* has thus accomplished this aim only at the price of making *mimesis* a permanent, if perpetually changing, feature of history.

Though Adorno will not *simply* adopt Benjamin's account of *mimesis*, and thus not *quite* follow Benjamin in his peculiar brand of "Marxist–Kantianism,"[16] this fragment will prove immensely important for him. Besides building on the natural-historical perspective he outlined in "The Idea of Natural-History" a year earlier – in part already a response to other of Benjamin's writings – Adorno inherited three specific points from Benjamin's discussion of *mimesis* that would inform his own: (1) *mimesis* has contributed at a fundamental and largely unconscious level to making society what it is; (2) *mimesis* is internally mediated through its historical forms, and thus it has been and still might be otherwise; and (3) the possibilities for mimetic transformation today exist within language, both in the sense of interpreting it so as to forge new correspondences between phenomena and in the sense of finding new forms for expressing these correspondences. It is especially regarding this last point that we find the beginnings of the theoretical importance of art for Adorno, for art makes possible a range of non-conceptual affinities and is in certain ways much like a language.[17]

Adorno's account of *mimesis* differs from Benjamin's in relation to the subject/object distinction. For Adorno, the permanence of transcendental conditions, even where historically mediated, has something of the mythological about them, and he is deeply suspicious of this. Benjamin's account of *mimesis* as the dynamic interaction between a natural mimetic faculty (a mimetic subject) and historical mimetic objects theorizes *mimesis* in terms of the subject/object relation, and insofar as it treats this form of *mimesis* as a transcendental condition of language,

16 Rosen, *On Voluntary Servitude*, 238.

17 *AT*, 54; *GSB7*, 86–7. *ND*, 18; *GSB6*, 29. Cf. Adorno, "Music and Language."

thought, and history, he makes this relation permanent. As we have seen, Adorno's turn toward the primacy of the object entails acknowledging that the subject is also an object; hence, the natural aspect of the mimetic faculty must be found to itself be an historical product.

If the mimetic faculty is produced historically, then either it is the product of some other, pre-mimetic drive, or *mimesis* is not originally a faculty, but something else that only becomes describable in terms of inherent faculties insofar as it becomes captured in the subject/object relation. Though these two possibilities need not be mutually exclusive, Adorno focuses on the latter and attempts to show *mimesis* to be a form of bodily comportment – an impulse (*Impuls*) rather than a faculty (*Vermögen*)[18] – that becomes tied up with concepts and identity-thinking as *imitation* (*Nachahmung*) through changes in what will become the human constitution. In this way *mimesis* is non-identical to the conceptual order of identity, and as such Adorno would turn toward it in an attempt to "make contact" with the mimetic element of non-identity, as he does with animality. However, Adorno sees two distinct possibilities leading from such contact: a regressive possibility, whereby conceptual thought is shunned in favour of mimetic myth-making, and a progressive one that would serve to displace and reformulate the conceptual order based on mimetic experience. Adorno's commitment to some version of Enlightenment thinking leads him to attempt to theorize the possibility of the latter.

Though Adorno claims that there is an "indelible mimetic element in all cognition and all human practice,"[19] *mimesis* is for him the desire to make contact with the object prior to there being a clear distinction between the object to be contacted and the subject making contact; as such, the mimetic impulse is irreducible to the subject/object distinction or to its particular instantiation in the human subject.[20] That is, while a mimetic impulse might be discernible in "all human practice," this claim should not be seen as indicating that it is exclusively human: *mimesis* is part of the other side of the conceptual order in which the human comes to be. It is, in this sense, animal. Yet it is the mimetic

18 *AT*, 90, 96, 118, 144, 162, 339; *GSB7*, 139, 148, 180, 217, 243, 503–4. It is also notable that Adorno again highlights the mediated – and hence non-foundational – character of this impulse in choosing the word *Impuls*, with its Latin root, rather than something "more German," such as *Drang*, or *Trieb*, with its Freudian connotations, or even Gehlen's *Antrieb*, which his translators also render as "impulse." See Gehlen, *Man*, 339.

19 *ND*, 150; *GSB6*, 153.

20 Recall Horowitz, "Adorno and Emptiness," 272. Cf. *AT*, 110, 329; *GSB7*, 169, 487.

desire for contact that facilitates the grasping that is the violence of the conceptual order, and in which the human will emerge. The desire for contact may propel one toward the object before there is a *one* to be propelled, but the *one*, the subject, is formed in this propulsion and contact so as to become conscious through contact with the otherness of the object. Where consciousness experiences the otherness of the object as a threat, as the human does the animal, there subject and object relate to each other antagonistically. The subject's attempt to reduce the perceived threat posed by the object to the subject is accomplished through the identification of the object with a concept, thus giving concepts the instrumental function associated with the preservation of the subject.

However, this displacement of *mimesis* by the conceptual order does not eradicate *mimesis*. Like Benjamin, Adorno holds that something of *mimesis* survives in the conceptual order,[21] though his account of how it comes to inform that order differs based on the pre-subjective status of *mimesis*. With Benjamin, we saw that it is through mimetic comportment that subjects become attached to the objects of their world: *mimesis* is what holds subjects and objects in thrall. For Adorno, however, the mimetic pull serves to constellate objects in such a way as to make possible the subject that is – the subject is thus posterior to the constellation of mimetic objects. Adorno thus distinguishes between *mimesis* and imitation, referring to the shape *mimesis* takes in the context of the subject/object relation in its reproduction of sociopolitical domination as *imitation*, rather than *mimesis* as such. *Mimesis* is thus non-identical to imitation, which is only its objectified form, a form that might be reversed.[22] Reversing the process of imitation amounts to the subjective release of objects and thus the possibility of their reconstellation so as to produce a new kind of subject.[23] This release involves a recovery of *mimesis*, of contact with the animality of the mimetic impulse *against* the reproduction of oneself as a human subject through the *imitation* of the objects given to imitate by one's society.

21 *ND*, 14; *GSB6*, 26; *AT*, 96; *GSB7*, 148.

22 See: "Mimesis was displaced by objectifying imitation [*Nachahmung*]" (*AT*, 162; *GSB7*, 243); "mimetic comportment does not imitate something but rather makes itself like itself" (*AT*, 111; *GSB7*, 169); the "doctrine of imitation [*Nachahmungslehre*]" might be reversed (*AT*, 132; *GSB7*, 199–200).

23 There is an affinity between the subjective release of objects and the life of these objects beyond the utility they had in maintaining a given subject. For a discussion that takes this point in a wildly different direction, see Vatter, *The Republic of the Living*, 109.

Yet, as noted above, Adorno is not trying to exchange the world of concepts for some primordial idea of *mimesis*, some pre-subjective relation to the world – his turn to animality is not reducible to a kind of nostalgia for the ape, or to a celebration of the "primitive." There is no pre-subjective world, pristine and conceptless, to which return is possible, and attempts to animate such an idea can only result in gross parodies of unreflexive nature and a return to mythological thinking. It is for this reason that Adorno will also on occasion employ *mimesis* pejoratively, referring to the "mimetic regression" involved in attempting to think the "Many" without subjective mediation, or to the "cave of a long-past mimesis" into which thinkers like Heidegger would "crawl."[24] For Adorno, recovery of *mimesis* is not an attempt to invoke a past prior to the transcendental subject of humanity, but rather an attempt to invoke a future that lies past such a subject, one constituted through a new relation to our animality. Yet how might one intervene in the pull exuded by *mimesis* between subject and object so as to break the spell that holds them in thrall? What words might be spoken, or what experience might there be, that could possibly allow for the release of the social objects to which a given subject is mimetically attached? And perhaps most importantly, how might such a mimetic transformation of the subject be accomplished in the progressive manner Adorno envisions, one that would represent a sublation of the transcendental subject as opposed to its repressive desublimation?[25]

The beginning of an answer might be found in Adorno's ideas on art and aesthetics. Adorno claims not only that art is "a refuge for mimetic comportment" but also that art makes possible a semblance of the reconciliation of reason and *mimesis*.[26] That is, artworks require both rational and mimetic comportment in their production and demand mimetic and rational reception, both as what Benjamin called "mimetic objects" and through their interpretation. In constellating *ratio* and *mimesis* in this way, art demands that reason be reconciled to animal impulses rather than to their simple repression, even while demanding that *mimesis* be directed toward rational ends, that is, the construction of a better world. The artwork, through its adherence to its own formal principles distilled through an antagonistic dialogue with its own history and the techniques on which it draws, distances itself from the objects that make up its sociopolitical context – its *material*. In

24 *ND*, 158, 131; *GSB6*, 160, 136.

25 To borrow a term from Marcuse. See his *One-Dimensional Man*, ch. 3.

26 *AT*, 20, 54; *GSB7*, 38, 87.

winning this degree of autonomy, the artwork comes to resemble *itself* rather than the material.[27] In this way the artwork presents itself as an example of mimetic activity alienated from the instrumental functions of imitation that serve to reproduce society as it is.[28] Through artworks, *mimesis* seeks contact with the nature that "does not yet in any way exist," its "non-existent" truth.[29] Artworks might thus make possible a liberation of the mimetic impulse that would reverse the conceptual capture of imitation, compelling reality to imitate art and making possible "the happiness of producing the world once over."[30]

In theorizing *mimesis* as central to the production *and* reception of art, and to the reproduction of society and the possibility of its transformation, Adorno thus invests the very autonomy of art – that is, its fundamental *distance* from morality and politics – with moral and political weight.[31] Through its relation to *mimesis*, art has potentially radical and far-reaching moral and political consequences, and these are in turn entwined with humanity and its future, along with the possibility of living in the present as if one were a good animal. I turn now to these threads and their unwinding.

## Morality and Politics

In taking animality as the starting point for the possibility of sociopolitical transformation and asking, with Adorno, how one might live so as to have been a good animal, it has been established that such a life, along with the desired sociopolitical transformation, is integrally connected to *mimesis*. Adorno theorizes *mimesis* as the comportment that serves to establish and reproduce the connections among social objects that make a subject possible. However, insofar as *mimesis* has been displaced or colonized by *ratio*, the subject produced through *mimesis* has been transformed into a transcendental human subject, one seen as the source of the web of social objects through which it is constituted rather than as their product. Recovery of the animality of *mimesis* is therefore necessary to undermine the power of this subject as well as the antagonism toward others it requires to sustain itself. This recovery, including the possibility of a reconciliation with reason rather than a rejection of it, is made possible through art, whose autonomy has for Adorno

---

27 *AT*, 104; *GSB7*, 159.

28 Cf. Menke, *Force*, 62.

29 *AT*, 132; *GSB7*, 199–200.

30 *AT*, 339; *GSB7*, 503.

31 On the possibility of aesthetic autonomy, see Menke, *The Sovereignty of Art*.

important moral as well as political consequences. It remains to elucidate what these consequences might be, and to this end, we must examine Adorno's thoughts on morality and its relation to politics.

The growing literature on Adorno's "ethics" has helped establish small niches for his work in a variety of disciplines, yet he remains relatively neglected as a political thinker. Part of the reason for this relative neglect may be that Adorno devotes little direct attention to the study of politics, even though it is difficult to find a work of his that is not touched by politics in some sense – indeed, Adorno claims that "politics is not a self-enclosed, isolated sphere" but must be understood as connected to all manner of social forces and their contest.[32] However, and perhaps more controversially, we might suggest that this emphasis on Adorno's "ethics" is precisely what has obscured the political dimension of his insights, insofar as these would examine his ethics independent of political consequence.[33] Adorno himself is sceptical of "ethics," preferring instead the term "morality," precisely for its perceived relation to politics.

In his lectures on moral philosophy, Adorno draws a distinction between morality and ethics through an appeal to their respective etymologies. Morality, from the Latin *mores*, concerns the customs of a community, the explicit and implicit rules that govern the common relations among people.[34] Ethics, by contrast, comes from the Greek *ethos*,

---

32 Adorno, "Critique," 281; *GSB10.2*, 785.

33 *Contra* Schweppenhäuser, who acknowledges Adorno's preference for the term morality, yet nevertheless reduces this and moral philosophy to "ethics." See Schweppenhäuser, "Adorno's Negative Moral Philosophy," 331–2. Cf. Vázquez-Arroyo's critical discussion of the "ethical turn" in political theory in *Political Responsibility*, ch. 1.

34 These *mores* can be found both in the word *Moral* (or *Moralität/Moralismus*) and in the *Sitte* or "custom" of *Sittlichkeit* (*PMP*, 9). That Adorno places *Moral* and *Sittlichkeit* together in opposition to ethics (*Ethik*), might perhaps indicate a further break with Hegel, for in Hegel's *Philosophy of Right*, *Moralität* and *Sittlichkeit* constitute discrete spheres, though the former is sublated by the latter. If *Moral* and *Sittlichkeit* can be conflated in the manner Adorno suggests, then the politics to which they point are something lying beyond the institutions of the state, which for Hegel constitute the realm of *Sittlichkeit*. Adorno's opposition to Hegel here is noted by Zuidervaart, though he misses Adorno's conflation of *Moral* and *Sittlichkeit*, thus taking Adorno to oppose *Moral* to *Sittlichkeit*, and so reject Hegelian *Sittlichkeit* in favour of Kantian *Moral*. But Adorno is not trying to return to Kant; rather, he is attempting to move beyond both Kant *and* Hegel – hence the opposition of *Moral and Sittlichkeit* to *Ethik*. See Zuidervaart, *Social Philosophy after Adorno*, 176. Cf. Adorno, *NSAV10*, 21–3.

which Adorno considers to be something more or less equivalent to nature, referring "to the way you are, the way you are made," though for the Greeks this also concerned one's fate and one's relation to the gods.[35] To live ethically then, is to live according to one's nature, according to one's fate, and so to live according to the laws of nature or the gods, whereas to live morally involves navigating the changeable rules of the community. Though one might object to Adorno's interpretation of the antiquarian roots of morality and ethics, the point here is to note that Adorno's use of the term morality is for him linked to the changeable structure of society in a way that ethics is not and so expresses a different set of possibilities in terms of relating the individual to the general. In this way, Adorno sees morality as being linked to reflection and the possibility of radical change, whereas ethics is bound up with the world of myth and the eternal return of the same. Morality and the reflections upon it gathered in moral philosophy thus have "a necessary connection with practical action," and the "crucial question of moral philosophy" is this: "What shall we do?"[36]

Though Adorno does not acknowledge it explicitly here, the historical resonance of this question hits a decidedly political note, recalling Lenin's "What Is to Be Done?" Despite Adorno's long-standing opposition to the Soviet Union and the Eastern Bloc, and despite his criticism of Brecht's "vulgar Marxism," one finds in writings unpublished in Adorno's lifetime surprisingly sanguine remarks about Lenin as late as 1956. In conversation with Horkheimer, he claims that against the "reified" thinking of Soviet bureaucrats, he has always wanted to "develop a theory that remains faithful to Marx, Engels and Lenin, while keeping up with culture at its most advanced," and that the manifesto he and Horkheimer were then attempting to write must be "strictly Leninist."[37] Moreover, he attributes to Lenin the idea "that people are products of society down to the innermost fibre of their being," an idea that has informed much of the preceding discussion of Adorno's understanding of humanity and its relation to animality.[38] Yet these comments are not enough to make Adorno a Leninist, at least not in any straightforward sense. The fact that the writing of this manifesto was ultimately abandoned undermines Adorno's apparent Leninist ardour, and moreover, the conversations in which Horkheimer and

35 *PMP*, 10; *NSAV10*, 23.
36 *PMP*, 2–3; *NSAV10*, 11.
37 *TNM*, 103, 94; *GSB14*, 69, 66.
38 *TNM*, 112; *GSB14*, 71.

Adorno recorded their ideas for this manifesto contain numerous contradictions, suggesting that these comments represent *possible* avenues for their thought rather than definitive statements of it. In this sense, Adorno's statements on Lenin here ought to be qualified by his other writings, which paint a rather different picture of the possibility of politics and its relation to morality.

As I have attempted to show in my discussion of Adorno's conceptions of progress and the global subject, Adorno is against advancing a universal conception of the good that requires the sacrifice of particular goods and the struggles tied to their advancement, theorizing instead a collective subject that exists only in the solidarity established at the level of particulars.[39] These conceptions are at odds with the direction taken by Lenin and Leninist parties and appear to offer a way of conceiving the organization of progressive political struggle different from the top-down model – that is, different from a revolutionary vanguard, organized under the aegis of a political party, leading the working class. Moreover, Adorno persistently rejected what he saw as an anachronistic strain of Leninism in the student movement of his day: the insistence that the unity of theory and praxis must guide political struggle. Vanguardist organizations sought to justify their programs through appeals to the unity of theory and praxis. However, Adorno sees this insistence on unity as denying the way in which theory is already a kind of praxis, thus serving to bury the objective possibilities of theory beneath the supremacy of a pre-given revolutionary subject.[40] For Adorno, it is no longer possible in the administered society of the West to rely on past modes of organization to guide political struggle, as if the possibilities available to political action had not changed with the defeat of the Sparticists. Thus, whatever might be left of Lenin must address a radically transformed terrain of political possibility, and it is for this reason that Adorno makes something very much like Lenin's famous slogan "the crucial question of moral philosophy," for therein morality and philosophy are pulled toward politics, even while politics is turned toward philosophy and morality.

In this way Adorno is subjecting Lenin to his own moral and philosophical roots: the question "What is to be done?" is "How ought I to live?" in a political crisis, during which philosophy cannot afford to be

39 *Contra* Hammer, *Adorno and the Political*, 178–80; and Zuidervaart, *Social Philosophy after Adorno*, 161; 177.

40 Adorno, "Marginalia to Theory and Praxis," 265; *GSB10.2*, 766; *PMP*, 4; *NSAV10*, 13–14.

an activity of the leisured, but rather seeks desperately to clarify the nature of the sociopolitical problems so that "total disaster" is not simply deferred, but averted through the transformation of the structure that has precipitated its possibility. Adorno's emphasis on the *moral* nature of this question ties it to questions of individual actions and how one relates to others, and it does so in a way that would obstruct the kind of political theodicy that sees violence as the evil necessary for salvation. When Lenin's question is made a moral one, the overarching structure of the party whose interests must be placed ahead of the individual is dissolved into moral demands on the individual, who can no longer use the party as a screen for obscuring these demands or as a vehicle for securing release from them.

Thus, while Geuss thinks it possible "to retain much of Adorno's analysis within a (revised) Leninist framework,"[41] without considerable elaboration of exactly what of Adorno might remain, and what revisions to Lenin might be necessary, it is difficult to see how exactly one could call Adorno's politics Leninist. Likewise, the moral dimension of Adorno's politics and their relation to knowledge seems to be lost on those who see him as endorsing the vanguardist view, and with it, the political authority of philosophers. Freyenhagen claims that Adorno thinks that, insofar as only "a few critical individuals" might have access to "genuine and unrestricted experience" in the world as it is, others must defer to and take direction from their authority as "the most progressive minds."[42] Adorno does indeed mention "the most progressive minds," or *consciousness* (*fortgeschrittensten Bewußtsein*),[43] and he does think that insofar as most people live without engaging in critical reflection they fail to see the veil that has been drawn over their eyes; but philosophical reflection can only ever be a partial solution, for, as Adorno claims, "if there really is no correct life in the false life, then actually there can be no correct consciousness in it either."[44]

If there is no correct consciousness, then there can be no definitive authority assigned to the philosopher concerning political matters, only a general demand that all engage in critical reflection. Adorno's insistence on this moral dimension to Lenin's question thus *impedes* rather than advocates the political authority of philosophers.

---

41 Geuss, *Philosophy and Real Politics*, 107n49.

42 Freyenhagen, *Adorno's Practical Philosophy*, 248–9. Cf. Zuidervaart, *Social Philosophy after Adorno*, 165.

43 *PMP*, 168; Adorno, *NSAV10*, 249.

44 Adorno, "Opinion Delusion Society," *CM*, 120; *GSB10.2*, 591.

Adorno explicitly links critique with the possibility of democracy and claims "intellectual autonomy" to be "the very core of the democratic ideal."[45] Yet even if only a few of the "most progressive minds" were to make this practice their own, *the most* that such individuals might offer through their attempts to clarify the sociopolitical problems that present themselves is *theoretical* leadership. That is, while philosophers may provide *theoretical* leadership by clarifying problems and providing conceptual tools that might be of use in political struggle, it is up to the participants in these struggles to reflect on them and do with them what they will. I see little evidence that Adorno thinks this *theoretical* leadership should translate itself into a political practice based exclusively on a pre-existent theory that would endow the theorist or his or her adherents with the authority to tell others what to do. Even Adorno's "democratic leadership," whose goal is to make "the subjects of democracy, the people, *conscious of their own wants and needs*" against their ideological variants, cannot be reserved exclusively for philosophers, for Adorno also criticizes leadership "severed from the people" and reminds us that authoritarian tendencies are always present where "power is wielded by a few over many."[46] The theorist or the philosopher might engage in political activity through theorizing, and perhaps even aid various political struggles in doing so, but nothing in this relationship would secure a position of privilege for the philosopher within political struggle, and this role would ultimately be subordinate to democratic leadership.[47]

In highlighting the moral dimension of Adorno's politics, I am not suggesting that Adorno reduces politics to morality, for in bringing politics into contact with morality, he is also trying to push morality toward politics. In fact, as we have seen in Adorno's opposition of morality to ethics, it is precisely morality's political potential that makes Adorno see it as the more promising of the two concepts. The dissolution of the

45 Adorno, "Critique," 281–2; *GSB10.2*, 785–6; Adorno, "Democratic Leadership and Mass Manipulation," 269. Though Adorno does not elaborate a positive theory of democracy, his insistence on the necessity of theory and the rejection of its synthesis with praxis together suggest a more open-ended and ongoing project of critical reflection than that typically thought possible within the framework of democratic centralism. For an attempt to formulate such a democratic theory, see Douglas, "Democratic Darkness," 819–36.

46 *GSB20.1*, 267–9.

47 This is not to suggest that there is no tension at all between theory, leadership, and democracy in Adorno. See Mariotti, "Adorno on the Radio." Cf. Chambers, "The Politics of Critical Theory."

Leninist party as the necessary locus of revolutionary political struggle must likewise spell the dissolution of the hard distinction between the demands of revolutionary politics and those of morality. That moral decisions are apolitical, or even anti-political, is an illusion that must be rejected, for morality, as the practical interpretation and navigation of social rules, already implies a politics. That is, morality already implies a position with respect to the creation or transformation of the overarching framework in which moral rules have force. Adorno confirms the political dimension of his own turn to morality in the conclusion to these lectures, where he claims: "In short, anything that we can call morality today merges into the question of the organization of the world. We might even say that the quest for the good life is the quest for the right form of politics, if indeed such a right form of politics lay within the realm of what can be achieved today."[48]

We must now ask: how does the proximity of morality and politics theorized by Adorno relate to art and his theory of *mimesis*? If morality concerns, as Adorno holds, the relation between the individual and the general that we find in interpreting and navigating the rules of the community, then it would appear there are two rather different kinds of moral activity. First, we can be said to act morally when we follow the rules of our community as we understand them, more or less unreflexively; and second, we act morally when we reflect on the rules of our community and try to give reasons that justify why one action is a more appropriate interpretation of a rule than another, or even when certain rules need not be followed. If, then, politics concerns "the organization of the world," that is, the order within which the rules of the community have force, and if one's moral disposition thus contains a political position, then these two moral dispositions result in a number of possible political positions. *Either* one upholds the political order as it is by following the rules of the community, be it unreflexively or for one's own reasons, *or* one contributes to changes in this order through practical adaption of the rules to personal circumstances, *or* one opposes this political order by not complying with the rules it attempts to guarantee, be it unreflexively or for one's own reasons.

Despite the possibility of considerable differences here between positions, especially with respect to activity that is "unreflexive" compared with activity that bases itself on explicit reasons, these moral dispositions and the political positions they entail have in common that they proceed from a subject. Their respective "starting positions," that is,

48 *PMP*, 176; *NSIV10*, 262.

the places from which moral activity or a political position is experienced, have already come to be as products of a particular constellation of social objects. Even if we grant that the production of this subject is ongoing, that moral decisions or political consequences can alter the social objects from which our subjectivity springs so as to make it possible to consciously change who we are, these decisions are always limited by the subjectivity from which they spring. We may be capable of consciously changing ourselves, but only according to the limits imposed on consciousness that constitute our subjectivity – only, that is, as the subjects that we are through a particular constellation of social objects. Put differently: we interpret the rules of our community and so act accordingly always already in terms of the subject we are through the particular constellation of social objects available to us in that community. In this sense, we tend to uphold the political order through our moral activity, even where we would oppose ourselves to parts of it through our interpretations of the rules, as we interpret and act in terms of the subjective possibilities already given by this order through the particular array of objects at our disposal.

Adorno's theory of *mimesis* is relevant here in that it concerns how we produce the relation between these social objects through our own thoughts and actions without direct intention. By attempting to address moral and political activity at the level of *mimesis*, one directs one's attention to the constitution of the moral and political subject that is irreducible to the conceptual order of reason, the rules of the community, or the political order in which their force is guaranteed. This approach can be viewed as *radical* in two senses: in the sense of attempting to alter the *root* of moral activity and its related political positions, and in the sense that the alteration of the relation between subject and social objects would create different ways of interpreting the rules of the community. Insofar as such dispositions would depend on a subject other than that produced through the simple reproduction of society, this moral activity would more likely be antagonistic to the political order. That is, through the mimetic transformation of the subject, moral activity is rendered politically radical.

Yet how, we might ask, is this kind of deliberate mimetic transformation possible, if *mimesis* is itself irreducible to reason, morality, or politics, though included in all? Through what register must such an intervention take place? As we saw in my brief outline of the relation between art and *mimesis*, it is through art that mimetic transformation might be possible, for Adorno holds art to be a reservoir for the mimetic impulse, and insofar as it might disrupt the subjective coordinates upon which morality and politics are based, art can thus be said to harbour inherently radical political potential.[49] It is precisely because of this radical political potential that Adorno thinks that art that directly and explicitly aims to make itself political actually places limits on its own radical political potential, for in adapting itself to the exigencies of struggle in the present it reifies these exigencies and the subject from which they emanate, rather than disrupting them with the possibility of their own otherness – with the possibility of a world organized otherwise, along with a different kind of subject. Conversely, then, it is precisely the art that aims at its own autonomy, at its fundamental *distance* from morality and politics, that most threatens to disrupt the subjective coordinates upon which morality and politics depend and thus possesses the most radical moral and political potential.[50] Thus Adorno writes that "politics has migrated into autonomous art" and claims that "an emphasis on autonomous works is itself sociopolitical in nature."[51]

In terms of the positive conception of humanity that serves as the central subject whose coordinates dictate what is morally and politically acceptable, disruption of these coordinates requires art that is most distant and strange to humanity – art that is *inhuman*. It is this inhuman art that Adorno sees as most threatening to the subjective coordinates entwined with the world as it is, and it is to the conditions and experience of this inhumanity, of this *animality*, that we now turn.

## The Inhuman Addendum

Let us summarize the key elements so far of this chapter's argument: Mimetic comportment serves to constellate the social objects through which a subject is produced, a subject that then maintains through moral and political activity a world in which a given set of social objects are available for mimetic comportment to constellate. In this way, the world as it exists reproduces itself through the activity of subjects; or, for Adorno: domination is reproduced precisely by means of the activity of the dominated, as their *expression*. The consequence of this view is that to simply be as one is, living according to one's desires more or less in accord with one's society, to "express" oneself through one's choices and life activity, is to reproduce the power structures of one's society,

---

49 Cf. Menke, who finds in aesthetic life a natural connection to freedom, though by way of an anthropological formulation that I avoid. See Menke, "Aesthetic Nature."

50 *AT*, 228, 242, 255; *GSB7*, 339, 358–9, 379. Cf. Adorno, "Reconciliation under Duress," 160.

51 Adorno, "Commitment," 318; *GSB11*, 430.

for what one *is* – one's personality and humanity – is a function of this society, not a pre-existing thing upon which society is imposed.

Adorno theorizes the possibility of breaking out of this cycle, and thus transforming this subject and this world, through an appeal to the mimetic comportment that serves to constellate the objects from which subjectivity is produced. Insofar as artworks serve to congeal mimetic activity, art appears to hold a position of privilege in this project – or at least those artworks do that disrupt the subjective coordinates that bind moral and political activity in the world as it exists, that is, in the world to which the human subject is reconciled. But here we must ask: what kind of experience might disrupt the subjective coordinates that fix us as human? How might the mimetic impulse be diverted from its role in imitation and so be turned against constellating the social objects of the world – a world from which a human subject will be reproduced in order to reproduce a human world reconciled to violence and domination? And what kind of art might make such experience possible?

For now I will bracket the question of what kind of art might produce this subjectively disruptive experience in order to focus on the experience more directly. Insofar as the mimetic impulse is an *impulse*, that is, a kind of corporal disposition to objects, a way of relating to them through bodily comportment that is both less than conceptual and less than voluntary, the human subject is in part constituted through an attempt to master this impulse in the figure of the body. The body is, for the human subject, the unruly matter that must be tamed and formed through the conceptual designs of the intellect, or at least through habits informed in some way by intellect – the body is the animal other lurking within human subjectivity that continually threatens human designs.[52] Commanding the mimetic impulse in this way is not impossible, but such commands are never wholly successful, and the involuntary aspects of our bodily comportment frequently repel such commands. An experience that might disrupt the subjective coordinates of the human and so allow one to attempt to live as a good animal would thus appear to involve an experience of the involuntary and corporal aspect of our human subjectivity. In this way, an object might be introduced into mimetic comportment that resists the particular constellation of objects that make up the human so as to enable it to produce something inhuman – a subject constituted through the experience of objects that

52 *DE*, 192–3; *DA*, 246–7. It is also, as we shall see, the other in me who is in the right – the other to whom solidarity is due. See Duttman, "Adorno's Rabbits," 186. Cf. *PMP*, 169–70; *NSAV10*, 251.

resists being constituted as human. We might find such an experience in what Adorno calls "the addendum."

In *Negative Dialectics* Adorno provocatively claims that "[a] new categorical imperative has been imposed by Hitler upon unfree mankind: to arrange thoughts and actions so that Auschwitz will not repeat itself, so that nothing similar will happen."[53] He further claims that this imperative cannot be dealt with discursively, but rather "gives us a bodily sensation of the moral addendum": it is only in the revulsion we feel when confronted with images or knowledge of Auschwitz that "morality survives"; it is only in this involuntary reaction, rather than for any possible reason we could give for calling what transpired in Auschwitz wrong, that a new subject might be constellated. Insofar as Auschwitz must be seen as a uniquely human creation – one that drew upon what have traditionally been conceived as uniquely human intellectual capacities and that was perpetuated according to uniquely human conceptual distinctions that served to divide different varieties of the human animal – arranging our "thoughts and actions so that Auschwitz will not repeat itself" demands the subjective reconstitution of the human being – it demands that we become an animal other than the human animal for whom Auschwitz was a possibility. To this end I must show that the addendum is an experience of animality and that cultivating this experience and thus producing the kind of animal for which Auschwitz would be an impossibility requires a certain kind of aesthetic education. In this way, Adorno revives classical notions of aesthetic education dating back to Plato and Aristotle, but he does so ironically, in that the subject he would produce is an animal opposed to the human rather than the exemplar of what is most divine in the human.[54]

Adorno uses the concept of "the addendum" (*das Hinzutretende*) to undermine the purity of the intellect as it is found in both Cartesian mind/body dualism and the Kantian will by claiming that a kind of "addition" or supplement would be needed to make sense of each, an addition whose existence would undermine or contaminate the very purity upon which these conceptual distinctions depend.[55] For Adorno

53 *ND*, 365; *GSB6*, 358.

54 Likewise, Adorno's insights here would radically historicize the contexts in which a given activity might be conceived as virtuous, or a given disposition, good. See Jaeggi, "'No Individual Can Resist,'" 71.

55 The addendum can also be seen as a polemical response to philosophical anthropologies that would theorize the sovereignty of human being, such as Scheler's conception of personality as the immediate "*domination over the lived body*," or Gehlen's conception of the "hiatus" that distances human actions from bodily

there is no mind that is not an embodied mind, no will that is not an embodied will, for both mind and will are historically mediated products of specific transformations in our bodily comportment. According to Adorno's natural-historical view, both mind and will are historical insofar as they can only be found embodied in historical objects, and in ways of viewing or acting upon these objects, which have themselves come to be – mind and will cannot be said to be unchanging and eternal any more than the historical objects in which they are found. Yet mind and will are at the same time natural, for they are not identical to historical objects: they depend on material that is never wholly produced or mastered by anything historical. The addendum is Adorno's way of illustrating this entwinement of history and nature in the concepts of mind and will as they are embodied.

The addendum is thus both natural and historical. It is natural in that it is a bodily impulse, a somatic tic that the intellect cannot wholly escape or master, so the intellect brands it as irrational in order to consolidate its mastery of the body.[56] Yet were the intellect to ever fully succeed in this mastery, it would be its death, for it is only through the body that the intellect came to be, and it is only through its persistence, through the addendum – that is, the traces of the bodily impulses within the intellect – that it might continue to confront its other and so be a recognizably different entity. Only entwined with the body does reason have life and some access to the world. Thus the concept of the will, of a particular faculty of the intellect that enables reason or consciousness to act upon the objects of the world and so change what exists, is for Adorno thoroughly dependent upon the involuntary bodily impulses of the addendum: as Adorno writes, "if the hand no longer twitched, there would be no will."[57]

Yet the historical dimension of the addendum must also be insisted upon, against a simple and reified conception of it as a set of natural impulses. Drawing on Adorno's claim that a sense of or even the *idea* of freedom depends upon the memory of an "archaic impulse" that precedes the ego, an impulse "not yet steered by any solid I" and so "later banished to the zone of unfree bondage to nature,"[58]

---

impulses, allowing for the voluntary nature of the former, and so the mastery of the human being as a self-creating and responsible entity. See Scheler, *Formalism*, 480; Gehlen, *Man*, 329–30. Italics in original.

56 *ND*, 228–9; *GSB6*, 227–8.

57 *ND*, 230, 241; *GSB6*, 229, 240.

58 *ND*, 221–2; *GSB6*, 221.

commentators have often described the addendum in a manner that suggests it is a neglected but basically unchanging and so perpetually available part of human experience. When one understands the addendum in this manner, it becomes a kind of natural human potential that Adorno is trying to actualize, obscured only by particular historical circumstance. Accounts of the addendum as a potential thus take on an ontogenetic character, making it the recollection of a natural part of any human individual's development, or a phylogenetic character, as the recollection or reflection of some natural state in which humans actually lived at some point in the past before reason became dominant among human capacities.

Cook takes the latter approach, writing that the addendum "points back to an earlier stage of history in which human behaviour was largely reactive and reflexive, but also points forwards to a stage where nature and mind may finally be reconciled."[59] Freyenhagen also emphasizes this phylogenetic side of the addendum, claiming that the memory of the "archaic impulse" serves to remind us of a spontaneous relation between consciousness and body that might be re-established through a social transformation whose material conditions have been brought to fruition by capitalism.[60] For their part, Habermas and Bernstein interpret Adorno ontogenetically: Habermas construes the lived bodily experience Adorno would incorporate into the idea of a free act to be the expression of the character that develops naturally out of an individual's lived history.[61] Bernstein takes a slightly different tack, dismissing the phylogenetic reading as "bad speculative anthropology"[62] and insisting instead that the addendum's function is one of immanent critique. However, in claiming it to be a piece of "anthropomorphic nature,"[63] he appears to leave the possibility open to an ontogenetic reading that would see the addendum as pointing back to a phase of individual development prior to a rigid distinction between mind and body.

The problem with these interpretations is that they treat the natural dimension of the addendum as a potential that pre-exists its particular historical instantiation and that persists as a possibility that might be recovered more or less unchanged through the sociopolitical changes wrought by history. In this way, they bring Adorno closer to Aristotelian

59 Cook, *Adorno on Nature*, 54.

60 Freyenhagen, *Adorno's Practical Philosophy*, 263.

61 Habermas, "'I Myself Am Part of Nature,'" 189.

62 Bernstein, *Adorno*, 258. Cf. *The Fate of Art*, 220.

63 Bernstein, *Adorno*, 254–6.

humanism and its anthropology than his philosophy actually sanctions.[64] However, if we are to follow Adorno's conception of natural history here, we must see the nature for which the addendum stands as being historically produced, an idea to which Bernstein comes closest when he refers to the addendum as an "excrescence of the pure will."[65] The addendum, *das Hinzutretende*, is precisely that: an *addition* (*Hinzu*), something *added onto* the will through the act of willing. The addendum is not an unchanging capacity, nor does it pre-exist the will; rather, it is *produced by the will* as that which is non-identical to the will, that which the will cannot master and so rejects as mere "unfree" nature, against which the will's own freedom is defined. What is prior to the will, the mimetic impulse, is fractured by the will and transformed, its remnants gaining shape in opposition to the will – *this* is the addendum. The addendum must thus be understood as the remnants of the mimetic impulse displaced and internally mediated by the sociopolitical transformations that shaped the human animal into one for whom actions depend upon a will.[66]

The "memory" of "archaic impulses" that survives in the addendum thus points not to a past that necessarily existed either as a moment in sociopolitical history or even as an individual's history, but rather to what is non-identical in the will as it exists, as a kind of mimetic resistance to its permanence. To retrieve these "archaic impulses" through an experience of the addendum is thus not to recover the kernel of a lost humanity, from which a new humanity might be born, but to seize upon the non-identical excrescence produced by humanity so as to oppose its subjective coordinates. The addendum marks the spot where the architecture of the human is most fragile, where the otherness it suppresses is closest to the surface: it is here where contact might be made with the remnants of the mimetic impulse that serve to constellate the social objects that produce the human subject. As I have shown, what is non-identical to the concept of the human, that which evades the violent dominance of the human and its particular capacities, is the animal. The addendum is thus a kind of animal wriggling through human concepts, itself produced as the excrescence of these concepts. To attempt to build a new subject around this experience, as Adorno's new categorical imperative demands, is to attempt to build

64 See especially Freyenhagen, *Adorno's Practical Philosophy*, 262, ch. 9.

65 Bernstein, *Adorno*, 256.

66 The addendum thus does not refer to "unmediated physical impulses," though it does, as we shall see, allow for a "deep concern with animal suffering." See Peters, "'The Zone of the Carcass and the Knacker,'" 17.

an inhuman subject – a new kind of animal out of suppressed and discarded impulses.[67]

Living so as to be capable of saying that one has been a good animal thus involves learning to allow one's willed actions to receive direction from the addendum, by these involuntary bodily responses to others and to the situations in which we find ourselves in contact with them. It is not, however, simply to forsake reason and reflection in favour of what are popularly known as "gut instincts" – to do simply what *feels right* to us – for these involuntary bodily responses are deeply ambiguous: they include impulses both toward affection and solidarity and toward aggression and dominance. It is for this reason that Adorno sees the role of reflection as being absolutely vital here, for we must continually interrogate our bodily responses and see how they relate to others, especially insofar as they might cause them pain, if the circuits of domination are indeed to be resisted and if one is to live as a good animal. Yet Adorno's turn to animality would also obstruct the capacity to ignore these impulses, for insofar as they are the repressed nature excreted by our society, they not only tell us about the structure of our society, about how it is reproduced and the possibilities for change therein, but also bring us into visceral contact with others in a way the bureaucratic machinery of modern society is often able to obscure.

Imagine, for example, that you are witnessing a man being apprehended on the street by the police. After being tackled hard to the ground he is now lying on his belly, hands above his head, legs splayed. The officer is crouched on top of him, his right hand weighing heavily on the man's head, pressing the side of his face into the pavement. With his left hand, the officer reaches for one of the man's outstretched hands while his knee digs into the small of the man's back, pinning him in place. The man thrashes a little, emitting pained and angered shouts as best he can with his face pressed against the road. There may be relatively good reasons for this treatment: perhaps the man had murdered a child on a school playground and had then killed the first police officer who had attempted to apprehend him. But you do not know this. The impulse to give reasons for this treatment, to identify with the authority of the police officer and construct a narrative in which this

67 This is also where Butler's interpretation falls short, for though Butler offers a nuanced account of the relation between human and inhuman, she makes the inhuman simply a moment of humanity, rather than the reverse, tellingly failing to make any mention of the animals inhabiting Adorno's texts and their relation to this problem. See Butler, *Giving an Account of Oneself*, 106.

treatment is acceptable *without knowing why* is what being directed by the addendum would oppose.

Through their conceptual capture, the impulses both to participate in this violence and to shrink from it become separated from suffering in a way that contributes to a certain subject maintained through this separation. When you identify with the police officer as a figure of authority, his violent activity becomes a kind of surrogate for your own aggressive impulses. In watching the violent activity of the police officer, your own aggressive impulses are discharged, without having to assume any responsibility for their consequences – it was, after all, not you who enacted this violence. This identification between yourself and the police officer opens a space between you and your own aggressive impulses that deadens the visceral affinity between you and the suffering you witness, establishing a stable order wherein your aggressive impulses can be expressed by proxy and so treated as if they were not your own. Insofar as the violent activity of the police officer is required in order for you to maintain your own distance from the suffering and thus maintain the particular form of subjectivity you are embodying, the impulse to shrink from this violence becomes attended by reasons for why you should not involve yourself, for why what you are witnessing is somehow acceptable, and in this way impulses toward solidarity are conjured away. To be directed by the addendum, conversely, is to deny the authority of these reasons and the separation they would establish between you and suffering. To persist in the crisis of one's visceral affinity to suffering is to be directed by the addendum, a persistence with which comes the demand for an interrogation of this crisis.

Interrogated in this way, the feelings of revulsion and the impulse toward solidarity one experiences when confronted with such violence might be mobilized so as to intervene against it. However, this kind of mobilization would not necessarily mean that there would be no forces of coercion, no police, or even that the man in our example would be released. These are political questions that demand critical scrutiny, reflection, and debate, and these would not be erased by opening ourselves up to the addendum, for the addendum prescribes no positive institutional arrangement. However, what we can say is that a society in which our reason was directed by the addendum to end violence when confronted with it, rather than to secure one's own safety, even in situations such as our example, could not operate as ours does – it would simply not be possible to accept police direction to "move along" and so ignore the man pinned to the pavement. Power in such a society would not have free hands, for its authority would be under perpetual scrutiny, and any coercion it would exercise would be continually subject to intervention.

We now see that what Adorno is trying to get at with the concept of the addendum is the disposition of the human subject toward suffering and power, and toward tipping the scales in favour of solidarity with suffering, as opposed to power. As I have argued, insofar as reason and the use of concepts evolved according to the exigencies of self-preservation so as to eventually come to dominate nature, reason has evolved entwined with power, and the human being is the product of this evolution. To attempt to live a life of activity directed by the addendum is to attempt to disentangle reason from power, to make decisions where reason is not directed toward maximizing benefits to the individual and so securing its survival or prestige, and thus to direct reason toward a different evolutionary path.

Reason would thus no longer hold the majority of seats in the parliament of the subject, but instead occupy a minority position: its role would become one of critically scrutinizing impulses, not directing them, and so would enter into a relation with animality that does not involve its mastery or suppression. To transform the role of reason in this manner is to alter the subjective coordinates of the human being. To privilege the addendum is to direct the mimetic impulse toward objects it would not be directed toward if guided by instrumental reason and thereby bring about a shift in the constellation of social objects from which subjects spring. The reason employed by a transformed subject is one that would perceive its interests differently than the instrumental reason that animates human survival, and thereby transform the manner in which this subject conceives of its relations to others, and thus its moral activity, along with the overarching structures that enable this activity – its politics. Only through this manner of subjective transformation that brings about a change in moral and political activity might one be able to say that one had been a good animal.

However, if the addendum concerns the bodily comportment involved in willing, in making decisions, we must now ask: how is it that we come to feel the way we do, when we do? What if we do not feel the revulsion we are supposed to feel, say, at images or knowledge of Auschwitz? If the involuntary reactions or impulses that make up the addendum stand for the repressed nature our society has produced, how might we ensure that this nature is produced so as to promote solidarity with suffering rather than identification with power? To gain a better idea of how this mimetic displacement of the subjective coordinates of the human might proceed, we must turn to Adorno's ideas on that reservoir of the mimetic impulse, art.

## Inhuman Art

As argued above, Adorno's concept of a "reconciled humanity" refers to what would be a different kind of animal than what the human being is: an animal constituted in struggle for whom the capacities that have enabled its self-preservation are aligned with sociopolitical domination. Furthermore, it has been argued that the passage toward this political transformation through which this new animal might emerge leads through the moral practice of attempting to live as if one were a good animal. This practice involves attempting to accommodate "animal impulses" in one's decisions and actions so as to displace reason from its role in self-preservation – which is to say, in maximizing individual benefits – in favour of fostering solidarity with others. The specific animal impulses that would be fostered here are what Adorno calls "the addendum," the bodily comportment entwined with willing. In this way, to allow oneself to be guided by the addendum is to allow for a different mimetic connection to the social objects of which one is subjectively constituted, and so to attempt one's own subjective reconstitution: indeed, to live so as to be able to say that one had been a good *animal*, as opposed to a person.

However, while Adorno claims in *Negative Dialectics* that the addendum has become part of the human constitution in response to the horrors of Auschwitz,[68] we must ask: how might the experience of the addendum contribute to solidarity, as opposed to something else – say, a corporal feeling of individual or collective power, such as that promoted by Nietzsche? How can Adorno ensure that untying "the historically tied knot"[69] of the person through the cultivation of the addendum will not result in a form of subjectivity and society much worse than that of the present? The short answer to these questions is simply: he cannot, for there is no such guarantee.

Adorno readily acknowledges that the removal of the conception of the person makes its "residue" easier to dominate[70] – the moral status of the person, demanding as it does some kind of individual

68 Moreover, Adorno views the basic substance of modern industrial capitalist society as continuous with Auschwitz. See for example, *TNM*, 13; Horkheimer, *GSB14*, 38. Or as Geulen writes, 1945 "marks the end and the break that changed everything, precisely because not enough changed … The truly disruptive effect of this break consists in the ensuing continuity." See Geulen, "Theodor Adorno on Tradition," 186.

69 *ND*, 276; *GSB6*, 273.

70 *MM*, 64; *GSB4*, 71.

responsibility imposed upon impulses, serves to obstruct not only the emergence of what Adorno considers a better organization of society, but potentially worse ones as well, as fascism makes only too plain. Consequently, Adorno needs some conception of pedagogy that would serve to educate, not the will, but its non-identical impulses, so that these impulses would recoil from violence. Insofar as Adorno theorizes art as a kind of reservoir for the mimetic impulse, art could prove to be an important means for this education. However, apart from a few radio lectures Adorno delivered in the 1960s concerning education, he makes no sustained attempt to develop such a theory or to explore the educational possibilities of art.[71] This is likely due in part to Adorno's insistence on the autonomy of art; however, as I will show, a politically progressive aesthetic education need not be at odds with artistic autonomy, for the attempt to establish art's autonomy in the manner Adorno theorizes is already politically progressive in a broad sense, as noted above.

The relation between Adorno's aesthetics and Hegel is often noted.[72] Others see also the influence of Schiller's concept of aesthetic education.[73] Though the question of the truth content of artworks appropriated from Hegel remains important to my discussion, I want here to expand this association with aesthetic education in order to see Adorno attuned to the problematic set out earlier by Aristotle. Thus certain of Adorno's ideas on art might be used to reanimate the classical idea of the aesthetic education of the impulses. However, this reanimation does not come without an ironic twist. The aesthetic education advanced here would not attempt to cultivate the animal so as to make it human, which would amount to drawing a division between reason and impulse and teaching reason to command and impulse to obey. Instead, this education would attempt to cultivate animal impulses so as to enable them to resist human capture and thereby facilitate the kind of displacement of the subjective coordinates that constitute the human by turning toward non-identity through the addendum. In this

71 He did, however, outline a research plan for such a study, though it was never completed. See Adorno, "The Problem of a New Type of Human Being," 468.

72 See for example, Geuss, "Adorno and Berg," 118; Paddison, *Adorno, Modernism, and Mass Culture*, 64. For more nuanced accounts of Hegel's role, at least in *AT*, see Weber Nicholsen, *Exact Imagination*, 130–3; and Zuidervaart, *Adorno's Aesthetic Theory*, 115.

73 Hullot-Kentor, "Back to Adorno," 17; Rancière, *Aesthetics and Its Discontents*, 8; 102; Hammer, *Adorno's Modernism*, 209, though Hammer also offers clear ways in which Adorno differs from Schiller.

way, Adorno's aesthetics can be seen to address the question of producing an *aesthetic* animal, in the sense of an animal being constituted not simply through the senses, through its bodily comportment towards objects, but through the arts.[74]

For Adorno, an aesthetic animal would be the subject found through aesthetic comportment, produced through the tutelage of two different kinds of aesthetic experience: a passive or *receptive* experience of artworks, in which one's subjective coordinates are displaced by the shock one receives through their sheer alien character; and an active or *productive* experience of artworks, wherein one must navigate the various technical problems foisted upon one by history in order to produce works of art. It is through the conjunction of these two kinds of experience that one might realign *mimesis* and reason and so alter the subjective structure of the human. These are the kinds of experience necessary in order to learn to live as a good animal, one whose morality would push against the order of domination and so bring about its transformation, thus making possible the emergence of a qualitatively new kind of animal.

In this subsection I elaborate on what I have called the receptive experience of the artwork. Specifically, I seek to show that a receptive experience of artwork can disrupt the subjective coordinates of the human in a manner analogous to the addendum and that certain kinds of artworks are more likely to disrupt in this way. Consequently, exposure to such artworks gives one a bodily experience of one's fragility and finitude – one's animality – combined with an impulse to reflect on this animality and its relation to others. Ongoing receptive experience of artworks might therefore foster the kind of disposition that I have called animal – that is, a disposition toward solidarity rather than individual benefit-maximizing, and with it an aversion to violence. It is not pretended, however, that such experience alone is enough to radically transform human subjectivity. For Adorno's idea of aesthetic comportment to push beyond the Aristotelian notion of aesthetic education, aesthetic comportment must consist not only in its receptive dimension but in a productive dimension as well.

Concerning this receptive experience of the artwork, we find an experience of the less than voluntary, less than conceptual, bodily reaction to artworks. This experience is closely related to the addendum; however,

---

74 Hellings characterizes the pedagogical dimension of aesthetic experience in Adorno as a "(mis-)education," though without connecting it to the Aristotelian problematic or the production of an aesthetic animal. See Hellings, *Adorno and Art*, 108.

the addendum, we must recall, is the mimetic impulse internally mediated through the moral will, produced through the moral will as its *excrescence*, its non-identical other. Though the receptive experience of artworks is likewise tuned to the mimetic impulse, this impulse will be mediated differently through artworks than through the moral will, and thus is articulated somewhat differently and will require a different name. The most common terms Adorno employs when describing the mediation of the mimetic impulse through artworks are the shudder (*der Schauder*), or shaking (*Erschütterung*), both of which evoke non-voluntary, non-conceptual aspects of a bodily reaction to artworks akin with the body's reaction to the moral decisions and actions with which it is confronted in the addendum.[75] These terms are, once again, heavily influenced by Benjamin.

In his essay "On Some Motifs in Baudelaire," Benjamin examines modernity according to its lived experience, according to what the modern age *feels like*, as new social objects are introduced into the mimetic comportment of the subject that serve to alter its corporal disposition. Specifically, Benjamin focuses on the experience of being jostled in a crowd on the street, and the experience of labouring with industrial machinery, claiming that both are experiences of "shock."[76] That is, the lived experience of modernity is one of shock, of continual exposure to rigid, even violent stimuli that demand particular bodily reactions. Both factory machinery and traffic signals demand a certain automatic deference to their operations by the subject confronted with them, and failure to comply with these demands can be met with serious physical injury or death – one cannot negotiate terms, one must simply react. To be the denizen of a world made of such objects is to mimetically assimilate oneself to their mechanisms, and thus to submit to their training, to the uniform and constant movement characteristic of a *drill* as opposed to a practice. As Horowitz notes, drills are without the rhythm that characterizes practice of all kinds: poetry, music, speech, and expression – drills possess virtually no rhythm at all.[77] Insofar as shock experience reduces the practices that make up lived experience to drills, the bodily experience of modernity is

75 *Convulsed* in this way by aesthetic experience, "the claims and needs of the empirical subject" are challenged. See Maharaj, *The Dialectics of Aesthetic Agency*, 154.

76 Walter Benjamin, "On Some Motifs in Baudelaire," in *Illuminations*, ed. Hannah Arendt, trans. Harry Zohn (New York: Schoken, 1969), 176. Cf. Benjamin, *GSB1*, 632.

77 Horowitz, *Ethics at a Standstill*, 111–12.

a radically impoverished form of experience,[78] one perhaps even describable as *inhuman*.[79]

Adorno assents to much of Benjamin's critique and to the central place of shock experience within modernity[80]; however, for Adorno it is precisely the inhumanity of this experience that, mediated through art, offers the possibility of sociopolitical transformation. Modern artworks make possible a transformation of the subject produced through shock experience by mimetically reproducing this shock;[81] in this way, the shock is alienated from its function in the reproduction of modern society and becomes instead poetic – it gains something like a rhythm. Of course, art must radically alter its received categories, forms, and techniques in order to render itself capable of expressing this shock, and the "rhythm" it produces in doing so is like no rhythm before it. Gone is the classical claim to wholeness and harmony – what is left are only twisted fragments: the wreckage of the world as it had been and of the rhythm that had animated it. What Adorno calls the shudder is shock experience reflected through the artwork: it makes directly palpable the truth of the experience of modernity that would be hidden by the primacy of the subject and the positive articulation of humanity, the person. Thus the truth of the work is revealed to the spectator "as if it must also be his own"[82] – the indigence and the distortion of the work reveal the indigence and distortion of the spectator. It is for this reason that Adorno refers to the shudder as "a memento of the liquidation of the I, which, shaken, perceives its own limitedness and finitude."[83] "Convulsed by art,"[84] the subject can no longer maintain its veneer of independence, and the object shines through the widening fissures.

This aesthetic rupture of the subject by its objectivity is, as we have seen, a turn to animality. Thus Adorno writes that "artworks win life only when they renounce likeness to the human,"[85] approvingly cites

78 Benjamin, "On Some Motifs in Baudelaire," 180; Benjamin, *GSB1*, 636. Cf. Rosen, *On Voluntary Servitude*, 243, 248.

79 Indeed, Benjamin will refer to the jostling crowd, fomenting as it does this shock experience, as "essentially inhuman." Benjamin, "On Some Motifs in Baudelaire," 172; Benjamin, *GSB1*, 626.

80 Cf. *MM*, 54; *GSB4*, 60–1.

81 Cf. *PMM*, 39; *GSB12*, 44.

82 *AT*, 269; *GSB7*, 401.

83 *AT*, 245; *GSB7*, 364.

84 *AT*, 269; *GSB7*, 401.

85 *AT*, 168; *GSB7*, 252.

Schoenberg's praise of Webern for having spurned "animal warmth,"[86] and lauds Baudelaire for his work that "wipes out any human trace."[87] However, disrupting the subjective coordinates of the human in this manner cannot be all the artwork has to offer if it is to contribute to sociopolitical transformation. Adorno is quick to point out that though the shudder reveals the human subject and its self-preservation to be semblance, the conditions from which this semblance is born persist. In other words: the receptive experience of art makes promises it cannot keep.[88] Moreover, as we have already seen in his critique of Aristotelian poetics, Adorno claims that overvaluing aesthetic effects runs the risk of making art into a form of "substitute satisfaction" to be manipulated and administered by the culture industry, thereby serving the forces of repression.[89] That is, the very power of *mimesis* reveals the truth of shock experience in its semblance, yet because it is an *aesthetic* semblance, distant to some degree from the actual shock experience of the crowd or the factory, it makes the aesthetic experience of these things *pleasurable.*

This is part of the reason why Adorno claims that "artworks tend a priori toward affirmation": artworks "bring forth another world," detaching themselves from the empirical world.[90] In this way, they reveal the truth of the object and so alienate the apparent naturalness of the empirical world and one's own subjective place in it, and they do so in a manner that gives the subject pleasure – thus anaesthetizing the subject to the suffering expressed in the work, which, as art, is enjoyable. Thus, artworks reconcile the aesthetic subject to the empirical world by way of the image of the other world they offer. Insofar as the experience of subjective displacement and alienation found in the shudder lasts but a moment, it is possible for the pleasure one receives from the work to annex the transformative moment the shudder reveals and thereby make it part of the work's overall effect, to be manipulated and administered. Instead of experiencing the dislocation of the social objects of

---

86 *AT*, 43; *GSB7*, 70; *PMM*, 118; *GSB12*, 113. Adorno, "Arnold Schoenberg, 1874–1951," 158; *GSB10.1*, 163. Adorno, "Vers une musique informelle," 309. What Schoenberg calls "animal warmth," a sense of comfort and familiarity, of surety in oneself and one's surroundings, is not animality in the sense I have been using it, but rather part of the positive articulation of humanity, the person, which his music would transcend.

87 *AT*, 21; *GSB7*, 39.

88 *AT*, 245; *GSB7*, 364.

89 *AT*, 238; *GSB7*, 354.

90 *AT*, 1; *GSB7*, 10.

which one's subjectivity is composed as a moment from which return becomes impossible, one instead comes to seek out those artworks that provide one with this affect, delighting in the *frisson* of inhumanity they provide as one does the tingling on the tongue one feels eating blowfish, touched as it is by poison.

Indeed, this particular mode of experiencing artworks Adorno polemically refers to as "culinary." Though *Aesthetic Theory* is replete with references to the culinary character of artworks,[91] for a definition one must look to Adorno's writings for Americans. In *Current of Music*, Adorno writes that the term "culinary" is used to denote musical qualities that provide instant and transitory sensual pleasure, serving to stimulate the senses.[92] The problem with producing music with culinary qualities, or with a listener seeking out the culinary qualities of a piece of music, is that in doing so one ignores the *truth* of the music and thus avoids those elements that might threaten one's personality. If art is indeed the unconscious writing of history,[93] then to experience the truth of an artwork is to grasp in some sense the truth of the movement of history as the possibility of redemption, as the possibility of a world not constituted by violence, in the fragment that is the individuality of the particular work.[94]

Thus the image of redemption that was found in philosophy to be a conceptual trick played at the expense of concepts is made palpable in the artwork – it becomes not simply a cognitive experience but a bodily one: it is the intimation of truth that makes one shudder. This is why Adorno claims that art that is experienced only in relation to who one already is, art that is classifiable into the world one already knows, is *not experienced at all*.[95] The truth of the artwork is not visible within the confines of the world as it is – that is, from the perspective of one's positive humanity. Just as "Utopia goes disguised in the creatures,"[96] so does the future come disguised in artworks: artworks are fragments of a future world that express themselves in the language of the present, and through this expression, the language of the present is

91 See for instance, *AT*, 157, 276, 334, 347; *GSB7*, 235, 411, 497, 516.

92 Adorno, "Radio Physiognomics," 123.

93 Adorno, "Those Twenties," 48; *GSB10.2*, 506. Cf. *PMM*, 43; *GSB12*, 47. Or in more Hegelian terms: "Artworks are enigmatic in that they are the physiognomy of an objective spirit that is never transparent to itself in the moment in which it appears" (*AT*, 128; *GSB7*, 194).

94 Cf. Geuss, "Form and 'The New,'" 143.

95 *AT*, 246; *GSB7*, 364–5. Cf. *AT*, 183; *GSB7*, 274.

96 Recall *MM*, 228; *GSB4*, 261.

transformed – it thereafter bears the imprint of the future toward which it now points. The "culinary" consumption of artworks amounts to the reduction of their truth to the terms of the human subject, which merely shores up the primacy of the human and provides sustenance to the ersatz experience it offers of the modern world.

What is needed, then, for the receptive experience of artworks to be capable of grasping their truth, is an active moment, an activity that remains receptive to artworks while resisting their culinary appropriation and persisting in the inhumanity of the subjective displacement found in the shudder. Hullot-Kentor provides a hint of what this activity might be when he equates Adorno's use of the Greek *thaumazein* in "The Idea of Natural History" with "shock."[97] *Thaumazein* in Aristotle is understood to be something closer to "awe" or "wonder" than the modern "shock," with its violent and mechanical associations; *thaumazein* informs philosophical activity – it is the wonder one feels in being confronted with nature that propels one to inquire and to reflect.[98] Though the harmonious experience of *thaumazein* as wonder has been transformed in modernity to the fragmented experience of shock that would turn one *away* from reflection, mediated through the artwork as the shudder, this bodily disposition toward objects might likewise provide an impulse to reflection, just as the addendum demands its own reflexive interrogation. It is worth recalling here that in *Politics* VII, Aristotle includes "study and thought [*theoria kai dianoeseis*]" among the components of a life of action (*bios praktikos*).[99] Adorno echoes this view in "Marginalia to Theory and Praxis" when he writes that "thinking is a doing" and that theory is itself a form of praxis.[100] That Adorno cites Aristotle here, noting both the ideological function of his emphasis on the life of contemplation and its truth content,[101] further illustrates the degree to which his treatment of these questions is bound up with the Aristotelian problematic.

While the *praxis* of *theoria* in Aristotle is specifically tied to the humanity of the human being and its separation from and superiority to other animals, in Adorno we find this theoretical praxis working in the

97 *INH*, 118; *GSB1*, 356. Cf. Hullot-Kentor, "Introduction," 107.

98 *Meta.*, 982b12–13.

99 *Pol.*, 1325b13–23.

100 Adorno, "Marginalia to Theory and Praxis," *CM*, 261, 277; *GSB10.2*, 761, 781. This point is frequently overlooked by commentators searching for a more direct relation between theory, praxis, and politics in Adorno. See for example Chari, *Political Economy of the Senses*, 161.

101 Adorno, "Marginalia to Theory and Praxis," *CM*, 267; *GSB10.2*, 769.

opposite direction. Adorno relies on the Aristotelian formulation of theory and praxis in order to turn it against itself, to turn it against the production of the human as master and the animal as pet, prey, or slave, which in turn involves the domination of some humans by others. The "irruption of objectivity into subjective consciousness"[102] in the experience of the truth of art equates with the animal shedding its human confines, thereby offering an image of its subjective possibilities reconstellated. The practice of theory is the active moment of the receptive experience of artworks that makes possible the grasping of their truth, and thus what establishes their greatness, for it is only insofar as an artwork is true that it can be said to be great. It is for this reason that artworks, "especially those of the highest dignity," can be said to "await their interpretation."[103] Interpretation, commentary, and critique are all internal to the artwork, to its process of becoming, for these serve to transform the artwork that has through expression captured a sociopolitical antagonism at a certain point in history.[104] The understanding of this sociopolitical antagonism and its place in history, and thus the understanding of future possibilities, and thus the possibilities one understands as informing one's own life, are thereby transformed through the interpretation of the work.[105]

---

102 *AT*, 245; *GSB7*, 363.

103 *AT*, 128; *GSB7*, 194; Adorno, *Aesthetics 1958–59*, 18, 129 154.

104 *AT*, 194; *GSB7*, 289.

105 This point is overlooked by Chari, who argues that certain artworks represent forms of "material critique" that "go beyond" Adorno, who privileges cognitive forms of critique to the detriment of political praxis. While there is a convergence between critique and artistic technique in the production of artworks, Adorno readily acknowledges this, and I argue below that this form of critique is closely related to political praxis. Yet from the receptive experience of artworks, can the works of Clare Fontaine cited by Chari be known as instances of "material critique" without Chari's own theorizing efforts, which are, of course, firmly rooted in cognitive-discursive means? How might Chari avoid the charge of engaging in "critique that is excessively cognitively centered," given that Chari's critique is not itself an instance of "material critique" in the manner of the works of Clare Fontaine, but rather proceeds entirely according to the "appeals to rationality, conceptuality, and thought" found in scholarly monographs? Insisting that "material critique" is "beyond" cognition-discourse, yet being unable to make this point without cognitive-discursive means, places the author in a performative contradiction whereby the place and relevance of her own theory is obscured. By acknowledging that interpretation is inherent to the artwork, however, this performative contradiction is avoided, for Chari's theoretical practice, like Adorno's, becomes part of what makes an artwork what it is. Clare Fontaine's works are not *immediately* material instances of critique; rather, the receptive experiences these material

In this way we find the receptive experience of artworks to indeed be capable of displacing the subjective coordinates of the human. But do all artworks enable this experience alike? If an artwork's greatness concerns the truth of its expression of a particular antagonism, which is itself determined through *critical reflection*,[106] how could there be a significant distinction between different kinds of artworks and their relative suitability for interpretation? Are not all works equally in need of interpretation, and thus equal in their possession of truth content? Though Adorno does indeed claim that truth content can assert itself through even the most ideological works,[107] and that art wholly free of ideology is probably impossible,[108] he nevertheless does hold that certain artworks do a better job of expressing a given historical moment than others, and thus that artworks possessed of certain qualities have greater truth content, where the relative truth content of a work is related to its power to disrupt the subject's coordinates.

Thus it is not simply a matter of the quality of the interpretation – Adorno does not, as Jameson would have it, wish "to reinvent a new kind of primacy of philosophy over artistic experience."[109] Rather, the truth content of works is entwined with the work itself and with the particular way in which its form reveals its material as content.[110] For instance, Adorno claims that though interpretation gives to artworks the life in which they become what they will be, in which the antagonism captured in the work at its birth is theoretically elaborated and grasped, this process is finite, in a sense. Eventually the work tends to be conceptually grasped such that its content and form are assimilated into the dominant constellation of social objects, at which point it ceases to be experienced as a work of art and no longer possesses the power to

---

objects provoke are deeply ambivalent and become instances of "critique" through the mediation of Chari's theory. As works, they demand interpretation, and their critical function will change according to their interpretation. See Chari, *Political Economy of the Senses*, 166–7, 173. Of course, this critical determination will not be without its non-identical remainder, namely the corporal experience of the work, which pushes against discursive assimilation. Cf. Hammer, *Adorno's Modernism*, 121, 129.

106 Cf. Hohendal, "Adorno," 78.

107 Insofar as ideology is itself "the distorted image of the true" (*AT*, 233; *GSB7*, 345–6).

108 *AT*, 236; *GSB7*, 351. *Contra* the notion that Adorno is a champion of art's "purity." See Rancière, *Aesthetics and Its Discontents*, 132; Wellmer, "Adorno, Modernity, and the Sublime," 124.

109 Jameson, *Late Marxism*, 208.

110 Cf. Paddison, *Adorno, Modernism, and Mass Culture*, 61.

dislocate the social objects that compose the subject, for it is among the objects that constitute the subject as it is. Or more bluntly: even inhuman art risks becoming human.

For this reason, art must perpetually reinvent itself in order to be experienced and so must continually invent ways to break from past forms and techniques that have become assimilated by the order of what is: art must be *new*. The necessarily antagonistic character of newness makes new artworks *dissonant*, in that they must disrupt the harmony established in the order of what is: their newness is heard as the torture of accepted forms. The new must also be *abstract*, for insofar as its innovation calls into being a world that does not exist, it is a world that is unknown, like "the secret of Poe's pit."[111] Opposing these are artworks that can no longer be experienced: artworks that have become "archaic."[112] However, Adorno insists that this process of ossification, this becoming-archaic, has no fixed trajectory, for "modernity is a qualitative, not a chronological category."[113] Rather, the process of becoming-archaic is fragmented, dynamic, and dependent upon the modern, upon the new, for new artistic innovations may appropriate the past in novel ways that breathe into it new life. Artworks of the past might live again by finding themselves in a new light, and it is their distance from this light that renders them invisible.

Thus important, even definitive examples of new or modern art for Adorno, such as Schoenberg's *Five Pieces for Orchestra*, Op. 16, called by Adorno the "oldest, boldest and most important" of large-scale atonal works,[114] today might be confused with parts of the soundtrack of *Planet of the Apes*. Yet even if the culture industry has managed to assimilate the most dissonant examples of modern art and transformed them into fodder for the reproduction of positive humanity, it has done so in large part by managing the contexts in which a subject is exposed to it. The experience of musical dissonance outside of the context of expressing the intensity or psychological distress of a scene in a film, that is, outside of a context in which it is expected and so forms part of the social objects in which personality is constituted, might still threaten to displace our subjective coordinates.

Imagine, for example, the confusion and even distress that might arise if Op. 16 were to be piped into the food court at a shopping mall. The

111 *AT*, 15, 20; *GSB7*, 29, 37–8. Together these three form the core of Adorno's modernism. See Osborne, "Adorno and the Metaphysics of Modernism," 36.

112 *AT*, 349; *GSB7*, 518.

113 *MM*, 218; *GSB4*, 249.

114 Adorno, "Vers une musique informelle," 291.

fact that Schoenberg could still today empty the food court lays bare the antagonism between the kind of experience captured in his work and the kind that supports the activities appropriate to a food court. Thus even the now century-old music of Arnold Schoenberg – considered by some passé even at the time of Adorno's writings – might be seen, thanks to the abstract and dissonant qualities of the work, as something like an undigested stone, even a tumour, in the bowel of the culture industry. Whether or not this tumour proves to be benign or malignant depends upon how it is articulated theoretically and appropriated by future art, but its availability for such appropriation is fundamentally different than for works that have never at one time been new.[115] Works that were once new thus embody a transformative capacity that carries with it moral and political possibilities, even though these works reject direct moral and political association.

In this way, the receptive experience of artworks that contributes to the emergence of the subject of aesthetic comportment is one wherein the bodily reaction to new artworks disrupts the subjective coordinates of one's personality – of one's humanity – and becomes mediated by reflection in a manner that resists re-establishing the subjective coordinates of humanity. This experience is without positive political content, yet when the relation between the subject and the objects of which it is constituted is undermined, and the subject is opened up instead to its own animality and reflection upon this animality, a wrench is thrown into the gears of society as it exists, opening up an interval from which transformation is possible. Yet just as man cannot live by bread alone, so the animal cannot be sustained merely by reflection on aesthetic experience.

If Adorno is to appropriate from Aristotle an idea of aesthetic education even while transcending Aristotle's manner of dividing higher and lower, human and animal, then he must also transcend Aristotle's aesthetic education based around the management of effects, around spectators assimilating themselves to social objects by way of aesthetic

115 A work can be said to never have been new if it was never the attempt to express an experience that necessitated innovation in artistic techniques, and whose own experience never served to displace the subjective coordinates of the listener/spectator. Works that lack sufficient contact with the material to require a transformation in their techniques fail to express the experience of the social antagonisms from which they were born; rather, these works would hide this antagonism with pseudo-experience. Such works are *born old* – they are already "archaic" the moment they hit the shops. For an attempt to apply Adorno's aesthetics to a more recent example of musical dissonance, see Campbell, "'Three-Minute Access,'" 278–95.

experience. So Adorno requires an aesthetic education that also includes subjects being capable of learning for themselves to produce the objects that will form part of the constellation of social objects from which they will in turn be produced. The practices needed to sustain the transformation of the human subject in this way must thus extend beyond the active moment in the receptive experience of artworks – reflection that, like *theoria*, makes the subject of receptive experience a *critic* – and connect to a productive experience of artworks, wherein the subject becomes an *artist*. To become an artist in this way is to enter into an active relationship with the techniques used to produce inhuman works of art. Thus while new works of art, as we have seen, disrupt the subjective coordinates of humanity, for Adorno to transcend Aristotle and so theorize the possibility of a truly aesthetic animal, he must incorporate the practices required to create these works. While the receptive experience of art disrupts and resists the subjective coordinates of humanity, truly aesthetic comportment that might actualize a practice of animality requires more direct engagement with the production of art.

## Animal Technique

In Adorno's conception of aesthetic comportment, the subject is one for which the relation between *mimesis* and reason has been radically altered so that reason is no longer a domineering force oriented toward maximizing individual benefits in the interest of self-preservation. Instead, reason is oriented toward inventing ways to express the mimetic impulse as contact and solidarity with others. The subject of aesthetic comportment is not human, but some other kind of animal, an animal that emerges through a kind of aesthetic education comprised of both receptive and productive experience of artworks. The receptive experience of artworks, discussed above, is comprised of a passive moment, the involuntary shudder that runs through a body confronted with the new, and an active moment of reflection upon the shudder and the works that invoked this reaction. The passive moment disrupts the subjective coordinates of the human; the active moment resists the reconstitution of the human, thus allowing for the persistence of animality.

But insofar as the receptive experience of artworks leaves the subject in a position of dependence upon artworks produced by others, there remains the division between critic and artist that is characteristic of the division of labour that has enabled sociopolitical domination. If this division is to be transcended, from Aristotle's distinction between action as speech and action as contemplation to the Leninist division between a revolutionary vanguard and the masses, a productive experience of artworks is required. This productive experience must be one wherein the inhuman subject of receptive experience learns to act according to impulses other than those of self-preservation even while producing the social objects from which new forms of subjectivity will spring. In this way the productive experience of artworks is a kind of alienation of alienated labour: it seeks to appropriate the most advanced productive techniques and the discipline necessary to employ them, but it is also turned toward the production of objects that lack the instrumental function of reproducing the world as it is.

In producing objects that are not immediately or obviously part of any system of equivalence, the subject experiences activity irreducible to what is necessary to reproduce the existing sociopolitical world, while also contributing truly individual objects to the sociopolitical constellation from which new subjects will be formed. In this way, "art becomes the schema of social praxis,"[116] for such works are expressions of the possibility of production organized otherwise than it is in the world of domination. Insofar as the experience of producing objects according to impulses other than those of instrumental reason amounts to a kind of education of the impulses and the rationality needed to express them, this productive experience must be seen as a moral one; and insofar as its products contribute to the order of social objects from which subjectivity emerges, it must also be considered political. So we must read Adorno's thoughts on artistic practice or *technique* as part of a kind of moral and political education, one where subjects engage in the activities that will produce a subject of a certain sort – in this case, *the good animal* of which Adorno has written, the actualization of subjective possibilities repressed by the human.

Like the receptive experience of artworks, productive experience consists of passive and active moments. The active moment of the productive experience of artworks concerns *forming* activity, that is, mastery of artistic material through techniques that dislodge it from the forms in which it is sedimented so as to make from it something new. Like the shudder, that is, the shock experience of modernity aesthetically pacified (see above), the aesthetic mastery expressed in form and technique reflects a kind of pacified mastery. The technical mastery of artistic material is a pacified image of the technological domination of nature, for the former is mastery without violence, mastery that expresses what had been trapped in the material and would otherwise

116 *AT*, 228; *GSB7*, 339.

have remained mute. In offering an image of non-violent mastery, the technical practices of artistic production provide an education of animal impulses so as to enable their articulation in a subject whose reason is the *agent* of animality rather than its censor. Understanding this non-violent mastery involves understanding its status in relation to concepts and reason.[117]

Just as concepts are for Adorno the means by which humans carve up and identify objects in the material world, so are forms the way in which artists have organized the plethora of possibilities available through artistic material, rendering it as content.[118] Forms are thus analogous to concepts without themselves being conceptual – we might say that forms are to *mimesis* what concepts are to reason. Forms and concepts are the means through which mimetic and rational impulses are bound up with the world: they are the point of contact where the body meets objects and is itself constituted as an object, capturing the world and in so doing being captured by it. Content is material given artistic form and thus *transformed*. The material as it existed in the sociopolitical world – what Adorno calls the "empirical world" – through artistic form acquires an individuality and a degree of distance, of *autonomy*, from the sociopolitical world. As we have seen, this autonomy is not so great as to render artworks incapable of being reintegrated into the sociopolitical world and so incorporated into its reproduction, and even this autonomy itself can be seen to harbour an ideological element insofar as it is possible for art's refusal of the terms of sociopolitical world to have a quietist dimension – hence the impossibility of "pure" art, art wholly free of ideology.[119] Nevertheless, even the tiny distance opened up between the world as it is and the world as it appears through artistic form is enough to inject new possibilities into the world as it is.

Adorno offers an example of new possibilities introduced through artistic form in his account of Morike's poem "Mousetrap Rhyme," wherein a child circles a mousetrap, calling for a mouse to come pay him and his cat a visit. The social material upon which this poem draws

117 For an account of the possibility of non-violent mastery from a psychoanalytical perspective, see Fong, *Death and Mastery*. Though my account differs from Fong's on numerous points, I broadly agree that Adorno's politics "was simultaneously an education that developed the capacities for autonomy necessary for political action" (107). Cf. Benhabib, "Critical Theory and Postmodernism," 335–6.

118 "Artistic form, when properly constituted, serves to liberate content from its chaotic and inarticulate state" as material. See Zuidervaart, *Adorno's Aesthetic Theory*, 128.

119 Recall *AT*, 236; *GSB7*, 351.

concerns the human practice of identifying some animals as friends or allies to be cared for (the cat) and others as vermin to be destroyed (the mouse). Reduced to its social material, the poem indeed appears to allude to this, concerning as it does the taunts of a sadistic child who is intent on seeing the triumph of human mastery. Yet Adorno claims that to interpret this poem as simply a taunt referring to this "miserable, socially conditioned ritual," that is, to reduce the poem to its social material, is precisely to overlook the poem as a work of art, and thus its form and content.

The poetic allusions to the mouse's capture, the child's claim that they will "sing" and "dance," transforms the violence of the social material into the ambiguity of poetic content, calling up "involuntarily" the "friendly image of child, cat, and mouse dancing, the two animals on their hind legs."[120] In this way, even an artwork that takes violent material as its content transforms this material into content whose meaning can no longer be reduced to what it was as material. Once appropriated by art, the material no longer has the last say: the "ritual" of which the child's taunt is a part becomes through artistic form a kind of counter-spell to invoke the liberation of the child, cat, and mouse from their socially determined antagonistic roles. Thus through the artwork, even the practice of destroying vermin can be recast as the utopian image of solidarity between animals.

The importance of technique here is twofold: (1) it is technique that imparts form to the material, transforming it into content and thus giving it the critical distance from the empirical world necessary to introduce new possibilities; and (2) technique serves as an example of activity that is both rational and without concepts.[121] That is, technique is activity that attempts to give rational expression to the non-identical as non-identical, as something that does not yet exist, rather than identify non-identity with a concept and so assimilate it to the conceptual order of the existing world. Artistic technique, as an activity, can thus be said to be both mimetic and rational. It is mimetic in that it makes contact with material and transforms it along formal rather than conceptual lines, and it is rational insofar as it is logical and calculating – artistic technique employs all the resources of cunning to invent means of expressing an experience of the material through a new form, instead of identifying it with a concept.

In this way, technique is a practice that is not human in the strict sense, for it demands a different relation between reason and *mimesis*

---

120 *AT*, 123–4; *GSB7*, 187–8.
121 *AT*, 213; *GSB7*, 317.

than that which constitutes the human. Humanity is born in the failed attempt to repress its mimetic impulses through the rational deployment of concepts; whereas artistic technique attempts to make reason an ally of *mimesis*. In this way, the artistic techniques deployed in the production of artworks can be seen as moral *praxis* in the Aristotelian sense, that is, as practice that engenders in the practitioner the kind of constitution capable of supporting certain values. Adorno, though, continues to resist Aristotle, by claiming that these practices are not aimed at values thought to be derived from what is naturally and necessarily human, but rather are linked to human animality, and that their practice encourages the emergence of a different subject, one opposed to the human. In this sense, artistic practices retain for Adorno an important affinity with critique: they are not aimed at identifying different actualizations of human animality with the concept of the human in order to reconcile the former to the latter; rather, they concern fostering an unruly profusion of individuality.

The practices that compose artistic technique are instances of critique through their engagement with the material and its history. Adorno writes that form "converges with critique,"[122] for the material itself is already the sedimented forms and contents of the past.[123] Material is thus already, in a sense, a graveyard of forms and their contents. Finding ways to give expression to the material is thus a means for individuating through redivision what is already artistic, historical, social, and political – it is a way, as noted earlier, of giving voice to a particular antagonism that their sedimentation has produced and, in so doing, acquiring a distance from this antagonism that might conjure up the image of its transcendence.

It is for this reason that articulating the new is a historical process, for in working through the material one is necessarily working through the ways in which past artists have employed different techniques in order to impart form to the material with which they were confronted. Producing an artwork that is new, one that might possess the power to disrupt the subjective coordinates of its audience, thus involves technical innovation in order to master the material, to transform the way in which it presents itself so as to be cast in a new light. The practice of applying these technical innovations and creating the new is moral in that it requires a particular kind of education of the impulses, and it can be called political insofar as it involves transforming the overarching

122 *AT*, 144; *GSB7*, 216.
123 *AT*, 144–5; *GSB7*, 217. Cf. Hullot-Kentor, "The Impossibility of Music," 182.

structure in which moral activity has its force, by producing new social objects that will enter the constellation constitutive of subjectivity.

But to accomplish this expression, the productive experience of artworks requires also a passive moment: form must not simply be imposed upon content haphazardly; technique must not simply be applied to material arbitrarily. Rather, both form and the techniques of which it is composed must themselves be responses to material necessity. It is thus only through a passive attunement to the material, to a sensitivity to its structure, that an artist might know how techniques might be employed and transformed to express it, and form might emerge out of the content rather than remain something antagonistic to the material.[124]

This passive moment limits the subjectivity of the artist, and makes this subjectivity the agent of the material's objectivity, and thereby ensures that the mastery learned through artistic practice is indeed non-violent. Thus, while Adorno will refer to technique as "mastery," and "repression," and even "domination," he also can claim that the artist mobilizes this domination against domination, for her domination of the material through technique is at once her submission to technical dictates emerging from the material.[125] He compares this reciprocal form of mastery to linguistic fluency: one can claim to have mastered a language only insofar as one has allowed oneself to be mastered *by* that language. Thus, if the logic of technique is one of "authentic control," then it must also include its opposite, "the education of the subjective sensibility to respond to the impulses of whatever is not the subject."[126]

In this way Adorno rejects the model of the artist as creator, both in its explicitly theological articulation and in its humanist echo, for in attuning herself to the material the artist accepts the technical demands necessary to express it and so makes herself something like the "extension of the tool," the means through which the potentiality of the work latent in the material is made actual.[127] The artist's reason, then, is neither God-given nor definitively human; rather, it is an animal impulse that might participate in the invention of forms to express this

124 *AT*, 142; *GSB7*, 213. Cf. Hullot-Kentor, "The Impossibility of Music," 183.

125 Adorno, "Reaction and Progress," 223.

126 Adorno, "Vers une musique informelle," *QF*, 319.

127 *AT*, 166; *GSB7*, 249. The speculation demanded by the antinomies of Adorno's aesthetic theory does not to my mind render them theological, as argues Hohendal. See Hohendal, *The Fleeting Promise of Art*, 61. Cf. Bernstein, *The Fate of Art*, 256; Gordon, *Adorno and Existence*, 195; Walzer, *In God's Shadow*, esp. ch. 10. For more comprehensive treatment of Adorno's relation to theology, see Brittain, *Adorno and Theology*; Cook, "Through a Glass Darkly"; and de Vries, *Minimal Theologies*.

animal and, in so doing, produce the new – the nature that does not yet exist. In the moral sense, this passive moment involves practising one's attunement to the objective animality that the receptive experience of artworks fosters, so that employing artistic techniques and producing artworks becomes a kind of mastery in service of animal solidarity. Read as political activity, then, artistic technique is the mastery of reason deployed to solve the problems that surround expressing the objective animality that the human world characterized by domination would suppress. Artistic technique is reason convulsed by the animal, reason driven to invent ways of enabling animal expression.

Moreover, by introducing new objects into the social constellation of which subjectivity is constituted, such activity might contribute to the creation of a new kind of subject. In this way, art, through the receptive and productive experiences of its works, cultivates resistance to the subjective coordinates of humanity and precipitates their transformation. The subject educated by these experiences, the subject of aesthetic comportment, is one for which violence is intolerable and who is compelled toward solidarity with suffering. Where this aesthetic comportment fosters solidarity between such subjects, a global subject might be constituted, one for which the intolerable status of violence makes it essential to transform the world so that the possibility of "total disaster" is no more.

It is for this reason that Adorno will claim that "watching over the artist's shoulder is a collective subject [*Gesamtsubject*] that has yet to be realized"[128]: the "I" that speaks in artworks is not the "I" of the individual ego of the artist, of his or her positive humanity, but the "We" of a collective subject.[129] The collective subject found in the image of reconciled humanity thus becomes the wound around which subjectivity is displaced – a wound that would only close with the positive realization of reconciled humanity. In this way, artistic activity pushes toward this image of a future humanity, which, as we have seen, is human no longer. It is by way of artworks and the techniques that produce them that the animal that is reconciled humanity weighs upon the subject, displacing this subjectivity and enabling its reconstitution around the experience of displacement – the experience of animality. Thus

128 *AT*, 231; *GSB7*, 343.

129 Hence another reason why reducing an artwork to its artist's intentions, motivations, or other characteristics, or even worse, making the artist into a celebrity who stands in front of the work, is to falsify its truth content. See Hellings, *Adorno and Art*, 89.

artworks "anticipate a nonexistent social whole," a "non-existent subject,"[130] the reconciled humanity that they call through the constellation of a global subject. In this radically transformed world, in the "nonexistent social whole" produced through the cultivation of animality, the human would become nothing more than a memory, the ancient nightmare of an animal that now finally wakes to life, eyes open.

What might such an animal be, one that was human but now, human no longer? What would such a society be like, where self-preservation and its violence no longer occupy the centre of gravity around which all else orbits? A society where none are dominated? What suffering would drive artistic expression, if suffering as the experience of one's mortality and fragility was without the razor's edge that accompanies life lived each against all? Adorno writes that art in such a society would be "wholly different" than it is in the society of the present, that its role would be transformed.[131] But transformed how? Would such animals "construct their edifices and works of art as birds build their nests and spiders spin their webs," or "perform musical concerts after the fashion of frogs and cicadas," as Kojève fancies? It is just as easy to laugh at such propositions as it is impossible to say. Violence is so deeply embedded in the human constitution that even displacing it from the centre of life's organization could mean introducing radically new ways of living. Radically *new*, even if this possible future already goes disguised in all the ordinary little fragments of peace we experience without even realizing it, entwined as they are with the different privileges particular to our societies.

Perhaps we might think of this possible animal future as a piece of music to be played with our bodies as the instruments. A work for the modern piano, say, Schoenberg's *Three Piano Pieces,* Op. 11, was already *physically* possible the moment the piano as it presently exists came into being. In this sense, Op. 11, and every piece for the modern piano before and after it, was inherent to the very construction of the piano as a physically possible combination of sounds. Yet it took the history of compositions for piano to produce the particular combination of sounds that is Op. 11, and its existence transformed what was known about the possibilities inherent to the piano and how it would be played thereafter. In this same way, while the animal agency that would transgress the rules of composition that is the human depends on a body whose most basic physiology has long been available, it has

130 *AT*, 167–8; *GSB7*, 251.
131 *AT*, 338; *GSB7*, 503.

required the conceptual history of humanity outlined in the Aristotelian problematic to make possible this animality and so make possible the subject that might reveal just how our understanding of what a body can do has been obstructed by our own understanding of its possibilities. I have argued that Adorno theorizes the possibility of the transformation of these obstructions – that a different animal is possible, one we might call *aesthetic*, not after the senses endowed by nature from which it might be thought to spring, but from the sense of a nature it will invent.

*Conclusion*

# Wither Humanity?

The rhinoceros king Archibald has a golden crown with a fat pearl and golden layers of skin over his eyes, but stands aloof from active government. He is having an affair with the giraffe "Gazelle," occasionally wears a silk-grey pair of pyjama trousers, and has published a pamphlet, the pan-humanist manifesto. It has appeared in the publishing house of the united jackals and hyenas. For years he has been working on his magnum opus. It is called "The Rhinoceros Whip," and is the theoretical groundwork of a human society that includes the animals.

– Adorno, in a letter to Horkheimer[1]

I have argued that Adorno's critical theory might be used to oppose the Aristotelian problematic, wherein the human is divided from and held superior to the animal. I have also argued that Adorno's critical theory might serve as a guide to recovering the repressed promise of that same problematic – the promise of a beautiful life lived in leisure, beyond the necessities of self-preservation – along with the idea that politics is not reducible to the human domain and that aesthetic experience can be marshalled to frame and transform political possibility. Paradoxically, while the Aristotelian problematic has been immensely influential on an entire tradition of political thinking, what I have called "the promise" of this problematic has largely been lost to that same tradition. Adorno does not present us with a return to Aristotle; rather, he recovers that promise transformed in a different constellation of sociohistorical objects. It is through Adorno, then, that we might think the possibility of a new subject, an *aesthetic animal* that might draw on

1 Cited in Müller-Doohm, *Adorno*, 240.

repressed animal potentials in order to reconstitute the subject in a way that no longer makes central the drives that have produced this animal as human, as one whose quest for self-preservation has been realized through violence and the domination of others.

However, the imperfections of my argument, like so many loose threads in a hastily knitted scarf, remain hanging from the article, no doubt irritating the reader, who might like to give one or two of them a good pull. I would thus like to conclude by addressing some of the more prominent of these insufficiently examined questions. These questions include: (1) How might this emphasis on the non-identity of the human subject and the recovery of its repressed animal potentials differ among human subjects classed according to different particularities such as gender, race, or sexuality? If the process of disrupting the reproduction of one's human subjectivity in the interest of becoming some other kind of animal is different for different kinds of human subjects, should I not be referring to aesthetic *animals*, not the aesthetic *animal*? Does not the subjective transformation I advocate neglect human plurality? And (2) what of the animal well-being and liberation movements relative to the subjective transformation I advocate? Am I not neglecting real pragmatic changes that can be accomplished here and now through political reform for some utopian dream of a post-revolutionary future? What about the alleviation of suffering that can be accomplished more or less immediately, irrespective of grand claims to subjective transformation? And if my more radical position is indeed merited, how does it relate to some of the other similarly radical positions articulated relative to the human/animal distinction and the problems it raises for politics?

The reader has undoubtedly noted that one is never simply human in general – one is only ever constituted as a human subject through a constellation of sociopolitical objects that differ not only according to the place of one's society in history and in the prevailing global order but also according to one's own particular place in that society. Consequently, one is constituted through this range of objects not simply as a human subject in general, more or less equal to all others, but as a classed, gendered, and racialized subject of a certain sexual orientation whose relation to the dominant concept of humanity will be different according to the particular ways in which power is exercised in one's society. So, while the animal is non-identical to the human subject, the process of turning toward the animal will differ markedly between human subjects whose humanity is constituted in different ways.

For instance, in societies in which the paradigmatic representative of the human subject is a white, heterosexual male, the identity of say, a black homosexual woman becomes non-identical to this concept of humanity. This is among the reasons why different kinds of human subjects have been in different times and places considered "deviant," associated with animals, and denied the rights and privileges accorded to those more clearly identifiable with the dominant concept of the human subject. From this perspective, the processes of affirming identities such as black, female, or homosexual may oppose the dominant place of the identities of white, male, and heterosexual and thereby potentially displace and even transform this concept of the human subject by insisting on a greater plurality of possible human subjects. This possible displacement of the dominant concept of humanity in the face of greater plurality might be seen as an important part of the progressive vector of identity politics.

However, such identity politics is also possessed of a regressive vector. As I have attempted to show, Adorno argues that the ways in which identities have been formed are bound up with the struggle for survival and with the violence and domination through which that struggle has been expressed in most human societies. Consequently, the identities of subjects in societies characterized by domination necessarily carry exclusion within their very structure – such identities *are* by way of excluding what they *are not*. Consequently, even the identity of a subject defined as black, female, and homosexual will exclude some other subjective possibilities in the course of affirming this identity (say, that of a transgendered person, or one who identifies as neither female nor male). More importantly, just as Adorno's negative conception of humanity as the opposition to violence was bound up with the violence it would oppose, along with the subject who would mask this violence, so are subjects constituted in this oppositional manner bound to that which they oppose. Thus, "black," "female," and "homosexual" in this instance are all the mirror images of the dominant subject against which they oppose themselves – as identities they are entwined with the dominant identity, and to assume them uncritically is to accept the range of subjective possibilities consonant with that identity in society as it exists. To actively identify with a *given* identity and the range of subjective possibilities *given* in the dominant order is thus to desire the amelioration of one's own position in that order but to otherwise accept that order in broad outline. In this way, the dominion of humanity remains one constituted through violence and domination, even if the humanity constituted through this violence is now a richer, more complexly plural subject.

This is not to say that the kind of identity politics sketched briefly above is to be rejected. Rather, its progressive vector found in the opposition to and displacement of the dominant concept of humanity must be accompanied by a second progressive vector: an opposition to and displacement of the fixed identity one assumes in opposing the dominant one. This later opposition or negation constitutes the utopian moment of the struggle: like Adorno's conception of reconciled humanity that displaces the permanence of the struggle between negative and positive humanity, the particular identities assumed in opposition to the dominant human subject must themselves be displaced by a utopian image of this subject transformed beyond the exigencies of the struggle for its survival if they are to avoid being trapped in a permanent struggle that ultimately maintains the dominant order. How exactly "black" or "female" or "homosexual" are to be imagined and given shape in utopian images, shorn of the violence to which they are subject in the present, is a matter to be decided by those who struggle through these identities – it cannot be imposed upon them. While others critically working through different sets of identities can offer their solidarity in these struggles – and *must* offer their solidarity, if a global subject is to be constituted so as to radically transform society – the particularities of these struggles beyond the basic aversion to violence must be navigated by those who are caught up in them.

Turning to animality, to what remains non-identical to one's constitution as a human subject, would necessarily take on a plurality of forms, for this turn involves working through the plurality of ways in which the human subject is itself constituted, along with various non-conceptual moments produced through different struggles and oppositions to that which is constituted as the dominant or paradigmatic representative of humanity in different societies and cultures. It thus makes little difference whether we refer to *the aesthetic animal* or *aesthetic animals*, for *the* aesthetic animal is always already a historically, socially, and politically situated possibility, and insofar as different societies and moments of history present different challenges to the realization of aesthetic animality, so this transformation will be different at different times and places. What allows these struggles to resonate with one another is the common movement toward a society free of domination, populated by subjects who are likewise not constituted through this violence.

There are wide-ranging views about the relevance of Adorno's work to feminism: some focus on its limitations or ambivalence; others view it as an important ally;[2] still others recognize in it the possibility of a

2 On Adorno's limitations in this regard, see Becker-Schmidt, "Critical Theory as a Critique of Society"; and Wilke and Schlipphacke, "Construction of a Gendered Subject." On Adorno's ambivalences, see Rebecca Comay, "Adorno's Siren Song";

transcendence of feminism's basic concepts.[3] But comparatively little has been written about how Adorno's ideas might be fruitfully cultivated in thinking about race.[4] While I have not in this study contributed to changing this state of affairs, I hope the above comments and the broad strokes I have painted concerning Adorno's ideas on humanity and animality will help clear the way for future studies of how Adorno's conception of identity might intersect in novel ways with various ideas concerning identity politics. It remains now to briefly engage the second set of questions concerning the loose ends I would, if not tie up, then at least call attention to here: those concerning animal well-being and liberation, and the relevance of my study to them and to other studies of the human/animal distinction not yet addressed.

I noted in the introduction that without Adorno's radical ideas concerning the philosophy of subjectivity and the subjective transformation that must accompany sociopolitical transformation, the kinds of reform-minded and consensus-building activities to which the animal well-being and animal liberation movements tend to direct themselves, and which theories of animal well-being and animal liberation would justify, are without, as it were, *teeth*. As I have attempted to show by way of Adorno, violence and domination are intimately linked to human evolution and the manner in which the "human" has been socially and politically established and perpetuated. To simply include animals as persons or selves within this order would be to overlook the violence that established and perpetuates this order. If animal liberation or the advancement of animal well-being is to succeed, it must be tied to broader sociopolitical goals that include the transformation of society so as to eliminate violence and domination as such.

As with the progressive vector of identity politics, the insistence upon a radical, utopian dimension here should not be understood as a rejection of more pragmatically oriented goals tailored to particular situations that might alleviate the suffering of different animals. Efforts by animal well-being activists and proponents of animal liberation to outlaw animal testing for commercial and scientific purposes, the successful campaigns in many countries to criminalize cruelty to

Leeb, *Power and Feminist Agency in Capitalism*, ch. 8; Marasco, "Already the Effect of the Whip." On a possible allegiance between Adorno and feminism, see Lee, *Dialectics of the Body*; and O'Neill, "Adorno and Women."

3 See MacCannell, "Adorno," 156.

4 For exceptions, see Dallmayr, "The Politics of Nonidentity"; Blake Emerson, "Dialectic of Color Blindness"; Varadharajna, *Exotic Parodies*; and Vázquez-Arroyo, "Universal History Disavowed."

non-human animals, the insistence on better treatment of animals that are harvested for their meat or milk or other products, and even the insistence that such harvesting be themselves outlawed, are all laudable projects that the utopian emphasis on radical subjective and sociopolitical transformation would not sacrifice for so-called greater aims, such as the radical transformation of society and its subjects. Indeed, these more immediate and pragmatic aims cannot be sacrificed, as we have seen through the way in which Adorno conceptualizes the relation between particular struggles and the constitution of a global subject. The kind of global subject that Adorno envisions transforming the objective and subjective dimensions of society could not be one that suppresses particular instances of resistance; rather, it must emerge out of these particular instances and allow them to resonate together through relations of solidarity.

When they lack this utopian dimension, the narrower efforts of animal well-being activists and their supporters fail to take into account the violence and domination whereby humanity is itself constituted. This failure is reproduced at the level of theory, perhaps most clearly in the particular variant of the rights-based approach advanced by Garner, who explicitly formulates his theory in a manner that excludes any utopian dimension. Garner distinguishes his theory from more radical theories that advocate "species-egalitarianism," focusing instead on developing a theory of justice *for animals* – one that will produce what he argues is "a politically achievable program."[5] While I am certainly sympathetic to Garner's goal of "eliminating animal suffering at the hands of humans,"[6] I simply do not think that such a goal can be realized without a more radical, utopian dimension that destabilizes the human subject.[7] Garner seeks to achieve his aim by appropriating the Rawlsian distinction between ideal and non-ideal theory and using these concepts as a test of his theory's validity (and also of the invalidity of theories promoting "species-egalitarianism"). Following Rawls, Garner excludes what he understands to be unrealizable as "utopian," yet he never specifies the balance of forces or political agencies whose contest might result in his program's goals

5 Garner, *A Theory of Justice for Animals*, 19.

6 Garner, *A Theory of Justice for Animals*, 18.

7 Another step in this direction is taken by Schmitz, who claims that the "resource paradigm" that shapes how humans see other animals must change for our treatment of other animals to change; however, Schmitz stops short of a concomitant re-evaluation of the concept of the human. See Schmitz, "Animal Ethics and Human Institutions," 47.

being achieved. Instead, he relies on a vague sense of prevailing opinions, existing institutions, and what he understands as natural human tendencies to delineate the possible. Thus, in his attempt to be realistic, Garner treats contemporary views on right animal treatment, human nature, and even the general institutional structure of his society as both static entities and conditions that a valid political theory must meet rather than challenge.

In this way, Garner assumes much of what one might hope he would attempt to illustrate and defend, repeating the liberal humanist *doxa* found in other theories noted above: he relies on "universalizable, non-alterable" traits of human nature to serve as theoretical trump cards, yet he never brings these traits under serious scrutiny; he considers persons inherently more complex and hence capable of more extensive suffering than non-persons, yet his notion of "complexity" remains excruciatingly arbitrary; and he treats justice as first and foremost a matter of "legal compulsion" rather than the result of collective political action or moral disposition.[8] This willingness to be fit to Rawls's measurements leaves him open to the same criticisms that have been levelled against Rawls: namely, that his theory is both insufficiently realistic and insufficiently utopian. Garner never specifies how the particular operations of power that characterize his society relate to his theory or its aims, and neither does he question the basic structure of that society.[9] The shortcomings of Garner's theory suggest that this radical, utopian dimension that challenges and displaces more moderate political goals actually *enables* these goals – it keeps more moderate political goals from becoming fused with the order of domination as their necessary opposite. To insist on a utopian dimension to the amelioration of the plight of animals that includes a transformation of the human subject is not to reject more modest political goals such as those advanced by Garner, but to reject the kinds of theoretical assumptions made by Garner that make the realization of his aims central to this struggle rather than a moment in its broader trajectory.

Another factor that tends to be overlooked, not only by rights-driven approaches to animal well-being such as Garner's, but also by advocates of the capacities approach, utilitarians, and animal liberation generally, is that the persuasiveness of the arguments they advance concerning the more or less essential commensurability of humans to other animals depends upon materialist and scientific

8 Garner, *A Theory of Justice for Animals*, 12, 15, 59, 165.

9 Geuss, "Realism, Wishful Thinking, Utopia," 246.

revolutions that have eroded previously dominant conceptions of the human being as an utterly distinct entity. The fact that the case for animal well-being and liberation, at least in its more moderate iterations, has come to seem so reasonable to so many in a world characterized by flagrant violations of human rights, including violations of these rights made in the very name of their preservation, should indicate the degree to which the metaphysical elevation of the human being has collapsed into a material subject, more or less reducible to a body to be manipulated or protected. Put differently: though the reduced status of the subject, or the fact that the human subject is now no more than an animal body, allows for other animals to potentially be included in the human category, the underside or obscene secret concealed here is that this is so because humans are being treated almost as viciously as other animals. To ignore this is to overlook the way in which violence and domination operate in contemporary societies.

The likelihood of being subject to such violence – to the violation of one's humanity, to being treated *like an animal* – is radically different for those of different positions in society and in different parts of the world. Consequently, a promulgation of animal well-being and liberation that fails to address the broader issues of sociopolitical violence and domination would mean a return to the possibility that being treated like a human or animal will depend not on species but on class, race, gender, and sexuality. Only the attempt to build on the gains of animal well-being and liberation by linking them to broader struggles against violence and domination might avoid the age-old problem of the affluent caring more for their pets than for the poor. Or more bluntly still: in a world where the majority of humanity suffers the scourges of poverty, malnourishment, preventable disease, and both random and systematic violence, a devotion to the welfare of other animals devoid of any intent to transform this basic state of affairs is not much better than a bourgeois affectation.

Yet as I noted at the beginning of this study, not all the positions taken up by recent work on the human/animal distinction fall beneath the liberal humanist umbrella – even as widely as I have opened it. In fact, a number of the criticisms I have levelled against thinkers such as Garner, Donaldson and Kymlicka, and Nussbaum and MacIntyre have been levelled in one fashion or another at other theorists and advocates of animal well-being and liberation. Moreover, thinkers such as Calarco have, on the heels of such a critique, taken aim at anthropocentrism "as such" and claimed that *"the human-animal distinction can no longer and ought no longer to be maintained,"* a statement with which I concur.[10] What then is different about the aesthetic animal, and how do my claims differ from those of these other positions?

A number of the theorists pursuing similar aims to those I have pursued here have taken their inspiration from Deleuze and Guattari's concept of "becoming-animal." While this is not the place for a thorough exposition of this difficult concept, for our purposes it suffices to note that for Deleuze and Guattari, becoming-animal involves humans becoming connected in new and unforeseen ways to animals in such a way that the human in question is compelled beyond the boundaries in which his or her subjectivity had previously resided. Perhaps the clearest example of becoming-animal offered by Deleuze and Guattari is that of Herman Melville's Ahab, who, through his intense fixation on Moby Dick, is propelled beyond the limits within which human life tends to circulate: in his pursuit of the unknown, Ahab leaves behind points of human subjectification related to family, country, and God.

Of course, the ultimately disastrous attempt to destroy a rare whale is not at first blush an obvious choice for non-violent transformation of the relations between humans and other animals. However, the desire to shed the human in favour of something new by shifting the points of human subjectification is common to both Deleuze and Guattari's project and my own. Where we begin to differ can be seen with a look at the larger project within which becoming-animal has sense: the overturning of the Western philosophical tradition that enshrined *the Being of the One* in favour of *the Becoming of the Many*. Becoming-animal is one of many concepts deployed by Deleuze and Guattari in support of this ontological upheaval, and as such is not really about animals at all, but about becoming, which they insist produces nothing beyond itself, and outside of which there exists no subject: "What is real is the becoming itself … not the supposedly fixed terms through which that which becomes passes."[11] Moreover, becoming-animal is but one becoming among many others and should not be accorded a privileged place among becomings. While Deleuze and Guattari hold that the politics of becoming-animal are "extremely ambiguous," this ambiguity seems to stem primarily from the different kinds of becoming-animal, two of which, the individualizing Oedipal becoming-animal and the categorizing mythic becoming-animal, use relations with animals to reaffirm the subjective

10 Calarco, *Zoographies*, 10, 3.

11 Deleuze and Guattari, *A Thousand Plateaus*, trans. Brian Massumi (Minneapolis: University of Minnesota Press, 1987), 238. Cf. *Mille Plateaux* (Paris: Les Éditions de Minuit, 1980), 291.

coordinates of the human within the spheres of the private, family realm and the public realm of the state, respectively. Only the third kind of becoming-animal, that which invents a relationship with a multiplicity of new directions, represents a truly innovative becoming that would move beyond human subjectivity.[12] Yet again, this is so because of the ontological privileging of the Many over the One, which Deleuze and Guattari, like Derrida discussed above, seem to find inherently liberating, rather than dependent on particular sociopolitical outcomes.[13]

While becoming-animal has been appropriated by those theorizing the human/animal distinction in a variety of ways, the emphasis on the ontological dimension and the inherently liberating power of ontological multiplicity have persisted as central themes in these appropriations. For instance, Calarco understands becoming-animal as an overcoming of the human through the "metaphysical reversal of human chauvinism," which he develops as a "zone of indiscernibility" in which humans discover a "shared mode of existence" with other animals that facilitates "developing modes of resistance to the established order."[14] This project of situating humanity within a common "plane" or "continuum" wherein other animals also dwell is shared by Massumi, who points to the animal as a tutor of the kind of play that might enable the human to overcome itself in the surplus of life. Though Massumi is much more explicit in this regard than Calarco, both follow Deleuze and Guattari's vitalist ontology in understanding life to be a multiplicity in perpetual creative flux, an endlessly proliferating series of becomings. Through segmentation and classification, human politics draw up the boundaries whereby the human might reproduce itself in perpetuity, more or less as a (however fictitious) unified and stable whole. In this way, the *being* of human politics is *anti-becoming*, and hence *anti-life*.[15]

---

12 Deleuze and Guattari, *A Thousand Plateaus*, 240–1; *Mille Plateaux*, 294–5.

13 As is well-known, Derrida's deconstruction of metaphysics was highly influenced by Heidegger's *Destruktion* of metaphysics, though unlike Heidegger, Derrida was extremely sceptical about deconstruction uncovering something more primal and original than metaphysics, as Heidegger's ontology claims to do. As examined above, in Derrida's writings on animals there is a privileging of the Many over the One; however, the degree to which this ought to be considered an ontological position is both debatable and beyond the scope of this study. For us it is sufficient to recall that Derrida misdiagnoses the problem, which results in an inadequate solution. See 62–3, above.

14 Calarco, *Zoographies*, 41; Calarco, "Being-toward-Meat," 206, 209.

15 Massumi, *What Animals Teach Us about Politics*, 69.

Given my arguments over the course of this study, it should be clear that I agree with such views concerning the goal of transforming humanity through a creative relation to animality. Yet to my mind the ontological bent of these approaches leaves human politics and society too abstractly theorized. *The Becoming of the Many* is not inherently more politically progressive than *the Being of the One*[16] – what decides the political effects of such terms is not ontology but politics, and to treat the principal evaluative measure of politics as the intensity of an experience[17] is to abandon political outcomes and ultimately the structure of society as primary sites of struggle. Though Deleuzeans like Connolly are right to note the dangers of "sociocentrism" in a world in which the lives of humans and many other animals and plants are being threatened by climate crisis, and hence right to insist on broader perspectives capable of accommodating the complexity of this situation,[18] it is ultimately through politics and the structure of societies that humans – or other animal subjects – might be able to address larger phenomena that cannot be reduced to conventional social or political categories, such as disappearing glaciers, rising sea levels, and species extinction. And while Adorno also tends to focus his critical eye on concepts and their deployment in a rather abstract fashion,[19] his tracking of the non-identity of concepts continually leads him back to their excessive materiality – to that which was and is excluded from their deployment, and hence to the various particularities and contingencies of their respective contexts.

In this way, Adorno's focus on the non-identical may perhaps do greater honour to "multiplicity" in the sense that in pointing to the context of a concept's deployment, he directs a critical lens toward new, unexamined territory, whereas the ontological approach, in seeking to specify the becoming in which particular entities are enveloped, risks making this becoming a transcendental condition of the possibility of these entities, and so falling back into the mythic world view that sees only endless continua of becoming wherein all that becomes is a permutation or combination of all that was. In this mythic or "tragic" view of the world there can be no historical break, no caesura through which

16 Recall Adorno: "The illusion of taking direct hold of the Many would be a mimetic regression, as much a recoil into mythology, into the horror of the diffuse, as the thinking of the One" (*ND*, 158; *GSB6*, 160).

17 Massumi, *What Animals Teach Us about Politics*, 41.

18 Connolly, *Facing the Planetary*, 15.

19 To the point where Deleuze and Guattari's own work has been seen as a radicalization of Adorno's work with Horkheimer. See Wolfe, *Animal Rites*, 177.

something genuinely new might emerge. Drawing on Adorno as I have done thus allows for a theorization of the world and society that leaves a place open for the new, and thus for the contingencies of political practice and the relations these might transform, instead of projecting into the future the structure of the world as it presently exists. In this way, the aesthetic animal that I find in the work of Adorno gives us a more practical approach to transforming the human subject, one concerned with political realities before ontological ones.

Yet why, one might ask, must this future agency that may replace humanity take the shape of a subject? Is this not to project the past into the future in the same way that I have just criticized the ontological approach for doing? And have we not learned, from Deleuze and others, that the subject is itself a category of domination to be done away with? To begin with the last of these questions, the idea that the subject may itself be a category of domination derives from Althusser's claim that subjects are a function of "ideological state apparatuses" that facilitate economic exploitation. For Althusser, individuals are always already "interpellated" as subjects and hence *subjected* to the various expectations and limits particular to a given ideological "apparatus," or set of social practices particular to a given sphere of ideology, such as the family, religion, school, law enforcement, participation in political institutions, and so forth. Insofar as the state is understood to be the ultimate power that serves to enable, limit, and coordinate these various apparatuses, and the state has itself been conquered by a particular class, that class (for Althusser, the bourgeoisie) expresses its power through these apparatuses by interpellating individuals as subjects. Hence, the duties specific to each ideological apparatus – being a daughter, a mother, a son, a brother, a religious adherent, a student, a teacher, a citizen, a voter, or even an electoral candidate – in their performance all fall within the bounds imposed by the power of a class and serve to reproduce the power of that class, even where these duties contradict one another.[20] Humanism, on this view, is an "ideological

---

20 Althusser, *On the Reproduction of Capitalism*, 136, 190, 194. Cf. *Sur la reproduction*, 109, 225–6, 229. It will be noted that my presentation is somewhat simplified: Althusser leaves the actual connection between ISAs and the state as a force of repression (physical violence), its class character, and how these relate to economic exploitation (including the idea of base/superstructure), highly ambiguous. Althusser worked within the conceptual framework of Marxist discourse endorsed by the French Communist Party, yet manipulated these concepts in an idiosyncratic manner that often left him at odds with the Party. While I do not believe the connections I have

makeshift [*ficelage*]"[21] that ties together the various ideological apparatuses, obscuring the machinations of bourgeois power and broader historical processes beneath the primacy of the individual and the concept of "Man," who, as the mirror-image of God, is the creator of society and of history. To reject humanism in this manner is to attempt to cut through ideological illusions and attain a theory of history as a process without a subject.

Althusser's anti-humanism as it relates to the concept of "subject" has been both highly influential and roundly criticized, though my own use of the term is not identical to his. In terms of this study, it is important to note that I have made a distinction between the subject and the human subject. On my view, subjects spring from constellations of objects, where "objects" are the conceptualizations of one's surroundings, the others in whose midst we find ourselves. In this way, the subject is the point at which an individual makes contact with others: it is an openness to others, a vulnerability to their impositions, both in terms of the actions these others demand and in the internalization of these demands in the form of beliefs, values, thoughts, and the characteristics that make up an "inner life" – we are, as subjects, *subjected* to others in this way. Yet at the same time, a subject is a manner of actively responding to these others through variations in one's actions and thoughts, both as individuals and in concert with others. In this sense, there are both individual subjects and collective subjects, and a given individual body is more than one – in modern society we participate in multiple subjectivities. The human subject, by contrast, is a particular way of compelling subjectivity to conform to certain boundaries considered both correct and natural. The most complete and influential iteration of the human subject, I have argued, is found in the Aristotelian problematic. The aesthetic animal draws upon the possibilities that have been made available by the Aristotelian problematic in order to invent a new shape of subjectivity, one not beholden to the same boundaries that divided the human subject and held it in thrall to violence and domination, though, as I have

---

drawn between Althusser's concepts misrepresents them, Althusser does solicit from his reader the imposition of a *Gestalt* that would be easy enough to deny is true to the author's intent. For the purposes of this study, what is most important is Althusser's attack on humanism and his equation of the subject as a necessary category of humanism. On Althusser as an author, some of the challenges involved in interpreting him, his conflict with the Party, and the material status of the texts in question, see Montag, *Althusser and His Contemporaries*, 2, 18, 100, 106, 142.

21 Althusser, "The Humanist Controversy," 253; Cf. "La querelle de l'humanisme," 469.

also noted, this aesthetic animal will take on different shapes relative to the particular contexts in which it emerges. While there are clear similarities between certain points of my analysis and those of Althusser – namely, the limiting function of humanism and the coercive dimension of subjectivity – that I see the subject to be also the point of action and agency, and that subjects are not reducible to human subjects, differs from Althusser.

This reliance on the concept of the subject is not to set the subject up as a condition of experience and thereby project the structure of society and politics as they currently exist eternally into the future, as the ontological approach risks doing. Unlike recent work on the problem of political subjectivity done by Martel, who uses Althusser to theorize political resistance in terms of the *failures* of interpellation, my theorization of subjectivity *does not* allow me to claim any necessary political affiliation for the subject, nor that it is and has always been multiple and decentred, and hence that the rebellion such multiplicity enables remains a resource for would-be rebels in perpetuity.[22] With these claims, Martel slides toward the ontological approach and the notion that the social world is lodged in unbroken continua of becoming, perpetually shifting and changing, whereas politics is a "steady stream of resistance and subversion."[23] The disposition of the multiple subject of this process is *amor fati* – the love of the fate that one cannot really change.[24] As I have argued above, such a disposition and the kinds of action it suggests are less political than moral, though Deleuzeans tend to shrink from this latter term.

As regards the subject, my claim is a historical one: the subject as I have outlined it has emerged through certain features of collective life that have arisen and been perpetuated in varying ways at different times and places, and are without guarantee of continuing indefinitely into the future. As such, there is always the possibility of a radical and unforeseen break that might transform the conditions that have made it possible to theorize the subject as I have done above. The aesthetic animal is not an eternal possibility but rather a shape the subject might assume made possible by the Aristotelian problematic and the history of its humanism, a shape the subject might assume that focuses on its agency, even in recognizing the limits of that agency and all that is non-identical to this shape of subjectivity.

---

22 Martel, *The Misinterpellated Subject*, 6, 8, 30, 271.

23 Martel, *The Misinterpellated Subject*, 23.

24 Martel, *The Misinterpellated Subject*, 136; 149; 153.

Yet if it is possible to retain the concept of the subject by distinguishing between it and the specifically *human* subject, might it be possible to distinguish between the particular humanism rooted in the Aristotelian problematic I have opposed in this study and some other, critical form of humanism, thus retaining the concept of humanism and "the human"? We find an example of such a splitting of humanism in Rancière's critique of Althusser. For Rancière, Althusser's approach to the question of humanism is hopelessly philosophical: Althusser concerns himself with humanism *as a theory*, notes its shortcomings and the obstacles it presents to knowing the truth, and from this claims that it is also politically pernicious. If one is to understand the political effects of humanism, Rancière instead claims that one would be better to focus on the political uses of humanist discourse.[25] In examining the history of proletarian struggles, Rancière finds that there is a humanism of the bourgeois and a humanism of the proletarian: while the bourgeois marshals the discourse of humanism to exclude the proletarian from his ranks, the proletarian draws upon humanist discourse to include himself in the category of those who decide, thereby to reclaim a share of the powers of which he has been deprived.[26] There is no single, stable philosophy of humanism; rather, humanism is itself a site of political struggle. In encouraging young intellectuals to abandon humanism as bourgeois ideology, the political consequences of Althusser's theoretical interventions include exacerbating the divide between intellectuals and other workers, who overwhelmingly continue to articulate their demands in humanist terms.

As I have shown in the preceding study, however, the aesthetic animal is part of a utopian moment that serves to displace the permanence of the struggle between the human and the inhuman. The aesthetic animal's opposition to humanism is the opposition found in transcending the opposition between humanity and inhumanity – its potential is to rupture this unity of opposites that upholds the order of domination. Hence, as we have seen with the discussion of both identity politics and animal well-being and liberation, this utopian moment insists on moving beyond the fixed terms of struggle and so compelling them beyond their place in the existing order and the appearance of stability and permanence this order lends to violence and domination. As such, the politics of an aesthetic animal do not necessarily preclude the use of humanist language for attaining narrower, pragmatic aims – all it

25 Rancière, *Althusser's Lesson*, 64, 85.
26 Rancière, *Althusser's Lesson*, 88, 90, 93.

precludes is that the narrow, pragmatic aims of humanist politics be considered the central and/or end point of the struggle. The politics of the aesthetic animal insists on pushing beyond the terms of humanist discourse, toward the construction of a truly global subject, but unlike Althusser's anti-humanism, it does not withdraw its solidarity from humanists where humanists combat violence and domination.

The importance of this utopian moment and the construction of a global subject for the displacement and transcendence of the terms of struggle found in humanism, and hence a limitation of Rancière's critique, is underscored, inadvertently, by Rancière himself. The humanist discourse of the proletariat that Rancière champions is a discourse of labour: "Man" is the rallying call of the worker and of his autonomy as a producer; his membership in this brotherhood assures him "the right to *work* [… and his …] right to collective organization."[27] While this "Man" is certainly opposed to the "Man" of the masters, functioning as a tool the workers can use *against* the masters, its use in Rancière's particular example comes with sexual and racial exclusion: the workers are men – *not* "negroes" and *not* women – and *it is for this reason* they ought to be treated with the same dignity as the masters.[28] The inclusion they demand with the word "Man" remains inseparable from other exclusions, which they perpetuate. Additionally, this "Man" of the workers affirms the basic structure of society wherein "Man" is essentially an *animale laborans*, a subject defined primarily through his struggle for self-preservation, rather than some *other, lighter, softer, swifter* animal, one that has yet to grace our world of blood and muck. The politics of the aesthetic animal serve to displace the terms of such humanist discourse, pushing beyond the struggle of labour and the existing order of violence and domination, opening up instead to the invention of the new.

I have argued that Adorno is the most apt guide to our current political juncture and the theorizing of its transformation, for he allows us to see our own animality as it has emerged through the history of humanism and to take the possibilities for transformation as beginning from this situation. Moreover, unlike those who might through their focus on ontology or even their focus on particular struggles inadvertently reify the current place of struggle in political life, Adorno shows us that we cannot get rid of the utopian dimension of political struggle. Rather, we must hold dear to this utopian promise, even if, as Adorno himself admits, the moment of its realization may never arrive.

27 Rancière, *Althusser's Lesson*, 90, 93.
28 Rancière, *Althusser's Lesson*, 88–9.

# Bibliography


Adorno, Theodor W. "The Actuality of Philosophy." In *The Adorno Reader*. Translated by Benjamin Snow. Edited by Brian O'Connor. 23–39. Oxford: Blackwell, 2000.

– *Aesthetics 1958–59*. Edited by Eberhard Ortland. Translated by Wieland Hoban. Cambridge: Polity Press, 2018.

– *Aesthetic Theory*. Translated and edited by Robert Hullot-Kentor. Minneapolis: University of Minnesota Press, 1997.

– "Alienated Masterpiece: The Misa Solemnis." In *The Adorno Reader*. Edited by Brian O'Connor. Translated by Duncan Smith. 304–18. Oxford: Blackwell, 2000.

– "Arnold Schoenberg, 1874–1951." In *Prisms*. Translated by Samuel and Shierry Weber. 147–72. Cambridge, MA: MIT Press, 1990.

– "Commitment." In *The Essential Frankfurt School Reader*. Edited by Andrew Arato and Eike Gebhardt. Translated by Francis McDonagh. 300–18. New York: Continuum, 2005.

– "Critique." In *Critical Models: Interventions and Catchwords*. Translated by Henry W. Pickford. 281–88. New York: Columbia University Press, 1998.

– "Democratic Leadership and Mass Manipulation." In *Theodor W. Adorno: Gesammelte Schriften*, vol. 20.1. Edited by Rolf Tiedemann, Gretel Adorno, Susan Buck-Morss, and Klaus Schultz. 267–86. Frankfurt am Main: Suhrkamp, 1986.

– "Education after Auschwitz." In *Critical Models: Interventions and Catchwords*. Translated by Henry W. Pickford. 191–204. New York: Columbia University Press, 1998.

– "The Essay as Form." In *Notes to Literature*, vol. 1. Edited by Rolf Tiedemann. Translated by Shierry Weber Nicholsen. New York: Columbia University Press, 1991.

– *Gesammelte Schriften*, vol. 1: *Philosophische Frühschriften*. Frankfurt am Main: Suhrkamp, 1973.

– *Gesammelte Schriften*, vol. 4: *Minima Moralia. Reflexionen aus dem beschädigten Leben*. Frankfurt am Main: Suhrkamp, 1980.
– *Gesammelte Schriften*, vol. 5: *Zur Metakritik der Erkenntnistheorie. Drei Studien zu Hegel*. Frankfurt am Main: Suhrkamp 1970.
– *Gesammelte Schriften*, vol. 6: *Negative Dialektik. Jargon der Eigentlichkeit*. Frankfurt am Main: Suhrkamp, 1970.
– *Gesammelte Schriften*, vol. 7: *Ästhetische Theorie*. Frankfurt am Main: Suhrkamp, 1970.
– *Gesammelte Schriften*, vol. 10.1: *Kulturkritik und Gesellschaft I: Prismen. Ohne Leitbild*. Frankfurt am Main: Suhrkamp, 1977.
– *Gesammelte Schriften*, vol. 10.2: *Kulturkritik und Gesellschaft II: Eingriffe. Stichworte. Anhang*. Frankfurt am Main: Suhrkamp, 1977.
– *Gesammelte Schriften*, vol. 11: *Noten zur Literatur*. Frankfurt am Main: Suhrkamp, 1974.
– *Gesammelte Schriften*, vol. 12: *Philosophie der neuen Musik*. Frankfurt am Main: Suhrkamp, 1975.
– "Gloss on Personality." In *Critical Models: Interventions and Catchwords*. Translated by Henry W. Pickford. 161–5. New York: Columbia University Press, 1998.
– *Hegel: Three Studies*. Translated by Shierry Weber Nicholsen. Cambridge, MA: MIT Press, 1993.
– "The Idea of Natural History." Translated by Robert Hullot-Kentor. *Telos* 60 (1984): 111–24.
– "Marginalia to Theory and Praxis." In *Critical Models: Interventions and Catchwords*. Translated by Henry W. Pickford. 259–78. New York: Columbia University Press, 1998.
– *Metaphysics: Concept and Problems*. Edited by Rolf Tiedemann. Translated by Edmund Jephcott. Stanford: Stanford University Press, 2001.
– *Minima Moralia: Reflections on a Damaged Life*. Translated by E.F.N. Jephcott. London: Verso, 2005.
– "Music and Language: A Fragment." In *Quasi una Fantasia: Essays on Modern Music*. Translated by Rodney Livingstone. 1–6. London: Verso, 1998.
– *Nachgelassene Schriften* no. 4, *Vorlesungen*, vol. 10: *Probleme der Moralphilosophie*. Frankfurt am Main: Suhrkamp, 1997.
– *Nachgelassene Schriften* no. 4, *Vorlesungen*, vol. 10: *Metaphysik: Begriff und Probleme*. Frankfurt am Main: Suhrkamp, 1998.
– *Negative Dialectics*. Translated by E.B. Ashton. New York: Continuum, 2007.
– "Opinion Delusion Society." In *Critical Models: Interventions and Catchwords*. Translated by Henry W. Pickford. 105–22. New York: Columbia University Press, 1998.
– *Philosophy of Modern Music*. Translated by Anne G. Mitchell and Wesley V. Blomster. New York: Continuum, 1985.

– "A Portrait of Walter Benjamin." In *Prisms*. Translated by Samuel and Shierry Weber. 229–41. Cambridge, MA: MIT Press, 1990.
– "The Problem of a New Type of Human Being." In *Current of Music*. Edited by Robert Hullot-Kentor. 461–8. Cambridge: Polity, 2009.
– *Problems of Moral Philosophy*. Edited by Thomas Schroder. Translated by Rodney Livingstone. Stanford: Stanford University Press, 2001.
– "Progress." In *Critical Models: Interventions and Catchwords*. Translated by Henry W. Pickford. 143–60. New York: Columbia University Press, 1998.
– "Radio Physiognomics." In *Current of Music*. Edited by Robert Hullot-Kentor. 41–132. Cambridge: Polity, 2009.
– "Reaction and Progress." In *Night Music: Essays on Music 1928–1962*. Translated by Wieland Hoban. Edited by Rolf Tiedemann. 218–29. London: Seagull, 2009.
– "Reconciliation under Duress." In *Aesthetics and Politics*. Translated by Rodney Livingstone. 151–76. London: Verso, 2007.
– "Scientific Experiences of a European Scholar in America." In *Critical Models: Interventions and Catchwords*. Translated by Henry W. Pickford. 215–42. New York: Columbia University Press, 1998.
– "On Subject and Object." In *Critical Models: Interventions and Catchwords*. Translated by Henry W. Pickford. 245–58. New York: Columbia University Press, 1998.
– "Taboos on the Teaching Vocation." In *Critical Models: Interventions and Catchwords*. Translated by Henry W. Pickford. 177–90. New York: Columbia University Press, 1998.
– "Television as Ideology." In *Critical Models: Interventions and Catchwords*. Translated by Henry W. Pickford. 59–70. New York: Columbia University Press, 1998.
– "Those Twenties." In *Critical Models: Interventions and Catchwords*. Translated by Henry W. Pickford. 41–8. New York: Columbia University Press, 1998.
– "Zu Ulrich Sonnemanns 'Negativer Anthropologie.'" In *Theodor W. Adorno: Gesammelte Schriften*, vol. 20.1. Edited by Rolf Tiedemann, Gretel Adorno, Susan Buck-Morss, and Klaus Schultz. 262–3. Frankfurt am Main: Suhrkamp, 1986.
– "On the Use of Foreign Words." In *Notes to Literature*, vol. 2. Edited by Rolf Tiedemann. Translated by Shierry Weber Nicholsen. 286–91. New York: Columbia University Press, 1992.
– "Vers une musique informelle." In *Quasi una Fantasia: Essays on Modern Music*. Translated by Rodney Livingstone. 269–322. London: Verso, 1998.
– "Why Still Philosophy." In *Critical Models: Interventions and Catchwords*. Translated by Henry W. Pickford. 5–17. New York: Columbia University Press, 1998.
– "Words from Abroad." In *Notes to Literature*, vol. 1. Translated by Sherry Weber Nicholsen. Edited by Rolf Tiedemann. 185–99. New York: Columbia University Press, 1991.

Adorno, Theodor, and Max Horkheimer. *Towards a New Manifesto*. Translated by Rodney Livingstone. London: Verso, 2011.

Agamben, Giorgio. *The Open*. Translated by Kevin Attell. Stanford: Stanford University Press, 2004.

Allen, Amy. *The End of Progress: Decolonizing the Normative Foundations of Critical Theory*. New York: Columbia University Press, 2016.

Althusser, Louis. "The Humanist Controversy." In *The Humanist Controvery and Other Writings*. Edited by François Matheron. Translated by G.M. Goshgarian. 221–305. London: Verso, 2003.

– "La querelle de l'humanisme." In *Écrits philosophique et politiques*, vol. 2. 433–532. Paris: Éditions STOCK/IMEC, 1997.

– *On the Reproduction of Capitalism: Ideology and Ideological State Apparatuses*. Translated by G.M. Goshgarian. London and New York: Verso, 2014.

– *Sur la reproduction*. Paris: Presses Universitaires de France, 1995.

Arendt, Hannah. *The Human Condition*. Chicago: University of Chicago Press, 1998.

Aristotle. *Aristotle's Nicomachean Ethics*. Translated by Robert C. Bartlett and Susan D. Collins. Chicago: University of Chicago Press, 2011.

– "Generation of Animals." In *The Complete Works of Aristotle*, vol. 1. Revised Oxford Translation. Edited by Jonathan Barnes. 1111–218. Princeton: Princeton University Press, 1984.

– "History of Animals." In *The Complete Works of Aristotle*, vol. 1. Revised Oxford Translation. Edited by Jonathan Barnes. 774–993. Princeton: Princeton University Press, 1984.

– *History of Animals*, vol. 1, bks 1–3. Translated by A.L. Peck. Cambridge, MA: Harvard University Press, 1965.

– "On Memory." In *The Complete Works of Aristotle*, vol. 1. Revised Oxford Translation. Edited by Jonathan Barnes. 714–20. Princeton: Princeton University Press, 1984.

– "Metaphysics." In *The Complete Works of Aristotle*, vol. 2. Revised Oxford Translation. Edited by Jonathan Barnes. 1552–728. Princeton: Princeton University Press, 1985.

– *Nicomachean Ethics*. Translated by Terrence Irwin. Indianapolis: Hackett, 1999.

– "Nicomachean Ethics." In *The Complete Works of Aristotle*, vol. 2. Revised Oxford Translation. Edited by Jonathan Barnes. 1729–867. Princeton: Princeton University Press, 1985.

– *Nikomachische Ethik*. Translated by Eugen Rolfes. Leipzig: Meiner, 1911.

– "Poetics." In *The Complete Works of Aristotle*, vol. 2. Revised Oxford Translation. Edited by Jonathan Barnes. 2316–40. Princeton: Princeton University Press, 1984.

– *Politics*. Translated by C.D.C. Reeve. Indianapolis: Hackett, 1998.

– "Rhetoric." In *The Complete Works of Aristotle*, vol. 2. Revised Oxford Translation. Edited by Jonathan Barnes. 2152–269. Princeton: Princeton University Press, 1985.

– "On the Soul." In *The Complete Works of Aristotle*, vol. 1. Revised Oxford Translation. Edited by Jonathan Barnes. 641–92. Princeton: Princeton University Press, 1984.

Arnhart, Larry. "Aristotle, Chimpanzees, and Other Political Animals." *Social Science Information* 29.2 (1990): 477–557.

Barnes, Jonathan. "Rhetoric and Poetics." In *The Cambridge Companion to Aristotle*. Edited by Jonathan Barnes. 259–85. Cambridge: Cambridge University Press, 1995.

Basnett, Caleb J. "Other Political Animals: Aristotle and the Limits of Political Community." *The European Legacy* 21.3 (2016): 290–309.

Bauman, Charlotte. "Adorno, Hegel, and the Concrete Universal." *Philosophy and Social Criticism* 37.1 (2011): 73–94.

Becker-Schmidt, Regina. "Critical Theory as a Critique of Society: Theodor W. Adorno's Significance for a Feminist Sociology." In *Adorno, Culture, and Feminism*. Edited by Maggie O'Neill. 104–18. London: Sage, 1999.

Benhabib, Seyla. "Critical Theory and Postmodernism: On the Interplay of Ethics, Aesthetics, and Utopia in Critical Theory." In *Handbook of Critical Theory*. Edited by David M. Rasmussen. 327–39. Oxford: Blackwell, 1996.

– *Critique, Norm, and Utopia: A Study of the Foundations of Critical Theory*. New York: Columbia University Press, 1986.

Benjamin, Walter. *Gesammelte Schriften*, vol. 1. Edited by Rolf Tiedemann and Hermann Schweppenhäuser. Frankfurt am Main: Suhrkamp, 1991.

– *Gesammelte Schriften*, vol. 2.1. Edited by Rolf Tiedemann and Herman Schweppenhäuser. Frankfurt am Main: Suhrkamp, 1977.

– *Gesammelte Werke*, vol. 1.2. Edited by Rolf Tiedemann and Hermann Schweppenhäuser. Frankfurt am Main: Suhrkamp, 1991.

– "On the Mimetic Faculty." In *Reflections: Essays, Aphorisms, and Autobiographical Writings*. Edited by Peter Demetz. Translated by Edmund Jephcott. 333–6. New York: Schocken, 1978.

– *The Origin of German Tragic Drama*. Translated by John Osborne. London: Verso, 2009.

– "On Some Motifs in Baudelaire." In *Illuminations: Essays and Reflections*. Edited by Hannah Arendt. Translated by Harry Zohn. 155–200. New York: Schocken, 1969.

– "Theses on the Philosophy of History." In *Illuminations: Essays and Reflections*. Edited by Hannah Arendt. Translated by Harry Zohn. 253–64. New York: Schocken, 1969.

Bennett, Jane. "Modernity and Its Critics." In *The Oxford Handbook of Political Theory*. 211–24. Edited by John Dryzek, Bonnie Honig, and Anne Philips. Oxford: Oxford University Press, 2008.

– *Vibrant Matter: A Political Ecology of Things*. Durham: Duke University Press, 2010.

Bernstein, J.M. *Adorno: Disenchantment and Ethics*. Cambridge: Cambridge University Press, 2001.

– *The Fate of Art: Aesthetic Alienation from Kant to Derrida to Adorno*. University Park: Pennsylvania State University Press, 1992.

– "Negative Dialectic as Fate: Adorno and Hegel." In *The Cambridge Companion to Adorno*. Edited by Tom Huhn. 19–50. Cambridge: Cambridge University Press, 2004.

Biro, Andrew. *Denaturalizing Ecological Politics*. Toronto: University of Toronto Press, 2005.

Biro, Andrew, et al., eds. *Critical Ecologies*. Toronto: University of Toronto Press, 2011.

Bloch, Ernst. *Avicenna and the Aristotelian Left*. Translated by Loren Goldman and Peter Thompson. New York: Columbia University Press, 2019.

Bowie, Andrew. *Adorno and the Ends of Philosophy*. Cambridge: Polity, 2013.

Braidotti, Rosie. *The Posthuman*. Cambridge: Polity, 2013.

Brassier, Ray. *Nihil Unbound: Enlightenment and Extinction*. New York: Palgrave Macmillan, 2007.

Breuer, Stefan. "Adorno's Anthropology." Translated by John Blazek. *Telos* 64 (1985): 15–31.

Brittain, Christopher Craig. *Adorno and Theology*. New York: Continuum, 2010.

Buchwalter, Andrew. "Hegel, Adorno, and the Concept of Transcendent Critique." In *Dialectics, Politics, and the Contemporary Value of Hegel's Practical Philosophy*. 61–82. New York: Routledge, 2011.

Buck, Christopher. "The Utopian Content of Reification: Adorno's Critical Social Theory of Nature." In *Second Nature: Rethinking the Natural through Politics*. Edited by Crina Archer, Laura Ephraim, and Lida Maxwell. 127–48. New York: Fordham University Press, 2013.

Buck-Morss, Susan. *The Origin of Negative Dialectics: Theodor W. Adorno, Walter Benjamin, and the Frankfurt Institute*. New York: Free Press, 1977.

Bull, Malcolm. *Anti-Nietzsche*. London: Verso, 2011.

Butler, Judith. "Foucault and the Paradox of Bodily Inscriptions." *The Journal of Philosophy* 86.11 (1989): 601–7.

– *Giving an Account of Oneself*. New York: Fordham University Press, 2005.

Calarco, Matthew. "Being-toward-Meat: An Analytic of Human–Animal Finitude." In *The Animal Inside: Essays at the Intersection of Philosophical Anthropology and Animal Studies*. Edited by Geofrrey Dierckxsens, Rudmer Bijlsma, Michael Begun, and Thomas Kiefer. 197–212. London and New York: Rowan and Littlefield, 2017.

– *Zoographies: The Question of the Animal from Heidegger to Derrida*. New York: Columbia University Press, 2008.

Campbell, Colin J. "'Three-Minute Access': Fugazi's Negative Aesthetic." In *Adorno and the Need in Thinking: New Critical Essays*. Edited by Donald Burke et al. 278–95. Toronto: University of Toronto Press, 2007.

Cavalieri, Paola, and Peter Singer. "A Declaration on Great Apes." In *The Great Apes Project*. New York: St Martin's Press, 1993.

Cavell, Stanley. *The Claim of Reason: Wittgenstein, Skepticism, Morality, and Tragedy*. Oxford: Clarendon Press, 1979.

Chambers, Simone. "The Politics of Critical Theory." In *The Cambridge Companion to Critical Theory*. Edited by Fred Rush. 219–47. Cambridge: Cambridge University Press, 2004.

Chari, Anita. *Political Economy of the Senses: Neoliberalism, Reification, Critique*. New York: Columbia University Press, 2015.

Chrostowska, S.D. "Thought Woken by Memory: Adorno's Circuitous Path to Utopia." *New German Critique 118*, 40.1 (2013): 93–117.

Comay, Rebecca. "Adorno's Siren Song." *New German Critique* 81 (2000): 21–48.

– *Mourning Sickness: Hegel and the French Revolution*. Stanford: Stanford University Press, 2011.

Connolly, William E. *Facing the Planetary: Entangled Humanism and the Politics of Swarming*. Durham: Duke University Press, 2017.

– *Identity/Difference: Democratic Negotiations of Political Paradox*. Ithaca: Cornell University Press, 1991.

– *A World of Becoming*. Durham: Duke University Press, 2011.

Cook, Deborah. *Adorno on Nature*. Durham: Acumen, 2011.

– "Ein Reaktionares Schwein? Political Activism and Prospects for Change in Adorno." *Revue international de philosophie* 1.227 (2004): 47–67.

– "Through a Glass Darkly: Adorno's Inverse Theology." *Adorno Studies* 1.1 (2017): 66–78.

Coyle, Lauren. "The Spiritless Rose in the Cross of the Present: Retracing Hegel in Adorno's Negative Dialectics and Related Lectures." *Telos* 155 (2011): 39–65.

Curran, Angela. "Feminism and the Narrative Structures of the *Poetics*." In *Feminist Interpretations of Aristotle*. Edited by Cynthia A. Freeland. 289–326. University Park: Pennsylvania State University Press, 1998.

Dallmayr, Fred. "The Politics of Nonidentity: Adorno, Postmodernism – and Edward Said." *Political Theory* 25.1 (1997): 33–56.

Deleuze, Gilles and Félix Guattari. *A Thousand Plateaus: Capitalism and Schizophrenia*. Translated by Brian Massumi. Minneapolis: University of Minnesota Press, 1987.

– *Mille plateaux: Capitalisme et schizophrénie* 2. Paris: Les Éditions Minuit, 1980.

Depew, David J. "Humans and Other Political Animals in Aristotle's *History of Animals*." *Phronesis* 40.2 (1995): 156–81.

Derrida, Jacques. *The Animal That Therefore I Am*. Translated by David Wills. Edited by Marie-Louise Mallet. New York: Fordham University Press, 2008.

– *The Beast and the Sovereign*, vol. 1. Edited by Michel Lisse, Marie-Louise Mallet, and Ginette Michaud. Translated by Geoffrey Bennington. Chicago: University of Chicago Press, 2009.

– *The Beast and the Sovereign*, vol. 2. Edited by Michel Lisse, Marie-Louise Mallet, and Ginette Michaud. Translated by Geoffrey Bennington. Chicago: University of Chicago Press, 2011.

– "Fichus: Frankfurt Address." In *Paper Machine*. Translated by Rachel Bowlby. 164–81. Stanford: Stanford University Press, 2005.

de Vries, Hent. *Minimal Theologies: Critiques of Secular Reason in Adorno and Levinas*. Translated by Geoffrey Hale. Baltimore: Johns Hopkins University Press, 2005.

Dews, Peter. "Adorno, Post-Structuralism, and the Critique of Identity." In *The Frankfurt School: Critical Assessments*, vol. 4. Edited by Jay Bernstein. 100–14. London: Routledge, 1994.

Donaldson, Sue, and Will Kymlicka. *Zoopolis: A Political Theory of Animal Rights*. Oxford: Oxford University Press, 2011.

Douglas, Andrew J. "Democratic Darkness and Adorno's Redemptive Criticism." *Philosophy and Social Criticism* 36.7 (2010): 819–36.

Dryzek, John S., Bonnie Honig, and Anne Phillips. "Introduction." In *The Oxford Handbook of Political Theory*. Edited by John S. Dryzek, Bonnie Honig, and Anne Phillips. 3–41. Oxford: Oxford University Press, 2008.

Duttman, Alexander Garcia. "Adorno's Rabbits; or Against Being in the Right." Translated by James Phillips. *New German Critique 97*, 33.1 (2006): 179–89.

Emerson, Blake. "Dialectic of Color Blindness." *Philosophy and Social Criticism* 39.7 (2013): 693–716.

Euben, J. Peter. *The Tragedy of Political Theory: The Road Not Taken*. Princeton: Princeton University Press, 1990.

Ferrarin, Alfredo. *Hegel and Aristotle*. Cambridge: Cambridge University Press, 2007.

Finlayson, James Gordon. "'Bare Life' and Politics in Agamben's Aristotle." *The Review of Politics* 72.1 (2010): 97–126.

Florin, Camila, et al., eds. "Special Issue on Adorno and the Anthropocene." *Adorno Studies* 3.1 (2019).

Fong, Benjamin Y. *Death and Mastery: Psychoanalytic Drive Theory and the Subject of Late Capitalism*. New York: Columbia University Press, 2016.

Foucault, Michel. *The Order of Things: An Archeology of the Human Sciences*. New York: Vintage, 1994.

Frank, Jill. *A Democracy of Distinction: Aristotle and the Work of Politics*. Chicago: University of Chicago Press, 2005.

Freyenhagen, Fabian. *Adorno's Practical Philosophy: Living Less Wrongly*. Cambridge: Cambridge University Press, 2013.

Fukuyama, Francis. *Our Posthuman Future: Consequences of the Biotechnology Revolution*. New York: Picador, 2002.

Gandesha, Samir. "The 'Aesthetic Dignity of Words': Adorno's Philosophy of Language." *New German Critique* 97, 33.1 (2006): 137–58.

– "Homeless Philosophy: The Exile of Philosophy and the Philosophy of Exile in Arendt and Adorno." In *Arendt and Adorno: Political and Philosophical Investigations*. Edited by Lars Rensmann and Samir Gandesha. 246–79. Stanford: Stanford University Press, 2012.

Garner, Robert. *A Theory of Justice for Animals: Animal Rights in a Nonideal World*. Oxford and New York: Oxford University Press, 2013.

Garver, Eugene. *Aristotle's Politics: Living Well and Living Together*. Chicago: University of Chicago Press, 2011.

Gehlen, Arnold. *Man: His Nature and Place in the World*. Translated by Clare McMillan and Karl Pillemer. New York: Columbia University Press, 1988.

– *Man in the Age of Technology*. Translated by Patricia Lipscomb. New York: Columbia University Press, 1980.

Gellrich, Michelle. *Tragedy and Theory: The Problem of Conflict since Aristotle*. Princeton: Princeton University Press, 1988.

Gerhardt, Christina. "The Ethics of Animals in Adorno and Kafka." *New German Critique* 97.33 (2006): 159–78.

– "Thinking With: Animals in Schopenhauer, Horkheimer, and Adorno." In *Critical Theory and Animal Liberation*. Edited by John Sanbonmatsu. 137–46. Lanham: Rowan and Littlefield, 2011.

Gerson, Lloyd P. "The Unity of Intellect in Aristotle's *De Anima*." *Phronesis* 49.4 (2004): 348–73.

Geulen, Eva. "Theodor Adorno on Tradition." In *The Actuality of Adorno: Critical Essays on Adorno and the Postmodern*. Edited by Max Pensky. 183–93. Albany: SUNY Press, 1997.

Geuss, Raymond. "Adorno and Berg." In *Morality, Culture, and History: Essays on German Philosophy*. 116–39. Cambridge: Cambridge University Press, 1999.

– "Art and Theodicy." In *Morality, Culture, and History: Essays on German Philosophy*. 78–115. Cambridge: Cambridge University Press, 1999.

– *Changing the Subject: Philosophy from Socrates to Adorno*. Cambridge, MA: Harvard University Press, 2017.

– "Form and 'The New' in Adorno's 'Vers Une Musique Informelle.' In *Morality, Culture, and History: Essays on German Philosophy*. 140–66. Cambridge: Cambridge University Press, 1999.

– "Outside Ethics." In *Outside Ethics*. 40–66. Princeton: Princeton University Press, 2005.

– *Philosophy and Real Politics*. Princeton: Princeton University Press, 2008.

– "Realism, Wishful Thinking, Utopia." In *Political Uses of Utopia: New Marxist, Anarchist, and Radical Democratic Perspectives*. Edited by S.D.

Chrostowska and James D. Ingram. 234–47. New York: Columbia University Press, 2016.

– "Suffering and Knowledge in Adorno." In *Outside Ethics*. 111–30. Princeton: Princeton University Press, 2005.

Gilroy, Paul. *Postcolonial Melancholia*. New York: Columbia University Press, 2005.

Gordon, Peter E. *Adorno and Existence*. Cambridge, MA: Harvard University Press, 2016.

Habermas, Jürgen. "The Entwinement of Myth and Enlightenment: Max Horkheimer and Theodor Adorno." *The Philosophical Discourse of Modernity: Twelve Lectures*. Translated by Frederick G. Lawrence. 106–30. Cambridge, MA: MIT Press, 1995.

– *The Future of Human Nature*. Translated by William Rehg, Hella Beister, and Max Pensky. Cambridge: Polity, 2003.

–. "'I Myself Am Part of Nature' – Adorno on the Intrication of Reason in Nature: Reflections on the Relation between Freedom and Unavailability." In *Between Naturalism and Religion: Philosophical Essays*. Translated by Ciaran Cronin. 181–208. Cambridge: Polity, 2008.

– "Theodor Adorno: The Primal History of Subjectivity – Self-Affirmation Gone Wild." In *Philosophical-Political Profiles*. Translated by Frederick G. Lawrence. 99–109. Cambridge, MA: MIT Press, 1983.

– *The Theory of Communicative Action*, vol. 1: *Reason and the Rationalization of Society*. Translated by Thomas McCarthy. Boston: Beacon, 1984.

Hall, Edith. "Is There a Polis in Aristotle's *Poetics*?" In *Tragedy and the Tragic: Greek Theatre and Beyond*. Edited by M.S. Silk. 295–309. Oxford: Clarendon, 1998.

Hammer, Espen. *Adorno and the Political*. London: Routledge, 2005.

– *Adorno's Modernism: Art, Experience, and Catastrophe*. Cambridge: Cambridge University Press, 2015.

Haraway, Donna J. *Simians, Cyborgs, and Women*. New York: Routledge, 1991.

Heath, John. *Talking Greeks: Speech, Animals, and the Other in Homer, Aeschylus, and Plato*. Cambridge: Cambridge University Press, 2005.

Hegel. G.W.F. *Elements of the Philosophy of Right*. Edited by Allen W. Wood. Translated by. H.B. Nisbet. Cambridge: Cambridge University Press, 1991.

– *The Encyclopaedia Logic: Part I of the Encyclopaedia of Philosophical Sciences with the Zusätze*. Translated by T.F. Geraets, W.A. Suchting, and H.S. Harris. Indianapolis: Hackett, 1991.

– *Hegel's Phenomenology of Spirit*. Translated by A.V. Miller. Oxford: Oxford University Press, 1977.

– *Hegel's Science of Logic*. Translated by A.V. Miller. New York: Humanities Press, 1976.

Hellings, James. *Adorno and Art: Aesthetic Theory contra Critical Theory*. London: Palgrave Macmillan, 2014.

Hohendahl, Peter Uwe. "Adorno: The Discourse of Philosophy and the Problem of Language." In *The Actuality of Adorno: Critical Essays on Adorno and the Postmodern*. Edited by Max Pensky. 62–82. Albany: SUNY Press, 1997.
– *The Fleeting Promise of Art: Adorno's Aesthetic Theory Revisited*. Ithaca: Cornell University Press, 2013.
Holloway, John. "Why Adorno?" In *Negativity and Revolution: Adorno and Political Activism*. Edited by John Holloway, Fernando Matamoros, and Sergio Tischler. 12–17. London: Pluto, 2009.
Honig, Bonnie. *Antigone Interrupted*. Cambridge: Cambridge University Press, 2013.
– *Political Theory and the Displacement of Politics*. Ithaca: Cornell University Press, 1993.
Honneth, Axel. *The Critique of Power: Reflective Stages in a Critical Social Theory*. Translated by Kenneth Baynes. Cambridge, MA: MIT Press, 1991.
– "A Physiognomy of the Capitalist Form of Life: A Sketch of Adorno's Social Theory." Translated by James Ingram. *Constellations* 12.1 (2005): 50–64.
Horkheimer, Max, and Theodor W. Adorno. *Dialectic of Enlightenment: Philosophical Fragments*. Edited by Gunzelin Schmid Noerr. Translated by Edmund Jephcott. Stanford: University of Stanford Press, 2002.
– *Dialektik der Aufklärung: Philosophische Fragmente*. Frankfurt am Main: S. Fischer, 2010.
– "Nachtrag zu Band 13: Diskussion über Theorie und Praxis." In *Max Horkheimer: Gesammelte Schriften*, vol. 14: *1942–1972*. 32–72. Frankfurt am Main: S. Fischer, 1989.
Horowitz, Asher. "Adorno and Emptiness." In *Subversive Itinerary: The Thought of Gad Horowitz*. Edited by Shannon Bell and peter kulchyski. 256–78. Toronto: University of Toronto Press, 2013.
– *Ethics at a Standstill: History and Subjectivity in Levinas and the Frankfurt School*. Pittsburgh: Duquesne University Press, 2008.
Huhn, Tom. "Introduction: Thoughts beside Themselves." In *The Cambridge Companion to Adorno*. Edited by Tom Huhn. 1–18. Cambridge: Cambridge University Press, 2004.
Hullot-Kentor, Bob. "Introduction to Adorno's 'Idea of Natural History.'" *Telos* (1984): 97–110.
Hullot-Kentor, Robert. "Back to Adorno." *Telos* 81 (1989): 5–29.
– "The Impossibility of Music." In *Things beyond Resemblance: Collected Essays on Theodor W. Adorno*. 180–9. New York: Columbia University Press, 2006.
– "Right Listening and a New Type of Human Being." In *The Cambridge Companion to Adorno*. Edited by Tom Huhn. 181–97. Cambridge: Cambridge University Press, 2004.

– "Suggested Reading: Jameson on Adorno." In *Things beyond Resemblance: Collected Essays on Theodor W. Adorno*. 220–33. New York: Columbia University Press, 2006.

Ionesco, Eugène. "Rhinoceros." In *Plays*, vol. 4. Translated by Derek Prouse. 3–107. London: John Calder, 1964.

– *Rhinocéros*. Edited by Reuben Y. Ellison and Stowell C. Goding. New York: Holt, Rinehard, and Wilson, 1961.

Jaeggi, Rahel. "'No Individual Can Resist': *Minima Moralia* as Critique of Forms of Life." Translated by James Ingram. *Constellations* 12.1 (2005): 65–82.

Jäger, Lorenz. *Adorno: A Political Biography*. Translated by Stewart Spencer. New Haven: Yale University Press, 2004.

Jameson, Frederic. *Late Marxism: Adorno, or, The Persistence of the Dialectic*. London: Verso, 2000.

Jarvis, Simon. *Adorno: A Critical Introduction*. New York: Routledge, 1998.

– "Adorno, Marx, Materialism." In *The Cambridge Companion to Adorno*. Edited by Tom Huhn. 79–100. Cambridge: Cambridge University Press, 2004.

Jay, Martin. *Adorno*. London: Fontana, 1984.

– "The Frankfurt School's Critique of Marxist Humanism." *Social Research* 39.2 (1972): 285–305.

– *Marxism and Totality: The Adventures of a Concept from Lukács to Habermas*. Berkeley: University of California Press, 1984.

Jenemann, David. *Adorno in America*. Minneapolis: University of Minnesota Press, 2007.

Kant, Immanuel. "Idea for a Universal History with a Cosmopolitan Purpose." In *Political Writings*. Edited by H.S. Reiss. Translated by H.B. Nisbet. 41–53. Cambridge: Cambridge University Press, 1991.

– "Perpetual Peace: A Philosophical Sketch." In *Political Writings*. Edited by H.S. Reiss. Translated by H.B. Nisbet. 93–130. Cambridge: Cambridge University Press, 1991.

Kateb, George. "Aestheticism and Morality: Their Cooperation and Hostility." In *Patriotism and Other Mistakes*. 117–49. New Haven: Yale University Press, 2006.

– *Human Dignity*. Cambridge: Belknap Press, 2011.

Kojève, Alexandre. *Introduction to the Reading of Hegel: Lectures on the Phenomenology of Spirit*. Edited by Allan Bloom. Translated by James H. Nichols, Jr. Ithaca: Cornell University Press, 1980.

Kontos, Alkis. "Domination: Metaphor and Political Reality." In *Domination*. Edited by Alkis Kontos. 211–20. Toronto: University of Toronto Press, 1975.

Kullmann, Wolfgang. "Man as a Political Animal in Aristotle." In *A Companion to Aristotle's Politics*. Edited by David Keyt and Fred D. Miller, Jr. 94–117. Cambridge: Blackwell, 1991.

Labarrière, Jean-Louis. "Imagination humaine et imagination animale chez Aristote." *Phronesis* 29.1 (1984): 17–49.

Laclau, Ernesto. "Why Do Empty Signifiers Matter to Politics?" In *Emancipation(s)*. 36–46. London: Verso, 1996.

Laclau, Ernesto, and Chantal Mouffe. *Hegemony and Socialist Strategy: Toward a Radical Democratic Politics*. London: Verso, 1985.

Larsen, Neil. "The Idiom of Crisis: On the Historical Immanence of Language in Adorno." In *Language without Soil: Adorno and Late Philosophical Modernity*. Eidted by Gerhard Richter. 117–30. New York: Fordham University Press, 2009.

Lear, Jonathan. "Katharsis." *Phronesis* 33.3 (1988): 297–326.

Lee, Lisa Yun. *Dialectics of the Body: Corporality in the Philosophy of T.W. Adorno*. New York: Routledge, 2005.

Leeb, Claudia. *Power and Feminist Agency in Capitalism: Toward a New Theory of the Political Subject*. Oxford: Oxford University Press, 2017.

Lemm, Vanessa. *Nietzsche's Animal Philosophy: Culture, Politics, and the Animality of the Human Being*. New York: Fordham University Press: 2009.

Levins, Richard, and Richard Lewontin. *The Dialectical Biologist*. Cambridge, MA: Harvard University Press, 1985.

Lloyd, G.E.R. *Early Greek Science: Thales to Aristotle*. London: Chatto and Windus, 1970.

– *Greek Science after Aristotle*. London: Chatto and Windus, 1973.

– *Magic, Reason, and Experience: Studies in the Origins and Development of Greek Science*. Cambridge: Cambridge University Press, 1979.

Lord, Carnes. *Education and Culture in the Political Thought of Aristotle*. Ithaca: Cornell University Press, 1982.

Luke, Timothy W. "Reflections from a Damaged Planet: Adorno as the Accompaniment to Environmentalism in the Anthropocene." *Telos* 183 (2018): 9–24.

Lyotard, Jean-François. *The Inhuman: Reflections on Time*. Translated by Geoffrey Bennington and Rachel Bowlby. Stanford: Stanford University Press, 1991.

MacCannell, Juliet Flower. "Adorno: The Riddle of Femininity." In *Adorno, Culture, and Feminism*. Edited by Maggie O'Neill. 141–60. London: Sage, 1999.

Madonald, Iain. *What Would Be Different? Figures of Possibility in Adorno*. Stanford: Stanford University Press, 2019.

MacIntyre, Alasdair. *After Virtue: A Study in Moral Theory*. 2nd ed. Notre Dame: University of Notre Dame Press, 1984.

– *Dependent Rational Animals: Why Human Beings Need the Virtues*. Chicago: Open Court, 2002.

Maharaj, Ayon. *The Dialectics of Aesthetic Agency: Revaluating German Aesthetics from Kant to Adorno*. New York: Bloomsbury, 2013.

Marasco, Robyn. "Already the Effect of the Whip: Critical Theory and the Feminine Ideal." *differences* 17.1 (2006): 88–115.

– *The Highway of Despair: Critical Theory after Hegel*. New York: Columbia University Press, 2015.

Marcuse, Herbert. *One-Dimensional Man: Studies in the Ideology of Advanced Industrial Society*. Boston: Beacon, 1991.

Marder, Michael. "Minima Potentia: Reflections on the Subject of Suffering." *New German Critique 97*, 33.1 (Winter 2006): 53–72.

Mariotti, Shannon L. "Adorno on the Radio: Democratic Leadership as Democratic Pedagogy." *Political Theory* 42.4 (2014): 415–42.

Martel, James R. *The Misinterpellated Subject*. Durham: Duke University Press, 2017.

Massumi, Brian. *What Animals Teach Us about Politics*. Durham: Duke University Press, 2014.

Maupassant, Guy de. *Afloat*. Translated by Douglas Parmée. New York: New York Review Books, 2008.

– *Sur l'eau: de St. Tropez à Monte-Carlo*. Paris: Encre, 1979.

McCormick, John P. "A Critical versus Genealogical 'Questioning' of Technology: Notes on How Not to Read Adorno and Horkheimer." In *Confronting Mass Democracy and Industrial Technology: Political and Social Theory from Nietzsche to Habermas*. Edited by John P. McCormick. 267–94. Durham: Duke University Press, 2002.

Mendieta, Eduardo. "Animal Is to Kantianism as Jew Is to Fascism: Adorno's Bestiary." In *Critical Theory and Animal Liberation*. Edited by John Sanbonmatsu. 147–60. Lanham: Rowan and Littlefield, 2011.

Menke, Christoph. "Aesthetic Nature: Against Biology." *The Yearbook of Comparative Literature* 58 (2012): 193–5.

– *Force: A Fundamental Concept of Aesthetic Anthropology*. Translated by Gerrit Jackson. New York: Fordham, 2013.

– *Reflections of Equality*. Translated by Howard Rouse and Andrei Denejkine. Stanford: Stanford University Press, 2006.

– *The Sovereignty of Art: Aesthetic Negativity in Adorno and Derrida*. Translated by Neil Solomon. Cambridge, MA: MIT Press, 1998.

– *Spiegelungen der Gleichheit*. Berlin: Akademie Verlag, 2000.

Montag, Warren. *Althusser and His Contemporaries: Philosophy's Perpetual War*. Durham: Duke University Press, 2013.

Morgan, Alastair. "A Preponderance of Objects: Critical Theory and the Turn to the Object." *Adorno Studies* 1.1 (2017): 13–30.

Müller-Doohm, Stefan. *Adorno: A Biography*. Translated by Rodney Livingstone. Cambridge: Polity, 2005.

Nagelhout, Marah. "Nature and the 'Industry That Scorched It': Adorno and Anthropocene Aesthetics." *symploke* 24.1–2 (2016): 121–35.

Nelson, Eric S. "Revisiting the Dialectic of the Environment: Nature as Ideology and Ethics in Adorno and the Frankfurt School." *Telos* 155 (2011): 105–26.

Neumann, Franz. *Behemoth: The Structure and Practice of National Socialism, 1933–1944*. Translated by Peter Hayes. New York: Octagon, 1963.

Nietzsche, Friedrich. *On the Genealogy of Morality*. Rev. Ed. Edited by Keith Ansell-Pearson. Translated by Carol Diethe. Cambridge: Cambridge University Press, 2008.

– *Thus Spoke Zarathustra: A Book for Everyone and No One*. Translated by R.J. Hollingdale. New York: Penguin, 2003.

Nussbaum, Martha C. "Beyond 'Compassion and Humanity': Justice for Nonhuman Animals." In *Frontiers of Justice: Disability, Nationality, Species Membership*. 325–407. Cambridge, MA: Belknap Press, 2006.

– *The Fragility of Goodness: Luck and Ethics in Greek Tragedy and Philosophy*. Rev. ed. Cambridge: Cambridge University Press, 2001.

– "Human Functioning and Social Justice: In Defense of Aristotelian Essentialism." *Political Theory* 20.2 (1992): 202–46.

Ober, Josiah. *The Athenian Revolution: Essays on Ancient Greek Democracy and Political Theory*. Princeton: Princeton University Press, 1996.

– *Political Dissent in Democratic Athens: Intellectual Critics of Popular Rule*. Princeton: Princeton University Press, 1998.

O'Connor, Brian. *Adorno*. London: Routledge, 2013.

– "Adorno and the Problem of Givenness." *Revue internationale de philosophie* 227.1 (2004): 85–99.

– *Adorno's Negative Dialectic*. Cambridge, MA: MIT Press, 2004.

– "Adorno's Reconception of the Dialectic." In *A Companion to Hegel*. Edited by Stephen Houlgate and Michael Baur. 537–55. Oxford: Blackwell, 2011.

O'Neill, Maggie. "Adorno and Women: Negative Dialectics, Kulturkritik, and Unintentional Truth." In *Adorno, Culture, and Feminism*. Edited by Maggie O'Neill. 21–40. London: Sage, 1999.

Osborne, Peter. "Adorno and the Metaphysics of Modernism: The Problem of a 'Postmodern' Art." In *The Problems of Modernity: Adorno and Benjamin*. Edited by Andrew Benjamin. 23–48. London: Routledge, 1991.

Paddison, Max. *Adorno, Modernism, and Mass Culture: Essays on Critical Theory and Music*. London: Kahn and Averill, 1996.

Panagia, Davide. *The Poetics of Political Thinking*. Durham: Duke University Press, 2006.

Peters, Mathijs. "'The Zone of the Carcass and the Knacker' – on Adorno's Concern with the Suffering Body." *European Journal of Philosophy* (August 2013): 1–21.

Pratt, Vernon. "The Essence of Aristotle's Zoology." *Phronesis* 33.3 (1984): 267–78.

Rancière, Jacques. *Aesthetics and Its Discontents*. Translated by Steve Corcoran. Cambridge: Polity, 2009.

– *Althusser's Lesson*. Translated by Emiliano Battista. New York: Continuum, 2011.

Rensmann, Lars. "National Sovereigntism and Global Constitutionalism: An Adornian Cosmopolitan Critique." *Critical Horizons* 17.1 (February 2016): 24–39.

Rocco, Christopher. *Tragedy and Enlightenment: Athenian Political Thought and the Dilemmas of Modernity*. Berkeley: University of California Press, 1997.

Rose, Gillian. *The Melancholy Science: An Introduction to the Thought of Theodor W. Adorno*. London: Verso, 2014.

Rosen, Michael. *Dignity: Its History and Meaning*. Cambridge, MA: Harvard University Press, 2012.

– *Hegel's Dialectic and Its Criticism*. Cambridge: Cambridge University Press, 1982.

– *On Voluntary Servitude: False Consciousness and the Theory of Ideology*. Cambridge, MA: Harvard University Press, 1996.

Rossello, Diego. "All in the (Human) Family: Species Aristocratism in the Return of Human Dignity." *Political Theory* 45.6 (2017): 749–71.

– "'To Be Human, Nonetheless, Remains a Decision': Humanism as Decisionism in Contemporary Critical Political Theory." *Contemporary Political Theory* 16.4 (2017): 439–58.

Savage, Robert. "Adorno's Family and Other Animals." *Thesis Eleven* 78 (2004): 102–12.

Schecter, Darrow. "Unity, Identity, and Difference: Reflections on Hegel's Dialectics and Negative Dialectics." *History of Political Thought* 33.2 (2012): 258–79.

Scheler, Max. *Formalism in Ethics and Non-Formal Ethics of Values: A New Attempt toward the Foundation of an Ethical Personalism*. Translated by Manfred S. Frings and Roger L. Funk. Evanston: Northwestern University Press, 1973.

– *Man's Place in Nature*. Translated by Hans Meyerhoff. New York: Noonday, 1970.

Schmidt, Dennis J. *On Germans and Other Greeks: Tragedy and Ethical Life*. Bloomington: Indiana University Press, 2001.

Schmitz, Friederike. "Animal Ethics and Human Institutions: Integrating Animals into Political Theory." In *The Political Turn in Animal Ethics*. Edited by Robert Garner and Siobhan O'Sullivan. 33–49. London and New York: Rowan and Littlefield, 2016.

Schweppenhäuser, Gerhard. "Adorno's Negative Moral Philosophy." In *The Cambridge Companion to Adorno*. Edited by Tom Huhn. Translated by Cara Gendel Ryan and Michael McGettigan. 328–53. Cambridge: Cambridge University Press, 2004.

– *Theodor W. Adorno: An Introduction*. Translated by James Rolleston. Durham: Duke University Press, 2009.

Shuster, Martin. *Autonomy after Auschwitz: Adorno, German Idealism, and Modernity*. Chicago: University of Chicago Press, 2014.

Silberbusch, Oshrat C. *Adorno's Philosophy of the Nonidentical: Thinking as Resistance*. London: Palgrave Macmillan, 2018.

Singer, Peter. *Animal Liberation*. 2nd ed. New York: Random House, 1990.

Sorabji, Richard. *Animal Minds and Human Morals: The Origins of the Western Debate*. Ithaca: Cornell University Press, 1993.

Steiner, Gary. *Anthropocentrism and Its Discontents: The Moral Status of Animals in the History of Western Philosophy*. Pittsburgh: University of Pittsburgh Press, 2005.

Taylor, Robert S. "Review of Nicholas Tampio, *Kantian Courage: Advancing the Enlightenment in Contemporary Political Theory*." *Perspectives on Politics* 11.2 (2013): 631–2.

Thomä, Dieter. "Passion Lost, Passion Regained: How Arendt's Anthropology Intersects with Adorno's Theory of the Subject." In *Arendt and Adorno: Political and Philosophical Investigations*. Edited by Lars Rensmann and Samir Gandesha. 105–28. Stanford: Stanford University Press, 2012.

Thompson, Evan. "Self-No-Self? Memory and Reflexive Awareness." In *Self, No Self?: Perspectives from Analytical, Phenomenological, and Indian Traditions*. Edited by Mark Siderits, Evan Thompson, and Dan Zahavi. 157–75. Oxford: Oxford University Press, 2010.

Thomson, Alex. "Polemos and Agon." In *Law and Agonistic Politics*. Edited by Andrew Schaap. 105–18. Farnham: Ashgate, 2009.

Tully, James. *Strange Multiplicity: Constitutionalism in an Age of Diversity*. Cambridge: Cambridge University Press, 1995.

Varadharajna, Asha. *Exotic Parodies: Subjectivity in Adorno, Said, and Spivak*. Minneapolis: University of Minnesota Press, 1995.

Vatter, Miguel. *The Republic of the Living: Biopolitics and the Critique of Civil Society*. New York: Fordham University Press, 2014.

Vázquez-Arroyo, Antonio Y. "Minima Humana: Adorno, Exile, and the Dialectic." *Telos* 149 (Winter 2009): 105–25.

– *Political Responsibility: Responding to Predicaments of Power*. New York: Columbia University Press, 2016.

– "Universal History Disavowed: On Critical Theory and Postcolonialism." *Postcolonial Studies* 11 (2008): 455–65.

Vernant, Jean-Pierre. *Myth and Society in Ancient Greece*. Translated by Janet Lloyd. New York: Zone, 1996.

– *The Origins of Greek Thought*. Ithaca: Cornell University Press, 1982.

Vogel, Steven. *Against Nature: The Concept of Nature in Critical Theory*. Albany: SUNY Press, 1996.

Waite, Geoff. *Nietzsche's Corps/e: Aesthetics, Politics, Prophecy, or, The Spectacular Technoculture of Everyday Life*. Durham: Duke University Press, 1996.

Walzer, Michael. *In God's Shadow: Politics in the Hebrew Bible*. New Haven: Yale University Press, 2012.

Webb, Dan. "If Adorno Isn't the Devil It's Because He's a Jew: Lyotard's Misreading of Adorno through Thomas Mann's Dr Faustus." *Philosophy and Social Criticism* 35.5 (2009): 517–31.

Weber Nicholsen, Shierry. *Exact Imagination, Late Work: On Adorno's Aesthetics*. Cambridge, MA: MIT Press, 1997.

Weißpflug, Maike. "A Natural History for the 21st Century: Rethinking the Anthropocene Narrative with Arendt and Adorno." Chapter 2 in *The Anthropocene Debate and Political Science*. London: Routledge, 2018.

Wellmer, Albrecht. "Adorno, Modernity, and the Sublime." In *The Actuality of Adorno: Critical Essays on Adorno and the Postmodern*. Edited by Max Pensky. 112–34. Albany: SUNY Press, 1997.

– *Endgames: The Irreconcilable Nature of Modernity: Essays and Lectures*. Translated by David Midgley. Cambridge, MA: MIT Press, 1998.

Wilke, Sabine, and Heidi Schlipphacke. "Construction of a Gendered Subject: A Feminist Reading of Adorno's Aesthetic Theory." In *The Semblance of Subjectivity: Essays in Adorno's Aesthetic Theory*. Edited by Tim Huhn and Lambert Zuidervaart. 287–308. Cambridge, MA: MIT Press, 1997.

Wolfe, Cary. *Animal Rites: American Culture, the Discourse of Species, and Posthumanist Theory*. Chicago: University of Chicago Press, 2003.

– *What Is Posthumanism?* Minneapolis: University of Minnesota Press, 2009.

Yack, Bernard. *The Problems of a Political Animal: Community, Justice, and Conflict in Aristotelian Political Thought*. Berkeley: University of California Press, 1993.

Zuidervaart, Lambert. *Adorno's Aesthetic Theory: The Redemption of Illusion*. Cambridge, MA: MIT Press, 1991.

– *Social Philosophy after Adorno*. Cambridge: Cambridge University Press, 2007.

# Index

www.ingramcontent.com/pod-product-compliance
Lightning Source LLC
LaVergne TN
LVHW041114090826

844660LV00062B/895/J

* 9 7 8 1 4 8 7 5 4 1 4 4 6 *